# Stand Together or Starve Alone

## Endorsements for
## Stand Together or Starve Alone

"Mark Winne charts the next steps integral to establishing a food movement in the United States where cooperation and collaboration are hallmarks and where hunger and food insecurity will not stand."

—*Cindy Gentry, Food Systems Coordinator, Maricopa County Dept. of Public Health*

"Unafraid to call out the role of money, funders, and larger-than-life personalities, Winne offers a sharp and informative analysis of the food movement. Read this book if you want to understand what drives the food movement, why it has fractured, and how it might unite."

—*Brian Depew, Executive Director, Center for Rural Affairs*

"I think Winne is right that poverty is the real issue, and I applaud this book's brave suggestion that we can solve this massive problem together!"

—*Jack Hale, Founding member of Hartford Food System and Hartford Food Policy*

"A crisp, engaging history of how [the food movement] got here, offering clear guidance on how we can move forward. A must-read!"

—*Janie Burns, Treasure Valley Food Coalition*

"Mark Winne provides those passionate about the food system an approach that can and does make a difference."

—*Gina L. Cornia, Executive Director, Utahns Against Hunger*

# Stand Together or Starve Alone

## Unity and Chaos in the U.S. Food Movement

### Mark Winne

*Foreword by Anne Palmer*

PRAEGER™

An Imprint of ABC-CLIO, LLC
Santa Barbara, California • Denver, Colorado

**Library of Congress Cataloging-in-Publication Data**

Names: Winne, Mark, 1950– author.
Title: Stand together or starve alone : unity and chaos in the U.S. food movement / Mark Winne; foreword by Anne Palmer.
Description: Santa Barbara, California : Praeger, [2018] | Includes bibliographical references and index.
Identifiers: LCCN 2017031923 (print) | LCCN 2017042619 (ebook) | ISBN 9781440844485 (ebook) | ISBN 9781440844478 (alk.paper : alk. paper)
Subjects: LCSH: Food security—United States. | Food supply—Political aspects—United States. | Nutrition policy—United States. | Agriculture and state—United States.
Classification: LCC TX360.U6 (ebook) | LCC TX360.U6 W56 2018 (print) | DDC 363.80973—dc23
LC record available at https://lccn.loc.gov/2017031923

ISBN: 978-1-4408-4447-8 (print)
       978-1-4408-4448-5 (ebook)

22 21 20 19 18    1 2 3 4 5

This book is also available as an eBook.

Praeger
An Imprint of ABC-CLIO, LLC

ABC-CLIO, LLC
130 Cremona Drive, P.O. Box 1911
Santa Barbara, California 93116-1911
www.abc-clio.com

This book is printed on acid-free paper ∞

Manufactured in the United States of America

We must hang together, or most assuredly we shall all hang separately.

—Benjamin Franklin

# Contents

# Foreword

When I stepped into the food system arena about 11 years ago, I was advised to seek counsel wiser than myself. My background was in public health, but I had no experience in food or nutrition, other than being an enthusiastic eater and an acknowledged nutrition nut. Before I left for my first Community Food Security Coalition conference in Vancouver, colleagues encouraged me to find Mark Winne and talk to him. And so I did. It took a little stalking, but I managed to schedule about 30 minutes with him, getting advice on a community food assessment and other reports I should read to ground my thinking. Mark has been a trusted advisor ever since and the Johns Hopkins Center for a Livable Future has benefitted enormously by our partnership with him.

I was one of the chosen few to read this book before it hit the shelves, and without divulging any of Mark's demographic details, history is best written by those who lived it. Mark weaves his personal experience into a comprehensive overview of how the movement started, who was involved, what were the struggles, and what it looks like now. Numbers can be daunting, but these numbers tell an impressive story that is worth understanding if you want to understand the historical context that brought us here and use that history to propel us forward.

Whose evidence (and numbers) do you use and how much do you need to know in order to move forward? As an attending midwife at the birth of food policy councils, Mark applies strategies that value inviting people from different walks of life, different professions, different sectors, and different beliefs to participate in a democratic process. Spending time with people outside of our circle of influence is a first step toward developing partnerships, partnerships that will allow us to share the burden of complexity. Too often we favor our approach to the problem as the solution rather than a solution that is contributing to the greater good.

All these steps prepare us to shift our thinking from linear to lateral and invite us to apply systems thinking in our work. I liken systems thinking to the realization that any one person cannot know all that there is to know about a complicated issue like food. We need to create spaces to discuss how the various food system components are connected and interrelated, ask what that means for our work, and attempt to anticipate how action in one sector would affect another. Mark uses systems principles and more to situate the book's thesis: that we need to work together if we want to build a better food system for everyone.

One of my favorite bumper stickers is, "Don't believe everything you think." Mark reminds us that we are learning new things about the food system and new things should help inform new thinking. Accepting that positions we have fought long and hard for are no longer accurate is difficult. Disagreements, debates, and differences can make us smarter, or they can tear us apart.

*Stand Together or Starve Alone* could well be an anthem for how the various food movements could move food together in a more coordinated fashion. While acknowledging that there will always be issues we cannot agree on, there are many issues we can agree upon—issues that provide mutual benefit to the food system writ large, to our institutions, to our collective well-being. Mark calls this sweet spot the "'radical center,' a place that is a little bit outside each other's comfort zones but where we might both find some new, but common ground."

So, what did I learn by reading *Stand Together or Starve Alone*? Listen more. Question authority and yourself. Prepare for change. Open your heart.

Anne Palmer
Program Director, Johns Hopkins Center for a Livable
Future and Research Associate, Health, Behavior and
Society, Bloomberg School of Public Health

# Acknowledgments

There are many people whose absence from my life would have made the writing of this book highly unlikely, if not impossible. The first, of course, is my mother who passed away in July 2016. Aside from the obvious role that a mother plays in bringing anything to life, Jean Obenchain would start every conversation of the year prior to her passing with, "So Mark, how's the book coming?" Since I was at least a year behind before I even started, I'd attempt to deflect these loving inquiries with something like, "It's coming, it's coming," and then move on to the weather. Well, it's done, Mom, and this one's for you!

Though a mother herself, Anne Palmer at the Johns Hopkins Center for a Livable Future deserves primary credit for making this book possible, not only for a being a critical reader and for writing the book's forward, but for giving me the leave and leisure to devote some of my "work time" to an enterprise whose enormity I underestimated by at least tenfold. Her colleague, Shawn McKenzie, and the center's numerous faculty and graduate students—the "brains" and "brains-in-training"—have been invaluable and thoughtful influences every step of the way. I also want to thank Brian Gunia, a professor at the Johns Hopkins Carey Business School, for his kind tutoring on the subjects of group dynamics and organizational development.

And then of course there is my son, Peter Winne, who called me up one day to tell me that he needed "a project" for his graduate school course on research methods, and would I be it. Since he's been one of my main projects for the past 31 years, I was glad to become one of his, even if for only a little while. His "just-in-time" survey intervention, shined with a little spit and polish from his New York University faculty advisor, gave this book that extra punch it needed.

Michael Burgan, himself a writer, good friend, and like myself, a fairly recent émigré from Connecticut to Santa Fe, New Mexico, saved my hide with his research and reference skills, areas where I never fully excelled. In addition, his mastery of the comma and semicolon has always left me in total awe.

There are of course dozens of other "food system players" you will meet on these pages to whom I am indebted for their time and wisdom. Every one of them is a character in their own right, but they all share one characteristic which is an undying devotion to this thing we call the food movement. I regard many of them as brothers and sisters in arms—people I would trust with my life—and I regard all of them as partners in the struggle for food that is healthy, sustainably produced, and affordable for all. No matter where and how we enter the struggle, may we all eventually embrace the same goals.

# Introduction

A small band of men and women were gathered in the atrium of the Hartford, Connecticut, South Congregational Church on a sunny autumn morning. They were a cheery bunch, many of them sporting a glow in their cheeks from the crisp New England air. Their smiles, while perhaps more ethereal than normal, were not uncommon among people who never fail to be dazzled by the season's flagrant display of red and gold maple leaves. But given the reason for the group's gathering, the upbeat mood might have seemed out of place, or even irreverent, if one paid attention to the dour portraits of the church's founding fathers staring down with eternal disapproval from the walls.

These folks were the members of a newly formed state organization meeting under the working name of the Connecticut Anti-Hunger Coalition. While they were still thrashing out the fledgling group's purpose—what does a coalition do that its individual members don't do?—each person standing in the atrium at that moment was highly motivated by a common and rising challenge. For the year was 1986, and with Ronald Reagan's second presidential term well underway, the decline in social services, the rise in housing costs, and the region's bleak employment prospects were driving an ever-surging tide of hungry people to the shores of Connecticut's emergency food pantries.

The growing demand was also expanding the number of pantries. The state's two food bank warehouses that supplied much of the food were not keeping pace with the hungry mouths that the pantries were valiantly trying to feed. Most of the people now moving from the atrium to the church's community room were good-hearted volunteers who had never imagined that they would one day be in the food business. With the exception of a few members of the state's clergy and a handful of social service professionals, the seats were rapidly filling with rank amateurs who were doing their God-given best to manage a brewing crisis.

Given the stress that this community of food providers and activists were under, a sense of dread should have consumed the swelling crowd. Whether buoyed by Fall's crackling brilliance or the fellowship of those who shared the same dilemmas, hardy handshakes and subdued merriment filled the room. And what made the warm vibe particularly perplexing was that none of the participants had yet glanced at the printed agenda then circulating around the table. Buried near the end of what was a lengthy list of topics was the question of what to do with an unexpected grant for $75,000 that had come the way of this undefined and pleasantly chaotic group.

The messenger for this dubious piece of news happened to be me. Even though I had been placed in the powerful position of determining how the money could be spent, I was inclined to let the members of the group decide for themselves—a concession to democracy that I approached with some trepidation. I had fallen into this unsought role, because, incidental to my work in organizing this coalition, I had been invited as the sole representative of the state of Connecticut to a conference in Los Angeles.

There, basking in the glow of the lights of L.A. and the aura of entertainment celebrities, 49 other state representatives and I set about the task of divvying up several million dollars. The source of this loot was the "profits" from what I hoped would be the last of its kind, a made-for-and-by-Hollywood event called "Hands across America." As a moderately successful but infinitely complicated fund-raiser and spectacle, "Hands" did raise some bucks as well as some awareness about the growth of hunger in America. And using a complicated mathematical formula that none of the attendees understood, various sums were quickly allocated to each state.

While the formula that guided this distribution was precise, the determination of who would spend the money was as loose as a roomful of drunks. I was sitting in the catbird seat only because a Hands' organizer knew somebody who knew somebody in Connecticut who knew me. Be that as it may, each "delegate" clutched a letter that guaranteed our state's prescribed share as we were shuttled back to LAX where we had landed barely 48 hours earlier. My marching orders were as murky as the contents of the nearby tar pits: spend $75,000 to end hunger in Connecticut.

While I was proud to carry this gift back home to my comrades, I knew this boon could easily go bust. Without the benefit of a clear vision and mission for our work, without the framework for an agreed upon decision-making process, and without staff or leadership other than a temporary chairperson, the still-very-wet-behind-the-ears Connecticut Anti-Hunger Coalition was about to make its first important decision. The determination on how to use these funds, valued at close to $200,000 in 2016 dollars, had as much potential to drown this neophyte group in acrimony as it did to raise it to a higher level of achievement.

Premonitions of both outcomes filled my thoughts as I introduced the agenda item to the group. After providing the background and the skimpy directions from Hands across America, I asked the group what they wanted to do. The first person to raise his hand was an earnest food pantry volunteer who, with help from his church, had been struggling to assemble and distribute food to hungry families one day a week. His suggestion was simple: 12 food pantries had been attending our meetings; divide $75,000 by 12 and give each one $6,250. "Boy," he said, "that would give me enough money to feed people for months!"

Trying to conceal my disappointment—it was definitely not the suggestion I was hoping for—I called on a young Congregational minister who was known for his "big picture" views. He reminded the group that this coalition did not yet have any staff, that the demand for food was growing, and that he had his doubts about how much of a dent $6,250 could make in the problem. After all, he noted, with just a whiff of the pulpit about him, that the federal government was letting us down and Connecticut's state government had done nothing so far to address the growing need. As an organized force with a presence at the state capital, couldn't we do more as a group than we could ever do alone?

I breathed an audible sigh of relief. The other 30 or so participants, including most of the food pantry representatives, nodded their heads slowly and murmured sounds of assent. Even though we had no formal rules of order, one person moved that we use the Hands across America funds to hire a coordinator for the Connecticut Anti-Hunger Coalition and that henceforth we work together to end hunger in the state through the public policy framework of the state of Connecticut. The motion was seconded because that was what we thought the occasion called for. The vote in favor was unanimous.

With the exception of a couple of people who spent some time working the state legislature on human service issues, no one in the room knew exactly what a public policy framework looked like. Perhaps they knew intuitively that the charity model they were working with had its limits. The justice model, a term not yet in common use, could shift responsibility for addressing the problems of poverty and hunger back to their cause. This creeping awareness that giving away food would not stem the tide of hungry people was starting to sink in. This new path suggested by buying into a strong anti-hunger coalition—a buy-in bought and paid for by the $6,250 that each pantry sacrificed for the greater good—was a more likely road to justice and a resolution of the hunger crisis.

The constructs were still vague, the plan of action needed work, and the glue that would hold the coalition together was still drying. But what was certain on that stellar New England day inside the austerely decorated church meeting room was that people present there did not have any idea what impact their decision would have. Over the course of the ensuing three decades, the Connecticut Anti-Hunger Coalition (which would later change its name to End Hunger Connecticut! (EHC!)) would have an enormous impact.

The number of EHC! staff and the size of its annual budgets would grow. Its outputs in terms of public funds committed to reducing food insecurity (a term for "hunger" not in the food activists' 1986 lexicon) in Connecticut would soar. In the decades to come, the coalition and its members would leverage tens of millions of dollars in public funds to increase funding for and participation in federal food programs like school breakfast, lunch, and summer feeding. Outreach efforts would accelerate the use of the food stamp program (later to become Supplemental Nutrition Assistance Program (SNAP)) by eligible residents. And as their understanding of the region's food system (a concept that also enjoyed very little understanding in 1986) expanded, they would diversify their public policy interests into programs that preserved the state's farmland, increased the purchase of locally grown food at farmers' market by lower-income households, contributed to the development of numerous state food organizations including the nation's first state food policy council, and even removed sugary soft-drinks from Connecticut's schools. The "return" on a $75,000 investment in terms of public investment in food security and the state's food system, if it had ever been recognized as a return, would be the envy of the most demanding venture capitalist.

The impact of EHC!'s work and the diversity of its policy portfolio reflected the variety of its members' interests and the swelling ranks of the state's food system stakeholders. But for the most part, an underlying commitment to collaboration, as embodied by the selfless but self-interested participants at the "$75,000 meeting" continued to inform the coalition's work, often in very unexpected ways. For instance, during a financial low point in EHC!'s history in the 1990s, the state's two major food banks agreed to pay membership dues to EHC! on behalf of all of the food banks' combined hundreds of food pantry members. Not only did this provide a sizeable contribution to the coalition's lean budget, it also gave those many emergency food distribution volunteers an opportunity to participate more directly in the policy-making process (unfortunately, this practice of the food banks sharing funds with EHC! to support policy work was suspended about 15 years later, offering evidence of a growing disunity in the state's food movement).

And just in case the reader might think that these were abnormally saintly times in the history of the food movement, or that the streets of Hartford were awash in the spirit of brotherhood, think again. Though some moments in history may be riper for collaboration and acts of selflessness than others, members of the food movement are never immune to the sins that all humans are heir to (a major point of this book that will be amplified in the following chapters). As a central participant in the events described earlier, putting my needs and those of my own organization (the Hartford Food System) ahead of others was never far from my mind; I, like any other nonprofit director, had a duty of loyalty to his organization. In public settings, we may wax eloquent about the need to work together for the common good (e.g., putting an end to hunger), but we inevitably and not-so-privately serve the mission of our group first. These are the realities that govern organizational life and perhaps society in general.

The devil followed me into church that day reminding me how much good that $75,000 could do for the Hartford Food System. Whether I ultimately stayed the course to collaboration because I heard the voice of some distant Sunday school teacher, or the anticipated outpourings of gratitude from those around the table, I can't honestly say. But just in case there is a larger concern that one's commitment to the common good may get you into heaven but won't get you your daily bread, allow me to share one final anecdote.

One year later, I was approached by a gentleman by the name of Mathew Melmed who ran the organization that would provide administrative support for the Connecticut Anti-Hunger Coalition for a few years. In that role, his organization received and administered the $75,000. He asked me if I would like to use about two-thirds of a federal grant that his organization received almost automatically each year. The amount was small, $35,000, but enough to enable me and an incipient farm and nutrition coalition I was working with (not the anti-hunger group) to start the Connecticut Farmers' Market Nutrition Program. By leveraging federal and state funds over the course of almost 30 years, this program, "seeded" by the $35,000, would provide millions of dollars in public funds for the purchase of fresh produce by hundreds of thousands of the state's lowest income families at Connecticut farmers' markets, a number that would climb from about 16 in 1987 to 130 in 2015.

Mr. Melmed's gesture was not gratuitous nor an obligatory discharge of an "IOU." If I had to characterize it in retrospect I would say it was a tacit recognition that we're all in this battle together; that each of us brings different interests, ideas, and talents to the table; that innovation should have an opportunity to be fairly tested and evaluated in the marketplace of solutions alongside existing programs and practices; and that a chain of functioning partnerships and strong networks is far better than numerous unconnected programs, policies, and organizations. We need more people like Mr. Melmed today.

## Challenges to the Movement

Suffice it to say that if the kinds of relationships I've described so far are the normal way that business is conducted in the food movement, there would be no reason to write this book. The unfortunate truth is that coordination, cooperation, and the gold standard of working together, collaboration, are the exceptions rather than the rule. While, for instance, we may find it a little easier to share a local sandbox where personal relationships are the currency we trade in daily, state and national sandboxes are bigger, less dependent on multiple food system stakeholders to play nicely together, and are politically and bureaucratically more complicated.

I may be able to "work things out" with local anti-hunger leaders and food program directors, but in Washington, D.C., where I have worked on numerous policy campaigns, national food organizations will block access to new participants if they perceive that an innovation is a threat to their pet programs. They can be barely collegial (and sometimes hostile) toward groups that propose new ideas such as the Community Food Project Grants program (1995) or the Women, Infant, and Children Farmers Market Nutrition Program (1989), which are funded at far less than 1 percent of their multibillion-dollar federal cousins, SNAP and Women, Infant, and Children Program (WIC), respectively.

Money is always a confounding variable in any relationship—personal, professional, or organizational. More partnerships have never been formed and more partnerships dissolved because someone didn't like the size of their slice of the pie. While it may seem like a harsh analogy, old movie images of unsavory pirates stabbing each other in the back while divvying up the loot do come to mind. Absent eye patches and gold teeth, members of the food movement and its kindred connections can be as ruthless as Blackbeard.

The funders who support members of the movement sometimes contribute to an environment of distrust and confusion as well. Only recently did I witness a major foundation fund two different organizations in the same small city for virtually the same thing. They did not inform at least one of the parties, but just as importantly, they did not attempt to promote coordination between the two recipients. Once publicly shamed, the funder "came clean" and has since worked to rectify the situation. More discussion on the role money plays in undermining collaboration will be found in the coming chapters.

Whom you take money from also matters in the food movement. The ethical arguments and snide accusations that ensue when someone accepts money from the "wrong" source have driven many a wedge between people and organizations. Remarks run from the catty, as in, "Just look at who he's getting money from!" to the cynical, "The only thing wrong with tainted money is there t'aint enough of it!"

The intensity of feelings reflects in part the underlying values of the food movement and the role they can play in cementing or destroying relationships. If the food movement exists to serve the common good and the health and well-being of people and places, then it is hard to countenance taking money, even with no strings attached, from those whose work runs directly against your values.

Perhaps the only force as powerful as money in the food movement is information. It carries multiple dimensions including expertise within a certain subject matter, who you know and how influential they may be, idiosyncratic knowledge about a place or an institution such as the politics of a particular bureaucracy, or simply facts that when revealed are capable of leveraging considerable action. Information is both a force for good as well as one that when withheld, strengthens the hand of its holder at the expense of others, including the common good.

One small, but positive example of the everyday power of information comes from a county one hour east of Nashville, Tennessee, that I visited in 2015. At a training workshop, I conducted for 35 local people interested in forming a food policy council, we were told by a participant who ran a meals-on-wheels program for homebound elderly in a rural area of the county that there were 150 people on a waiting list. These were people who needed the service, but due to lack of funds, could not yet be served. The entire room was shocked by this information. Even though they all lived and worked in the same county, they were unaware of the extent of the need or the potential harm to those not being served. Prior to this meeting, the woman who shared the information didn't have a supportive audience who might be able to take action. The sharing was sufficient to catalyze the formation of a county food system working group (an early-stage coalition) to address the waiting list issue as well as other rising food concerns.

In other cases, information is so closely held or so cloaked in nonsense that its nondisclosure stymies progress. A humorous example of this comes from an old community at the eastern end of Long Island that had the opportunity to convert the last undeveloped 10 acres of private farmland into a community-owned, nonprofit farm. The action would have preserved badly needed open space as well as some local food production capacity. At a town hearing regarding the parcel's disposition, I heard debate rage back and forth as to what to do with the property.

Reasonable and decidedly unreasonable arguments were made by both sides. But the one argument that became the most prevalent was the claim that one's deep roots in the community somehow granted a person greater wisdom. One man in his late fifties proclaimed that because his family has been in this town for *15 generations* that he automatically knew that converting the private farm to a community farm was a bad idea. Not to be outdone, another gentleman, this one a little older, announced that his family's roots went back *16 generations*, and therefore he knew that preserving the farm for community use was better than the construction of 10 one-million-dollar homes.

By my rough calculations, each man's ancestors must have landed on the shores of Long Island in Viking long boats. Regardless, none of them presented facts or information to buttress their position. Others joined the debate by also exploiting lineage and longevity to draw righteous lines in the sand. As a result, there were no results. No coalitions were formed; no plans were made to enable the community to move forward. The names of long-dead ancestors whose bones moldered in the nearby marsh were invoked to drown facts, reason, and vision. The community remained divided, and to the best of my knowledge, lost its remaining farmland.

In easily the best and most horrific example in modern civilization of the consequence of information being withheld, China lost 36 million people to famine between 1959 and 1962. In his book *Tombstone*, Yang Jisheng chronicles in excruciating detail what happens when a country's control of its food system is centralized, there is no free press to disseminate unbiased information, and those with opposing points of view are suppressed, often through execution. The sense of the country's tragedy is heightened by the realization that it was not drought, floods, or even war that were responsible for such rampant hunger; it was denying the opportunity for stakeholders, from the capitol to the provinces to the villages, some modicum of democratic participation in solving problems.

Many coils of concertina wire separate people, organizations, and sectors from one another in the food movement. The reasons are so many and complex that regiments of psychologists and sociologists could be kept busy for ages unraveling their mysteries. Within the space available, future chapters will discuss, diagnose, and where possible offer remedies with the intent of building a food future we can all live with and a future that will enable us to live.

## A Note about the Author and His Methods

As can be easily detected from the preceding events that took place in Hartford, I have been an active participant in the food movement, having virtually grown up with it. Starting in 1971, when I began a breakfast program for low-income children and a community food coop while attending college in Lewiston, Maine, I have played numerous parts on the ever-expanding food system stage. Many of the stories and experiences from my work have already been recounted in my first book, *Closing the Food Gap: Resetting the Table in the Land of Plenty*. I will take a solemn vow to you, my reader, to not repeat those tales here. However, for better or for worse, it is the sum total of 45 years of food system and food movement work that informs this book. As such, that will be the lens through which I view and consider both the opportunities and challenges to having the biggest possible impact on our food system.

The number of hands-on food projects and public policy experiences that I've been associated with are numerous. They have ranged from gardens and farms, to kitchens and supermarkets, to places where public policy is made including city halls, state capitols, and Washington, D.C. The journey has allowed me to work with thousands of good people from all walks of life. In addition to being racially, ethnically, educationally, and professionally diverse, they are also people who are from communities that are affluent as well as those that are socially and economically distressed.

But what has inspired this book more than my experience in food program and policy work has been the training, consultation, and writing I have done over the past 15 years. By working with hundreds of organizations in nearly every state (the Dakotas being the only exceptions for some reason unbeknownst to me) and four countries, I have become acutely aware of the rising wave of food movement energy flowing across North America. And at the same time, with no small amount of chagrin, I see that wave fail to gain the force necessary to have the necessary impact.

Though the power of experience and observation has been my primary tool for learning, teaching, and action, it has been sharpened in recent years by a growing encounter with research, data, and the good writings of others. The marriage of practice to research and its application to theory has also been aided by a few years as a visiting scholar and part-time advisor with the Johns Hopkins Center for a Livable Future, which has generously allowed me time to pursue this book. This relationship has enabled me to spend time in the company of academics who approach the problems of the day with a penchant for evidence and a resistance to easy answers.

As such, I've reached beyond my experience to consult as many sources as I could without sacrificing my allegiance to experience. The citations and references that follow attest to that effort, one that may fall short of more traditional academic rigor, but nevertheless speaks to a respect for the research and ideas of others. But to augment my own experience, I have consulted dozens of other practitioners and a few academics through interviews. Unless I note otherwise, their statements will be found in quotation marks and are derived from face-to-face interviews, e-mails, or phone calls.

So, I come unabashedly to this project as a food system practitioner who is grateful for the million-and-one moments of experience. But I am equally grateful for the opportunity to pass those moments through the sieve of careful thought and analysis.

# CHAPTER ONE

# What's at Stake?

I began work on this book the same day (September 8, 2015) that the U.S. Department of Agriculture (USDA) released the results of its annual food security survey. The news wasn't good. According to what is the best count we have of hungry Americans, 48 million people, or 14.3 percent of us, are considered "food insecure" or have "very low food security." The first category refers to people who, to put it as simply as possible, experience uncertainty as to where their next meal is coming from. The second category, which includes 18 million Americans, or 5.6 percent of us, is of people who suffer more severe and frequent forms of uncertainty (Coleman-Jensen, 2015).

These numbers sound bad, and they are, but they are even worse when you look back to the beginning of this century when the 2000 USDA food security census placed 10 percent and 3 percent of us, respectively, in these categories (ibid.). In other words, the richest country in the world has not only made no progress in reducing the number of people who struggle to feed themselves, but is going backward.

But food headlines don't stop with hunger. As many of us know, exceeding a healthy weight—referred to as obesity and overweight—has essentially eclipsed tobacco consumption as the nation's number one public health concern. According to the Centers for Disease Control and Prevention, 36.5 percent of adult Americans are obese. This condition reduces the quality of their lives, or worse, cuts their lives short. This rate of obesity exceeds the 1994 level of 23 percent by half. One result: about 10 percent of Americans are diabetic (for the recipients of private and public food aid, those who have been the object of a huge amount of public largess, the rate is 33%) (Centers for Disease Control and Prevention, 2016).

There is one more important element of our national food story that claws its way into our consciousness on a daily basis, and that is the consequences of industrial-scale food production and manufacturing. Though they have been accused of almost everything short of terrorist jihad, so-called Big Food producers and manufacturers load our air and water with toxic levels of pollutants and animal waste, fill livestock with unnecessary amounts of antibiotics, and transform raw food ingredients into products often packed with unhealthy quantities of chemicals, salt, sugar, and fat. The Environmental Protection Agency found, for instance, that the number of impaired water bodies had risen to 42,898 in 2016, and that agricultural nonpoint pollution is the greatest source of impairment in lakes and rivers (Environmental Protection Agency, 2017). Though we are now hearing with some frequency how food corporations are reforming their practices, for example, reformulating food products to reduce the sugar content, they have a long way to go before their practices and products are healthy, humane, and sustainable.

This is the state of our food system at the midpoint of the millennium's second decade. It is the place where we produce, process, distribute, and consume the essential nutrients for life, but the problems associated with our food supply affect nearly every one of us somewhat and many of us severely. As we look at today's data and cast an eye back at yesterday's, we have to ask ourselves why, if the so-called food revolution has been underway for 50 years, so little progress has been made.

Yes, there is a strong argument that the food system has failed us, that "it" is responsible for a host of evils that only the most sainted and self-reliant among us could avoid. This is a claim I partially accept, and one I will discuss further. But I want to explore another idea, one I've come to reluctantly embrace as a result of working for and with numerous food organizations, campaigns, and causes for 45 years, and it is that *we have failed the food system*. By "we" I mean the vast army of individuals, organizations, and agencies that have claimed a stake in making good, healthy, and fair food available to all.

I don't mean to imply that any one person or entity has necessarily performed his or her tasks in a slipshod manner, but I do believe that there has been a failure to achieve long-term, lasting, and comprehensive success because of the food movement's inability to collaborate. While we may each do a heck of a job running a food pantry, organizing a farmers' market or advocating for Congress to add more money to the Supplemental Nutrition Assistance Program (SNAP, formerly known as food stamps), when it comes to working together, we are like a rookie rowing team whose oars are splintered and hopelessly tangled as the coxswain calls out contradictory instructions every few seconds.

This lack of exchange and interface between groups leads to another roadblock to collaboration: we become overly committed to our strategies abjuring the kind of critical analysis of our own programs, which can lead to necessary reform. This kind of parochialism is evident, for instance, with SNAP. As a program historically rooted in racist assumptions that poor people, particularly people of color, can't be trusted to responsibly manage cash forms of public assistance, it has evolved into a uniquely American and relatively large form of the nation's social welfare policy, unlike anything else in other developed nations. Its defenders and advocates have of course pushed back relentlessly at any attempt to reduce funding, but they have also treated its basic tenets as unassailable and its role within a larger food movement as separate and apart.

Granted, on a sector-by-sector basis, the food movement's efforts can look enormously impressive. The local food movement is booming with over 8,500 farmers' markets (there were barely a few hundred in the 1970s), and over 40,000 schools are buying food from nearby farmers (nary a local carrot had found its way into school cafeterias until the late 1990s) (Farmers Market Directory Search, 2017; Farm to School Census, 2015).

At some of the country's most elite institutions of higher learning, a national, student-run organization called Real Food Challenge has secured commitments from hundreds of colleges and universities to collectively purchase at least a billion dollars of food annually that is defined as "healthy, fair, and green" by 2020 (Real Food Challenge, 2017). But as we have seen time and time again in the food movement, good intentions to right the food system's wrong often ignore the creeping demons of its failures. Since 2011, almost concurrently with the rise of the Real Food Challenge, over 500 college and university food banks have been established to serve a growing number of hungry students and staff (College and University Food Bank Alliance, 2017).

Though a dubious measure of success, over 200 very large food bank warehouses dot the American landscape, distributing billions of pounds of free or nearly free food annually to over 60,000 emergency food sites (Feeding America, 2017). Again, a short historical view tells a tale: not a single warehouse or regionally oriented food bank existed prior to the late 1970s. Today, both their number and growing size often make them the most visible and dominant nonprofit organization in many communities.

With the intent of reducing obesity and improving local economies, local and state governments have started to play a more prominent role in correcting the failings of the food system. According to a 2012 survey of municipal food policies conducted by Michigan State University, and a follow-up survey in 2015, more and more American cities and towns are playing significant roles with respect to food system activity in their respective jurisdictions (Michigan State University Center for Regional Food Systems, 2013). The National Conference of State Legislatures reviewed the food policy activity of state legislative sessions from 2012 through 2014 and found that 36 states had enacted over 90 bills that created various measures to improve food access and promote food security (Essex, Shinkle, and Bridges, 2015, 1).

As charity feeding sites proliferate, and federal food spending escalates, it is true that tens of millions of Americans are kept from hunger's door. But unfortunately, all of this private and public largesse has not turned the ship around; in fact, it has to throttle up its engines ever harder to just stay even in the face of an ever stronger current of demand. This lack of progress was further affirmed by a Feeding America research brief that used data from 61,000 food client interviews to conclude that "families no longer visit 'emergency food' sources for temporary relief, but rely on food pantries as a supplemental food source" (Echevarria et al., 2011, 7). When we have cash and enough SNAP benefits on our electronic benefit transfer (EBT) card, we go to Walmart. When we don't, we turn to the local food pantry.

Explanations for the lack of progress abound, one being that we live in unprecedented economic times. The Great Recession's wrecking ball scattered us like tenpins before the crushing weight of private greed and inadequate government regulation. As a result, the number of people receiving SNAP benefits soared from 26 million in 2006 to 49 million at the recession's peak. Yet even today, at the end of 2015, with the recession's aftershocks reduced to the barest of tremors, about 45 million Americans remain on SNAP. And while unemployment has dropped below 5 percent as of 2017, almost one-third of all U.S. workers live on wages that are at or below 185 percent of the poverty level, which makes them eligible for some federal nutrition programs (Supplemental Nutrition Assistance Program, 2017).

Recent mortality research by the 2015 Nobel Prize–winning economist, Angus Deaton, and his colleague, Anne Case, puts a tragic face on the declining fortunes of a growing class of Americans. They identified a dramatic rise in death rates for middle-aged white U.S. males due largely to suicide, drug abuse, and physical pain. These growing rates were associated with low education and poor job prospects (Case and Deaton, 2015). More frequently we are finding that hunger, bodies worn down before their time, self-abuse, ill health, and suicide are rife and rising in no-wage or low-wage America.

As far as obesity goes, we have been fighting the battle of the bulge with billions of public and private dollars for nearly 20 years. In spite of Michelle Obama's best dance moves and her tenacious insistence that school meals become healthier, we've only seen a small tick downward in childhood obesity rates.

A Republican Congressional majority that is too ready to trash improved school nutrition standards, and the glacial pace of change from the food industry are both worthy of blame. But as I gaze in disbelief at my home state of New Mexico's overweight and obesity rates for 3rd graders (2015)— 50 percent for Native Americans, 36 percent for Hispanics, 34 percent for African Americans, and 22 percent for whites—I'm depressed by the distance we must travel to reduce such enormous racial and ethnic health disparities (New Mexico Department of Health, 2016).

Though the efforts have been worthy, the results have been troubling. More fundamental and lasting progress will not be made until the numerous submovements that make up the larger food movement learn how to collaborate far better than they do now. We, and I count myself as a participant, must find a way to set common goals and a shared understanding of the problems; we must agree on what progress looks like, which means creating a shared measurement system; our activities don't have to be the same, but they should be mutually reinforcing; the groups, submovements, and major sectors must be in continuous communication so that everyone knows what everyone else is doing; and, ideally, there needs to be a backbone organization that serves as a hub so that the spokes can do their job. What I've described is the collective impact model, which with only a few local and state exceptions does not exist in any meaningful way in the U.S. food movement.

There are many impediments to implementing a collective impact approach, but none of them is insurmountable. For instance, we see the continuing reluctance of national anti-hunger groups—from food banks to SNAP advocates—to upgrade the nutritional quality of emergency food (e.g., more fresh produce at food pantries) and aligning federal food benefits with healthy dietary guidelines (e.g., restricting the use of SNAP benefits to purchase sugary soft drinks). But when groups have gathered at the local and state levels to discuss these issues, increasingly there is a consensus around what needs to be done, and in some cases (e.g., Minnesota Food Strategy, Michigan Food Charter) a common agenda emerges. The growth in local sales taxes on sugary soft drinks is one example of cities taking matters into their own hands.

Another challenge to linking arms for the common good is knowing what counts for each of us, and what each of us counts. If I think that the food movement's success is determined by such things as how many varieties of goat cheese are available at my farmers' market, and your indicator of success is how many pounds of food your pantry gives away, then it's not likely we'll have much incentive to work together. But if we can agree that healthy food for all and a vibrant local farm economy go hand-in-hand, we can devise mutually supportive program strategies that are measurable, thus enhancing our collective impact.

At the national level, groups have been struggling for two decades to join agriculture, environmental and climate, food security, and human health issues into one "joined-up" food policy, most likely through the "Farm Bill." While the realization of that goal could be light-years away, a glimmer of hope came during the spring of 2015 (and faded shortly thereafter) through another national policy moment, which is the five-year update of the nation's Dietary Guidelines. Among its many progressive and insightful features, the expert government panel stated, "Meeting current and future food needs will depend on two concurrent approaches: altering individual and population dietary choices and patterns and developing agricultural and production practices that reduce environmental impacts and conserve resources . . ." (Dietary Guidelines Advisory Committee, 2015). In other words, eat like your life and the life of the planet depend on it.

Additional dietary recommendations addressed household food security and access to healthy and affordable food in so-called food deserts. Nothing this far-reaching in the annals of national food policy had ever been uttered before, and because the sugar, meat, and dairy industries are solidly arrayed against making these scientifically based linkages, the recommendations are not likely to find their way into national policy anytime soon.

Money matters in other ways as well, not just with respect to how it shapes national food policy. Having the financial capacity to take on the wrongs of the food system and to create alternatives is essential. But as the Bible says, money can also be the root of all evil. Private and public funders who do not require meaningful collaboration between like-minded grantees, or at the very least, don't fund the capacity building necessary to develop effective collaborations, are sowing the seeds of fragmentation. Sometimes funding the "glue" that might promote cohesion among many groups is far better than funding a single program activity or organization.

A recent conversation I had with a foundation program officer in Pittsburgh illustrates the dilemma. She noted that her foundation wanted to support collaborative work between its region's food organizations, but at the same time the foundation was swamped by requests from an ever-growing number of these groups. She was particularly perplexed by out-of-state organizations that were seeking multimillion-dollar commitments to replicate models in the foundation's region that had been developed elsewhere, but not necessarily with the collaboration of local organizations.

Each submovement—for example, local food, anti-hunger, community-based food education—has evolved its own methods and tools over time through an uncoordinated and underevaluated process of trial and error, and sometimes each with its own distinct subset of funders, conferences, and professional associations. While this sometimes-crude application of good old American entrepreneurism has led to some powerful innovations, it has also hindered the development of a shared understanding of the causes of our food problems.

With the intent of digging down to root causes, I feel some urgency that we recognize that the single greatest indicator of hunger—and, to a lesser extent, obesity and the ills of the industrial food system—is American income and wealth inequality. As Thomas Piketty's tome *Capital in the 21st Century* (2014) has made abundantly clear, America is the most unequal nation on earth, and it is neither morally nor economically sustainable for the top 10 percent of a nation's income earners to gobble up 50 percent of the income. If current economic policy trends continue, capital accumulation (the top 10 percent control 72 percent of the nation's private capital) and the income divide will only grow greater (p. 264).

The consequences of income and wealth inequality are not limited to how many houses and yachts the nation's top income earners and wealth holders can buy. Keep in mind that America's top 1 percent of income earners is 2.6 million people who can and do exercise a disproportionately large amount of social and political power. They and their elected representatives keep taxes low, suppress the popular will's urge to increase the minimum wage, and maintain a chokehold on the public purse. The lack of financial resources is a good reason that this country's public transportation, educational system, and renewable energy efforts often lag behind those of other developed nations.

If, for instance, we could raise the minimum wage to just $10.10 per hour—an amount already out of date in comparison with cities like Los Angeles and Seattle that are well on their way to $15 per hour—we would reduce SNAP enrollment by 3.1–3.6 million people and the program's cost to the taxpayer by 4.6 billion dollars (West and Reich, 2014). As it stands now, our social and economic policies don't hold the private sector accountable for paying living wages and instead shift the burden for such things as feeding people to the public sector.

Just as Piketty says, "it is hard to imagine an economy and society that can continue functioning indefinitely with such extreme divergence between social groups," it is hard to imagine a food movement functioning effectively without embracing the fight for far greater income and wealth equality (p. 297). To date, a deeper and more robust incorporation of inequality issues into the food movement's agenda has not proceeded much beyond lip service.

In spite of my bleak assessment of the current state of food organization functionality, there are bright spots and opportunities to build on. One promising venue for developing more collaboration is food policy councils (sometimes called "food councils" or "food system networks"). Their numbers have increased by nearly 250 percent in the last five years to 246 in the United States (there are about 50 also in Canada, and they are starting to pop up across Europe), partly due to the growing realization that there is a need to coordinate the work of so many local and state food and food-related organizations (Johns Hopkins Center for a Livable Future, 2015a). As indicated earlier, the local and state governments are stepping up to the food policy plate through thousands of administrative and legislative actions that address specific food system needs. Food policy councils (FPCs) are often the catalyst for these actions. Many local FPCs (e.g., Indianapolis) have also utilized the collective impact model, and some state FPCs (e.g., Massachusetts) have developed statewide food plans.

Some food banks are showing promise as well. Assembled under the progressive umbrella of the "Closing the Hunger Gap" conference, hundreds of creative emergency food activists have met three times over the last five years to discuss how food banks can engage more stakeholders and conduct public policy advocacy that addresses systemic causes of hunger. One example is the North Alabama Food Bank led by the visionary Katherine Strickland. As she put it at the 2015 Portland, Oregon, conference, "the food bank's mission has evolved to shoulder the risk to address poverty," not just treat its symptoms (Closing the Hunger Gap Conference, 2015). To that end, they are employing economic development strategies that provide financial credit to their region's farmers, training farmers in food safety and handling methods, and operating a food hub that has generated $500,000 in local farm sales to schools and the food bank itself.

But only serving one's organizational mission rather than working for a larger common vision is still the norm. Government bureaucracies have yet to break free from silos, academic departments avoid interdisciplinary work, and nonprofit organizations defend their turf with the tenacity of an irritable linebacker. Transformative breakthroughs that can resolve the problems of food security, diet-related illness, and agro-industrialization will only come when the players are aligned like a well-coached team.

Right now, the food system landscape resembles the small town American square which only has room for one statue whose noble presence reinforces the myth that we owe our salvation to a miniscule number of courageous individuals. Just as we must give our sculptors the license to imaginatively represent the common enterprise of the many—raising the "we" above the "me," collaboration among food system stakeholders must be recognized, rewarded, and supported. It is demanding and often frustrating work, but without a commitment to collaborative effort and the principles of collective impact, we can only look forward to a kind of never-ending warfare with hunger and poverty, where the shape of the battlefield shifts from year to year, but a lasting peace is never achieved.

# CHAPTER TWO

# Growth Brings Challenges

Where and when did the food movement begin? Without consulting the Book of Genesis—and to avoid a protracted debate—let's just say it wafted in on some 20th-century breeze making landfall on a relatively undisturbed portion of the American coastline (specifying which one might also start an argument). There, it eventually found fertile ground in the warm heart of a young man disaffected no doubt by his mother's cooking and a persistent bowel irritation traced back to a steady diet of Twinkies. Finding a female companion whose soul was filled as much by a desire for joy as by the same simmering discontent, the first revolutionary food couple turned their backs on their local A&P supermarket and roadside diner.

Somehow, they managed to stay warm that winter by feeding ripped pages from their mothers' *Good Housekeeping Cookbook* into a rusty woodstove. Wide-eyed and innocent, they planned a spring garden, which to them was only a concept they had overheard from their grandmothers. A Garden of Eden it wouldn't be, but what did bear fruit that first season was less a story of bounty and nourishment than a story of human agency. Together, they had rejected a convention that, at worst, contained a destructive power that was only just becoming known, and at best was so overwhelmingly mediocre that acceptance would consign their spirits to the pale ash-bin of a paltry life.

This is my food movement creation story, and in spite of the lack of evidence, I'm sticking to it. Disgruntlement balanced against hope; failure offset by a fire in the belly and an untiring urge to innovate. The words of Mark Twain always ring true, "All you need is ignorance and confidence: success is sure to follow." We must maintain a faith that the seed, planted somewhere, sometime, by someone we don't know, had both a purpose and a vigor to not only bear good fruit but to change, adapt, and set forth an unending chain of resilience and diversity.

Those who claim membership in the food movement abhor the status quo and flock to change like moths to light. Passing through New Haven, Connecticut, during the warmer seasons you'll find City Seed Mobile Farmers' Market. In what now seems like an age-old struggle to get good food to every underserved corner of America, the continuum of innovation has taken us from the development of cooperatives, supermarkets, and farmers' markets to small-scale, laser-sharp methods of bringing food to the people.

In New Haven's case, several lower-income neighborhoods continue to defy efforts to find cost-effective access to affordable and healthy food. The mobile farmers' market is nothing more than a single-axle, 12-by-6-foot trailer that supports a perfectly adorable, custom-made farm shed whose side panels open up to a full display of Connecticut-grown produce. The farm stand finds its way to neighborhoods with insufficient population density and purchasing power, to say nothing of being victims of racism and neglect, to support even a small farmers' market.

For 15 weeks in the summer and fall, the farmers' market makes its rounds to 16 different sites in the city where it takes cash; Women, Infant, and Children Program (WIC) and Senior Farmers Market Nutrition Program vouchers issued by the State of Connecticut; and EBT/food stamp cards, whose value is doubled by private foundation funding. The produce is sourced from several area farms including the Common Ground Charter School, which has a one-acre teaching farm, and Hall's Farm, one of Connecticut's oldest organic farms. In 2014 the mobile farmers' market sold over $17,000 of produce, 15 percent more than 2013. That represented 13,000 pounds of fruits and vegetables purchased from Connecticut farmers. The program includes cooking demonstrations and other food and health-related enrichment activities (personal communication with Caitlin Aylward, mobile market coordinator).

But what the mobile farmers' market stands for is yet another progression in a long line of innovation, learning from others, and connecting the dots. It brings together knowledge of place and community, smart social enterprise thinking, and an aggressive use of public policy to level the playing field. The policies themselves are a product of a continuous evolution that began in the 1980s with the development of special produce vegetable vouchers programs funded by state and federal governments. Designed to serve lower-income mothers and children, later lower-income senior citizens, and then Supplemental Nutrition Assistance Program (SNAP) recipients, the most recent public policy variation on this theme of improving the nutritional health of at-risk groups is the Food Insecurity Nutrition Initiative (FINI) created in The Agricultural Act of 2014 (also known as the "Farm Bill").

Some big projects are the culmination—though I suspect there are never any final culminations—of years of pilot projects, mistakes, and stumbling forward until some partial vision is realized. Such may be the case with a Louisville, Kentucky food hub, touted as the largest in the nation that will provide a virtual one-stop selling destination for farmers and access point for restaurants, processors, and food banks (Rohleder, 2014).

At the other end of the size scale is Aly Lewis in Del Ray Beach, Florida, whose up-by-the-boot-straps nonprofit is turning surplus beeswax from a local beekeeper into lip balm sold in local drug stores. The profits will be used to start community gardens with SNAP recipients and a nearby food bank (personal communication). Seeds are planted, projects emerge, morph, sometimes die, and are reincarnated in some similar but different form. "Let the shapes arise!" as Walt Whitman said.

The food movement has a history that defies a precise assignment of cause and effect. It is reactive, adaptive, and nonlinear. More like evolutionary biology, though moving at a much faster pace, the food movement can change its costumes with the speed of many actors in a Broadway play. Though the movement may be in perpetual motion it does have a history. Consult Michigan State University's Good Food Timeline (http://foodsystems.msu.edu/resources/local-food-movement-setting-the-stage), and you'll be astounded by the volume and diversity of growth. Besides the growth in farmers' markets, food policy councils (FPCs), and farm-to-school projects, the timeline also charts the astronomical growth in SNAP enrollment and the abject failure of the minimum wage to stem the growth in poverty or reduce hunger.

But even here, the food movement strives to keep pace by embracing the cause of low-wage food chain workers and passing innovative legislation such as FINI. The litany of programs and policies is endless, in part due to the openness of innovators and developers to share their wisdom with the next generation of entrepreneurs. This diffusion of ideas and energy across a wide landscape has expedited the process of program reproduction without resorting to cookie-cutter approaches. Each person in his or her own way has assimilated the lessons learned from others and applied them to his or her own place and circumstances.

## Food Movement Participant Survey

As dynamic and flexible as the food movement has been, I wanted to determine if its participants felt it could be strengthened with the hope of increasing its impact. To determine the level of concern about the lack of cooperation and coordination among food movement participants, I conducted a survey of food system activists and academics. I also wanted to know if participants recognize different needs and strategies when thinking about local level versus national work. The survey was sent to nearly 1,800 subscribers to my blog www.markwinne.com. From this group, 193 people responded to a short deadline—about 40 percent of the total number of subscribers who typically open my postings. Though not counted because they did not meet the deadline, a few dozen more responded late. I have summarized the report's findings here (Winne, 2017).

The survey was in two parts: a series of single choice questions (agree/disagree along a five-point spectrum), and open-ended responses to the same questions. The respondents were staff or volunteers at nonprofit food organizations (50%), employees of government agencies (9%), students/staff/faculty at a college or university (15%), workers for a commercial food operation including farms (9%), and "other" (17%).

The following are the compilation of responses to the single choice questions:

- Sixty-seven percent of the respondents currently belong to a food coalition, food network, or FPC.
- Sixty-four percent said their awareness of the work of other food organizations in their region has increased "a lot" as a result of belonging to one of the above groups.
- Fifty-seven percent said that belonging to one of these groups has helped advance their own organization's mission.
- Eighty-seven percent either strongly agree (61%) or somewhat agree (26%) that their region would benefit from organizations working together more closely.
- Eighty-nine percent either strongly agree or somewhat agree that the nation's food movement would be improved through greater food organization cooperation.
- Respondents said that conferences (57%), online forums (54%), and more extensive leadership (69%) would improve cooperation among food organizations.

That over two-thirds of the respondents reported that they did belong to some kind of coalition is an indication that food activists are certainly active outside of their own organizations or institutions. They benefited from belonging to these kinds of organizations since nearly two-thirds responded that they had increased their awareness of the work of other groups, and 57 percent indicated that belonging to a coalition also served to advance the mission of their own organization. But in spite of what appears to a strong interest in "joining up" with others, respondents registered a strong affirmation (87% regionally, 89% nationally) of the need for more coordination and cooperation between food organizations. From a little over half to two-thirds of the respondents identified conferences, online forums, and better leadership as the ways to achieve those ends.

The data indicated that respondents generally agree with this book's premise that the food movement would benefit from greater levels of coordination, especially at the national level. Respondents offered a wealth of suggestions on how to encourage cooperation, differing slightly on regional versus nationwide tactics. At both the regional and national levels, respondents frequently commented on a need to increase opportunities for *communication and sharing of information*. At both levels, but particularly the regional, respondents commented on a need for stronger *leadership*. At both levels, but particularly the national, they expressed a need for better ways of *organizing and integrating different stakeholders* in the food movement. Especially at the national level, respondents commented on a need for *policy and/or systemic social change*. Especially at the regional level, they expressed a desire for more *funding*.

Respondents generally had favorable opinions of the FPCs they belong to (129 of the 193 respondents indicated they belonged to an FPC), but offered many ideas for how their functioning could be improved. Respondents frequently mentioned that the functioning of their FPCs would improve from better ways of *organizing and integrating different stakeholders*, increased opportunities for *communicating and sharing information*, and more *funding*.

Suggestions for improving the functioning of FPCs most frequently fell under the categories of needing to better *organize and integrate stakeholders* and needing to be more *inclusive of diverse voices*. Multiple respondents remarked on including the perspective of the private sector: "We need to involve more farmers, restaurants, and businesses in order to have an accurate picture of our food system and for better communication between all sectors." Others commented on a desire for more diverse membership: "Ensuring the diversity of people that comprise FPCs results in a policy framework developed by a broader base of people with strong potential for generating a more integrated approach to change." Some commented on the need for FPCs to reach across barriers to access: "We must maintain a strong commitment to engaging with the community's most disenfranchised."

A need for *increased resources and funding* was the second most frequently mentioned theme. These comments often spoke to the challenge of running an organization with volunteer-only personnel: "We would hugely benefit from funds to hire a part-time or full-time staff position. Everyone has full-time jobs and participates because they know it's important, but they don't have extra time to organize meetings and projects." Some respondents lamented time challenges: "The biggest struggle is finding time when everyone can meet and contribute to developing the council."

Responses also frequently mentioned a need to increase *opportunities for communication and sharing information*: "Listservs, webinars, and workgroups work well to keep people connected and active on a continuous basis. Conferences and workshops are also helpful." Others commented on a need to *educate the public* about the work FPCs do: "Much needed is a means to educate municipal and community partners about food systems." Another recurring theme was the need to *monitor* the results of FPC initiatives and hold their participants *accountable* for results: "As one of the more established organizations in the group, I often feel as if we are giving more than we are getting from our participation in the group which makes it hard to participate when things get really busy." Another wrote: "We need surveys and tools to measure effectiveness."

A large number of respondents (108) answered "yes" when asked: "Are there any other place(s) outside of your organization besides a food coalition/network/policy council where you turn to for help in advancing your organization's mission (excluding funding sources)?" From their answers, eight recurring categories emerged. Respondents most frequently answered that they turn to *other organizations* (48%). Organizations listed included large NGOs, local food nonprofits, social service providers such as homeless shelters and workforce development programs, and nonprofit-for-profit partnerships such as farmers' markets. The second most frequent category was *academic sources and/or experts in the field* (32%). This category included university departments and professors doing food-related research, the Johns Hopkins Center for a Livable Future, local research institutions, experienced professionals in various fields, and scholarly texts.

Another recurring theme was the need for improved *leadership*: "The challenge is always leadership. We are so busy with our own organizations that it's hard to exercise leadership in these coalitions." Another respondent pointed to *training* and mentoring as a way to better utilize food leaders: "There are many people who have been working in advancing more sustainable and equitable food systems; shifting these people from a direct-action role to a training/mentoring role, particularly across organizations, might be a great way to catalyze cooperation."

The conclusion I draw from the survey, albeit small in size and somewhat selective in scope, is that the urge for connection is high and that the recognition of the power of collective impact is strong. People are finding ways of working together and securing resources, both financial and technical, but they often come up short. There is a strong consensus that much more needs to be done to pull together the various elements of the food movement, both locally and nationally, to create a more cohesive force for change.

The food movement has had something of the energy and innovation of Silicon Valley and the dot.com explosion. The hallmarks of the food movement include continuing evolution of ideas, projects, and policies; diversification of strategies and products; learning from others and an environment of near-transparency, and a kind of imaginative social entrepreneurism that never seems to find a boundary or final resting place; and publicity and press that would be the envy of any professional marketing campaign.

But with this growth, often chaotic and rarely coordinated, comes a surge of energy that sometimes threatens to blow out the grid. While generally avoiding fast food, the food movement is moving so fast that you sometimes feel as if the burgers and fries are coming at you faster than they do at a downtown McDonald's at lunchtime. So, like a writer whose desk is about to collapse from the weight of too many documents, we are forced to select, define, and ultimately give our attention to only a small portion of them.

## Taking a Look at the Numbers

### Digital

Between February 8 and 14, 2016, I received 82 unduplicated e-mails that each represented a distinct, food-related meeting, event, publication, e-magazine, news summary, upcoming conference, request to take action, or announcement. And yes, "unduplicated," meaning that I am not counting multiple e-mails for the same item, for example, reminders of a meeting or a second and third nudge to take action, spam, junk, Facebook notifications, or personal e-mails from friends and colleagues.

After analyzing the "personal" category, I must confess to some embarrassment when I realized how my social life had merged with my professional life. Separating the two was not easy as my counting enabled me to discover. More of my socializing time with colleagues—the beer (or two) after work, an evening reception or special fundraising dinner for a nonprofit food organization, and even political events that enable you to cultivate policymakers' interest in food issues—have become a larger part of how I fill the space between official work time and sleep.

I also belong to five food-related list serves that during the same week sent me 95 *separate* notices about upcoming conferences, new reports and studies, requests for information, or simply alerting me to something the sender considered interesting, important, urgent, or dangerously close to doomsday. As with my regular e-mails, these messages did not include multiple postings on the same subject or exchanges that might have ensued between listserv members on the same topic—the so-called thread. And as a curmudgeonly baby-boomer with a sometimes-antisocial attitude toward social media— I started my professional career with manual typewriters, mimeograph machines, and rotary dial phones with no buttons—I am not counting Tweets, Instagram, or texts in the onslaught of information.

On February 10 of that week, I counted all the pages of food-related attachments, e-magazines, newspaper articles, reports and studies, and other substantive documents (not the e-mail cover page, forms, or other incidental items) that I received on that one day. This is material that is at least of tangential interest to me, and that I would make a good faith effort to at least scan or selectively read. They totaled 176 pages. There was nothing unusual about this day or the entire seven-day period of this sample week. In other words, I would submit that this is a "normal" informational week for me on food topics. For some colleagues of mine who inhabit the dark caves or stratospheric heights of the 24/7 cyber food cycle, this would be considered a light week.

## Listservs

The Community Food listserv, popularly known as "Comfood," is one example of how listservs have loaded the food movement's airwaves with a near infinite number of communication vectors. Like most lists, Comfood's origins were humble and served an emerging need for more efficient communication between a relatively small number of people, that is, to "network" those working in various parts of the food movement who had no or limited opportunities to meet face-to-face.

Following a Northeast regional food summit held in Hartford, Connecticut in 1997, the organizers, who included myself, Hugh Joseph and Molly Anderson of Tufts University, and Kathy Ruhf from the New England Small Farm Institute, were wrestling with ways to retain and channel the energy generated by the 200 or so summit attendees. They had come from nine Northeast states and were eager to "stay in touch," learn from one another, and possibly develop a common regional food system agenda. The technology to create and operate listservs was just emerging, and so the organizers decided to apply it to this opportunity in hopes that it would nurture a regional network. With technical support from Tufts, the Northeast Food ("NEFood") listserv was launched. I can recall how pleased we all felt when NEFood's subscriber list reached 300 by the year 2000.

Almost as soon as NEFood was up and running, the Community Food Security Coalition (CFSC) adopted the same technology to connect people in the growing community food security movement, but this time on a national scale (eventually to become international). As with NEFood, Tufts and Hugh Joseph provided the "know-how" and leadership for Comfood. It started with a few hundred subscribers and didn't reach 3,000 until 2009, but jumped to 5,000 in 2011. It now stands at over 6,200. Absent other venues to reach significant numbers of people in the food movement, Comfood became the "go-to" place for community food practitioners, researchers, and students to place queries, notices, share knowledge and "how-to" information, and of course the occasional rant. Its size as well the variety of postings, especially in a few categories, required at least one "subdivision." The large number of employment postings led to the creation of a separate list in 2012 called ComfoodJobs, which passed the milestone of 10,000 subscribers in May 2016. That number certainly reflects the strong interest in food system careers and, to a lesser degree, the growth in food system employment (more later on what those jobs look like).

There are many more such lists that target the food movement, and many people are on multiple lists. One Chicago-area food activist reports that in addition to being on the two Comfood lists, she's also a member of Chicago Advocates for Urban Agriculture (2,100 subscribers), Sustain Evanston (130), Illinois Local Food Coalition (253), the Johns Hopkins Center for a Livable Future Food Policy Networks (1,100), and the Women, Food and Agriculture Network (372) (personal e-mail contact, 2015).

The digital flow of food information represents only a few ice crystals glazing the proverbial iceberg. These examples are noted here because they affect me immediately and provide evidence that the size of the food movement has exploded in depth and breadth. But beyond the stuff splattered across my computer screen, more substantial documentation of the food movement's evolving complexity must also be noted.

Staying with the connections between food and agriculture, health and nutrition, public policy, programs and projects, community development, environment and climate change, sustainability, labor, access, poverty, security and insecurity—the boundaries roughly prescribed by this book—we see a torrent of food-related activity that shows no evidence of abating. Even holding aside such prolific categories that are narrowly devoted to cooking, diet and weight loss, or gardening—topics that this book does not address directly—the rate of growth is significant.

## Books

In the book category, there has been a steady increase in food issue titles published since just 2005 (by "issue" I mean a substantive area of food-related concern such as health, hunger, or agriculture). The following five categories, which themselves could be broken down into numerous subcategories, provide some examples and illustrations.

(Note: An Amazon search was conducted in February 2016 to identify how many titles within five food-related categories were published that year; the numbers, therefore, are not cumulative but simply apply to that year's releases. But Amazon searches are an imprecise research tool depending on how much one wants to narrow or widen any particular search. If a search was expanded to "food," for instance, thousands of titles appeared for 2005. If it was limited to "food systems" only 52 appeared for that year. In the interest of being conservative, I narrowed the searches as much as possible. Even then, these numbers should not be regarded as exact data sets but as an indication of general trends. And lastly, our understanding of how to define an issue, and therefore categorize a book, changes over time. "Food System," for instance, is a term that was not well understood or even commonly utilized in 2005, but as its use grows so does its understanding.)

## Food System Category

2005:    52
2010:    217
2015:    372

Sample Titles and Authors: *Earth Democracy: Justice, Sustainability, and Peace* by Vandana Shiva; *Food Security Governance: Empowering Communities, Regulating Corporations* by Nora McKeon; *The Chain: Farm, Factory, and Fate of Our Food* by Ted Genoways.

## Food Movement Category

2005:    13
2010:    54
2015:    103

Sample Titles and Authors: *Food First: Selected Writings from 40 Years of Movement Building* by Teresa K. Miller and Tanya M. Kerssen; *Organic Struggle: The Movement for Sustainable Agriculture in the United States* by Brian K. Obach; *Human Rights and Food Sovereignty Movement: Reclaiming Control* by Priscilla Claeys.

## Food Policy Category

2005:    53
2010:    136
2015:    241

Sample Titles and Authors: *Food Policy: Looking Forward from the Past* by Janel Obenchain and Arlene Spark; *Soda Politics: Taking on Big Soda (and Winning) (1st edition)* by Marion Nestle; *The Food Activist Handbook . . .* by Ali Berlow and Alice Randall.

## Hunger Category

2005:    148
2010:    231
2015:    929

Sample titles and authors: *Growing Up Empty* by Loretta Schwartz-Nobel; *The Stop* by Nick Saul.

## Food Justice Category

2005:    2
2010:    11
2015:    27

Sample Titles and Authors: *Food Justice* by Robert Gottlieb and Anupama Joshi; *Just Food: Philosophy, Justice and Food* by J.M. Dieterle (Editor); *Food Deserts in Vermont: Rural Justice, Equity, and Access in the Green Mountains* by Jesse C. McEntee.

## Sustainable Agriculture Category

2005:    168
2010:    454
2015:    587

Sample Titles and Authors: *Permaculture for the Rest of Us . . .* by Jenni Blackmore; *One-Straw Revolutionary: The Philosophy and Work of Masanobu Fukuoka* by Larry Korn.

The number of food book titles, their growth and volume to say nothing of their near-limitless diversification in topics, speaks not only to the size of the food movement book market but also to the challenge of building the movement. If many people read only a few titles such as they did in the 1970s with *Diet for a Small Planet* by Francis Moore Lappé for instance, or in the first decade of the 21st century as they did with *The Omnivore's Dilemma* by Michael Pollan, then life might be simpler. We'd be inspired by more or less the same thing and would be more likely to act in unison. But the human experience doesn't accept a status quo; it's dynamic and always in flux. One successful entry into a new, yet untested market is soon followed by many entries that attempt to build and expand on their predecessors' success. In doing so, of course, they hope to illuminate new territory, shed light on new knowledge, or catalyze a new cause or variation on an existing cause. Whether driven by ego, ideology, or a genuine urge to add to the store of human knowledge, the human quest to express oneself in books or any other appropriate media is never sated.

As our understanding of the food system grows and our need to apply that understanding increases, our knowledge strains at the confines of single volumes or the space limitations of book shelves. Hence the need to compile, catalogue and consolidate information. The yearning for knowledge that is indeed encyclopedic will, not shockingly, eventually produce an encyclopedia. This was the case in 2015 when *The SAGE Encyclopedia of Food Issues* appeared in three volumes spanning a combined 1,664 pages and selling for $395. The reach of its topics is considerable, though their individual treatment is not comprehensive which, of course, is what you'd expect from an encyclopedia. While you can find almost anything that you might imagine about food issues between its six covers, the major contribution of such a publication to the food movement and food issues is its mere existence—we have built a mountain of knowledge from a trillion scraps of experience and expression.

I learned, for instance, that in 1997 "Chowhound" lays claim to being the first food blog. As of 2013, there were 18,000 blogs on all aspects of food (this author included among them), and most likely there are more today (Szymanski, 2015, 136–140). Their diversity of opinions and followers, like the proliferation of listservs and e-mail flows, tweets, and Facebook posts, are a testament to the size and complexity of the food movement. But they also point to what is the downside of human interaction in the age of the Internet—an inadvertent slide into a narrowing of choices and a selection of interactions rather than a widening of our social and intellectual spaces. We may interact frequently with more people on the Internet, but those people are more like us and more likely to share our opinions. This process of self-selection has the equal and opposite reaction of erecting barriers between us and others. *New York Times* columnist Frank Bruni wrote, "We construct precisely contoured echo chambers of affirmation that turn conviction into zeal, passion into fury, disagreements with the other into the demonization of it," with result that we question their wisdom, even their system and find safe-harbor with the "group-think of micro-communities, many of which we've formed online" (Bruni, 2016).

## Books and Food Policy

SAGE has entries on federal food assistance programs that started with the first version of the food stamp program in 1939 designed to reduce agricultural surpluses, increase farm prices, and provide some food relief to the poor. Though suspended during World War II, it would be revived and reinvented by an executive order of President John F. Kennedy and then by an act of Congress in 1964. The food stamp program, later renamed the SNAP would be joined over the ensuing years by 15 additional nutrition assistance programs including the National School Lunch Program (actually established by President Harry Truman in 1946) and the Women, Infant and Children Program (signed into law by President Richard Nixon in 1972). These programs would collectively come to cost the taxpayer well over $100 billion annually, and would be authorized by Congress, generally every five years, in what are generically referred to as either the Child Nutrition Act or the Farm Bill (Hall, 2015, 625–630).

SAGE tells me that the first Farm Bill in 1933 was 24 pages long. The most recent version that passed in 2014 was 357 pages, a fact that has implications beyond increased printing costs (Lehrer, 2015, 453–458; U.S. Department of Agriculture (USDA), 2014). Collectively the 12 titles that now make up the Farm Bill are the heart and soul of our nation's food and agriculture policies and, to a lesser extent, our health and welfare policies. But less obvious to those who may only follow these issues from a distance are how they represent a rapid evolution in public awareness, our understanding of human health and nutrition, the politics of public spending, and again, a diversification and growth in specialized interests. The advocacy organizations and professional associations spawned by this growth and segmentation of programs—and who fuel the program's growth as well—don't necessarily work to ensure a consistent and unified response to critical human needs; they primarily serve their mission, which is to protect, expand, and enhance their respective program(s).

The extraordinary compilation of food facts in the SAGE encyclopedia will certainly help students and journalists write papers and articles about various segments of the food system. For others, the information merely constitutes the stuff we use to amuse and amaze our friends with. But when we examine the many parts of the food system that are described or catalogued separately throughout the encyclopedia, trends emerge, which deserve interpretation and analysis. Let's take the subject of "local food," which is sometimes associated with organic and/or sustainably produced food, but more importantly has been integral to what, if not a true food revolution, is at least a major insurrection.

Within the section on community-supported agriculture (CSA), we locate some historical roots in Japan where a group of women in 1965 grew concerned enough about the loss of farmland and traditional (local) food sources to band together with farmers to form a kind of cooperative (*teikei* being the Japanese word that best defines CSA). In 1984, the first application of this concept in the United States can be found at Indian-Line Farm in western Massachusetts and the Templeton-Wilton Community Farm in New Hampshire. Like every food or agriculture innovation that results from a newly planted seed, many varieties, shapes, and sizes will spring forth, often without bearing much resemblance to the mother plant. So just 25 years later, in 2009, the CSA count in the United States had reached 2,932 representing many hybridizations of the original (Spurling, 2015, 266–270).

If the local food movement has an iconic face, it's the farmers' market with its pop-up tents and pick-up trucks arranged around the town square. Before their steroid-like growth of the past two decades, the number of farmers' markets and their variants (e.g., public market places) had been steadily declining since the beginning of the 20th century. The best estimate at the nadir in the early 1970s of that rustic, outdoor, direct from the farmer shopping experience was 340 locations across the country (Brown, 2002).

Today, according to the USDA, which conducts an annual count of farmers' market, the number is well above 8,500 (USDA, 2017). During the years of accelerated growth and rising popularity, different interests have argued over the true definition or "authenticity" of farmers' markets, especially with regard to the source of goods sold in them (e.g., were the goods grown by the farmer/seller or by someone, somewhere else?). But the issue that has provoked ongoing controversy and precipitated the most responses have been whether farmers' markets are nothing more than an elitist shopping arcade, a kind of Nordstrom's of food, or do they truly serve all income levels need for healthy, affordable food.

Due in large part to this debate, nonprofit advocates and sometimes private institutions have partnered with local, state, and federal governments to create publicly funded programs such as the WIC/Farmers Market Nutrition Program, the Seniors/Farmers' Market Nutrition Program, the FINI, and the expansion of the Electronic Benefit Transfer program (swipe-card payment technology for SNAP recipients) to farmers' market sites. Usually at a smaller scale, private and philanthropic initiatives have also supported and funded similar incentives, "Double-up Bucks" that increase the value of SNAP benefits used at farmers' markets being the most notable. Various state and national groups have organized at different times to support the development of farmers' markets, and in particular, to advocate for a couple of policy initiatives at both state and national levels. At the state level, the New Mexico Farmers Marketing Association is one good example, while nationally, the Farmers' Market Coalition is the most recent incarnation of various efforts to educate and advocate the needs of farmers' markets (New Mexico Farmers' Market, 2017; Farmers Market Coalition, 2017).

Lastly, as yet one more manifestation of the fervor stirred up over "local food," the farm to school movement has emerged as a powerful force in opening up institutional markets for regional farmers. The simultaneous benefit of course has been bringing fresh, locally grown food into the school cafeteria. The first formal farm to school efforts were in Santa Monica, California and North Florida in 1997 (personal communication with Rodney Taylor and the North Florida Growers Coop). (While it has failed to find its way into the literature, this author ascertains that he and his colleagues at the Hartford Food System organized the farm to school program in the Hartford, Connecticut public schools in 1998, which is notable for the fact that this was the first non-year around, cold climate growing region to develop farm to school.) But what stands out more than these modest beginnings is the fact that there are now over 42,000 schools in the country, K through 12, that have some form of a farm to school programs. That's over 42 percent of all the nation's public schools, and according to the USDA, the collective farm to school initiative has made a local and regional economic impact of slightly under $800 million (USDA, 2016). Initially founded and nurtured by the CFSC (more on CFSC later), a national entity now called the National Farm to School Network has emerged as a highly competent nationwide organizer and proponent for farm to school.

Many other submovements like CSAs, farmers' markets, and farm to school have similarly evolved over past three decades. They include food hubs, which are brick and mortar facilities or simply sites that aggregate larger quantities of food from multiple sources, primarily local farmers, and then redistribute the food to larger buyers such as schools. The National Good Food Network was founded in 2007 (the same year as the National Farm to School Network (NFGN)) to support development of food value-chain activity and food hubs. From information gleaned from the NFGN website, there appear to be over 300 food hubs, and since the term itself has evolved to mean different things to different people, it is difficult to say where and when the first one was established. It's reasonable, however, that their growth mirrors that of other submovements (Michigan State University Center for Regional Food Systems, 2016).

Stepping outside of the local food ring we find an arguably older submovement, which is referred to as emergency food, food banks, or sometimes anti-hunger. Its trajectory in terms of numbers and velocity exceeds those of all others combined. This submovement's first manifestation was settlement houses which were established in large cities as early as the 19th century. The rise of soup kitchens and related charitable services, for example, the Salvation Army, followed a similar historical path. But it wasn't until 1967 when the world's first food bank was founded in Phoenix, Arizona (Power, 2015, 553). Since then, so-called emergency food programs have skyrocketed. Over 60,000 food pantries and soup kitchen facilities exist across the country, many of them supported by over 200 giant warehouse facilities called food banks (Feeding America, 2017). Collectively, this effort gave rise to the national organization first known as America's Second Harvest, but later to change its name to Feeding America, whose membership essentially comprises the large food banks.

We'll leave this enumeration and description of food submovements for now. The point of providing this partial list (many large segments have been left out for now, e.g., obesity reduction and healthy eating initiatives, the plight of farmworkers and other food chain workers) is to underscore a process that has occurred repeatedly over the course of the food movement's evolution: projects, usually small in scale, develop to meet a need or to address a problem in a specific place (community, city); these projects are replicated elsewhere, often introducing some variation and innovation; these projects, having spread out across the country, begin to join together as an affinity group to support skill development and knowledge sharing, and to develop a common agenda, usually funding or policy-related, that enables further growth and replication; local, state, or regional associations are formed, often followed by a national association.

Though this process undoubtedly strengthens the individual initiative (submovement) and draws an ever-growing number of followers to at least one sector of the larger food movement, it also defines a turf, an idiosyncratic language or jargon, and a set of goals that are unique to its own existence and expansion. Like biological organisms, these systems of social organization form their own means of protection, survival, differentiation, and enhancement, and even create their own ecosystems. But the ecosystems consist largely of their own members thus lacking the rich diversity of inclusion with other submovements. While there are some lines of communication between the respective submovements, mutual support and identification of common goals between them are limited or nonexistent.

Does this matter? The hypothesis of this book is that it does matter because the resolution of profound food problems like the ones we face today require the collective action of all the submovements. In other words, they require a systems approach because the problems have a uniquely intersecting set of relationships that need to be understood and acted upon in a coordinated fashion by all groups. Creating numerous fiefdoms that share a broad and varied food system landscape but devote all their resources to their own perpetuation will not win the larger war. Yes, they may grow stronger individually, but without a plan for mutual defense or cooperation they will fail to realize a much larger food system vision, which is increasingly necessary to be defined and then implemented. Even worse, their lack of solidarity leaves them susceptible to being picked off one at a time like chickens in the night by the wily fox who has found his way into the hen house.

## Food Films

For sheer mass appeal and for bringing the masses into food movement's house of worship, nothing has succeeded like documentary films, especially those that take on the industrial food system. *Food, Inc.* was among the top five grossing documentary films in 2009 (Nash Information Services, 2017). Over the past few years, commercial food films, to say nothing of noncommercial films made for a variety of educational, public interest, and community benefit purposes, have become a popular part of the local food scene. No food event or conference would be complete without a screening of one or more food films (as a speaker at many such events I have lost count of how many times I've had to sit through another showing of *Food, Inc.*).

No attempt to list, review, or catalogue the hundreds of food films is made here because a separate book would be required to fulfill that task. Just the list of "Best of . . ." or "My Picks . . ." was daunting. Grist has its list of "26 Food Films You Have to Watch." Epicurious has its "Top 10 Food Films." Serious Eater has "12 of Our Favorite Food Movies." And Lettuce Eat Kale has its "10 Top Documentary Food Films." With little effort, I found a dozen more such preferential proclamations.

Popularization of a subject, especially via media, can have its beneficial effects. Millions of Americans have gained at least some knowledge of the threats to the food supply, and many have certainly altered their food choices. Consumers are flocking to retailers such as Whole Foods and their local farmers' markets in search of food that does not bear the sins of the industrial food system, at least as they are portrayed in film. The world's largest food corporations are reducing sugar, salt, and fat content in response to consumers' heightened awareness over the health risks associated with these ingredients. But even those dietary concerns are eclipsed by eaters more dominate interest in the sources of their food—"where and how was it produced?" is now a bigger question than "what's in my food?"

This shift, not necessarily sanctioned by scientific evidence, is due in large part to mass media's oversimplification of complicated food, agriculture, and health issues. A 60-minute film renders large food corporations as purveyors of poison; the corporations retaliate in-kind with massive ad blitzes touting the safety of their products and the need to feed a hungry world; and government experts and professionals who can normally be counted on to render objective opinions are caught in the cross-fire between political, advocacy, and industry groups. Truth is hard to find, science and data are misused, and fear and emotion rule the day. We now have a condition where many more people than in the past have a little bit of knowledge about different parts of the food system and food supply, but not enough evidence-based, comprehensive information and analysis to make the best choices possible (the communication problem will be discussed in more depth later in this book).

In my home community of Santa Fe, New Mexico, a small but vocal group of citizens had viewed several anti–genetically modified organism (GMO) films at the same time that a national anti-GMO advocacy organization had come into the state. That organization had a single agenda, which was to pass legislation that would ban GMO ingredients and crops and require mandatory labeling of food products. The citizen group had prevailed upon some Santa Fe City Councilmembers to sponsor an ordinance that would require all food products sold in Santa Fe to carry a GMO label if they contained such ingredients. The ordinance would have also banned the use of GMO seed in the County. They had also prevailed upon a state senator to introduce a similar statewide bill in the New Mexico legislature.

I'm personally in favor of providing as much product information at point of purchase as possible even though the evidence doesn't necessarily support labeling's efficacy. But all of the proposals by the citizen group and the outside organization were illegal, impractical, or politically unfeasible. When the Santa Fe Food Policy Council (I am a member of that body) attempted to widen, and reframe the discussion to include a proactive plan to raise up the value of locally produced food and to place equal weight on consumer information regarding fat, sugar, and salt, the anti-GMO citizens group adamantly said, "No." They were single-mindedly focused on banning GMOs because the films and the advocacy organization had made that the only issue that mattered.

In an ideal world, people would use films to augment their information from what might be considered less entertaining, but more objective and comprehensive sources. In the same way that an avalanche of food books has hindered the creation of a unified food movement, food flicks have oversimplified complex problems, divided groups into camps, and ratcheted up emotions to a fever pitch, which can, at certain times, undermine a group's credibility.

These developments may portend a larger and deeper cultural problem with respect to how people are getting their information today. As one Alabama food organizer told me, "The people I'm working with won't read anything. If you want to impart information, you can't use more than a two-minute video." Taking the statement at face value, I must ask if this is simply the popularization of one medium over another, a fad, a reaction to too much stimuli from too many sources, or some kind of dumbing down of education and thought. Taken together, they have potentially troubling consequences for unifying a more powerful food movement, and perhaps even more ominous outcomes for American society in general.

## Food Studies

California food activist and colleague Hank Herrera joked with me once that "Colleges and universities are afraid of losing their accreditation if they don't have a food studies program." While it may take more than the lack of food courses to sully their academic reputations, he is right that institutions of higher learning have become a hotbed of food activity. From food departments to programs to courses to student farms to demands for dining services food that not only tastes good but is sustainably and fairly sourced, at times it seems that food is supplanting football as the number one diversion on the nation's campuses.

The full-page *New York Times* advertisement made it clear what the University of California San Diego's priorities were with title and subtitle lines that read: "Food Solutions for the 21st Century: Improving Food Supply in a Warmer World; Feeding Bodies and Minds with Urban Agriculture; Breeding Drought-Resistant Plants to Feed the Planet" (*New York Times*, May 31, 2015, p. 5). As colleges and universities pile on food courses and programs, presumably in response to a perceived market demand, it's not surprising that they will find multiple ways to pitch themselves to the minds, hearts, and stomachs of prospective students. There is the one that combines noble purpose, science, and a great career such as UC San Diego is doing, but there is also the more generalist, liberal arts, and even social justice appeal of the food studies programs that are flourishing across the country.

The following description from the University of Oregon's Food Studies Program website is fairly typical of this second appeal since it offers young people an opportunity to develop a more unified and systems-based approach to food issues.

> Food is central to human life. It is therefore no surprise that the research interests of faculty and students across a wide range of disciplines relate to food in some way. In the social sciences and humanities, for example, scholars examine issues including food access and affordability as well as the cultural significance and representation of food and agriculture. In the natural and applied sciences, researchers explore the biological and ecological dimensions of food systems and food-related health issues. For decades, scholars working in these various fields have highlighted important aspects of food's key position in the human experience over time and across space. Too often though, these streams of inquiry have stayed relatively isolated from one another.
>
> The UO Food Studies Program developed out of a growing recognition that an integrated perspective on food matters is vital to developing fuller understandings of complex food-related issues. Food Studies brings the power of an interdisciplinary approach to widely varied food themes and topics. (University of Oregon Food Studies, 2017)

I began my own "career" (I put the word in quotes because over my 45-plus years of food work, it has always lacked the kind of intentionality I normally associate with a genuine career plan) with food issues during my first weeks as a college freshman (see *Closing the Food Gap*) long before the concept of food studies was even a glimmer in some academic's eye. My work was done in the community because there was absolutely no place to do it in the classroom. That was nearly 50 years ago, and it wasn't until the late 1990s that New York University and Boston University started what are arguably the first formal academic food studies programs in the United States, which were highly differentiated from conventional agriculture colleges at the time where young people typically went to prepare themselves to become a "modern farmer."

According to a 2015 survey of 50 separate U.S. university public health programs by students at the Johns Hopkins Bloomberg School of Public Health, 23 have food system courses (though academics will argue over precisely how many angels can balance on the head of a pin, "food studies" and "food system courses" are roughly similar). The Association for the Study of Food and Society lists 22 U.S. colleges with food study programs. Law schools such as Harvard's and UCLA's have food policy law clinics, which utilize law students to assist communities and nonprofit organizations with food issues. Courses with such titles as "Food Studies: Harvest to Health (University of Washington)," "Obesity Prevention (University of North Texas)," and "Eat, Pray, Regulate: An Analysis of the Current Food Regulatory System (University of Minnesota)" are proliferating. Even my small alma mater, Bates College, jumped boldly into the food studies pond in 2010 when it received an anonymous private gift of $5 million to support the study of food (a two-year, campus-wide meditation called Bates Contemplates Food is described in my book *Food Rebels, Guerrilla Gardeners, and Smart-Cookin' Mamas*). And, of course, none of these programs, surveys, or lists captures the most traditional form of "food education," which we find in the nation's agriculture schools, most of which have vastly augmented their standard offering of crop, animal, and nutrition courses with more cutting-edge programs in economics, public policy, and sustainability (Johns Hopkins Center for a Livable Future, 2015b).

Where does all this study and training lead? In a world increasingly smitten with the notion that the primary purpose of higher education is to train students for the current job market—antithetical in other words, to the "knowledge for knowledge's sake" ideals of a liberal arts education—a broader, multidiscipline food studies education is not the fast track to lifelong prosperity. One review by the North American Food Systems Network of ComfoodJobs' postings for 10 months in 2012 found a total of 576 jobs (private communication with Hugh Joseph, ComfoodJobs list administrator, 2015). However, one-third of these jobs were no-pay or low-pay (internship and volunteer positions) or short-term positions such as AmeriCorps Vista. The rest appeared to be fairly stable jobs at reasonable wages, including educators, researchers, project managers, and nutritionists. But the ComfoodJob site, as stated earlier, has 10,000 subscribers, which implies a significant imbalance—nearly 20 to 1—between job seekers and actual job opportunities.

While not an exact comparison but one that brings up interesting contrasts, the industrial side of the food system coin finds that food and agriculture technology startups are now a $4.6 billion industry. They are drawing heavy investments from the likes of Monsanto and Google. These companies are taking on projects that are trying to reduce food waste, build underground farms, and create lab-grown meatless meat. The USDA has projected that 60,000 high-skilled jobs, including systems analysts, robotics and automation technicians, and GPS and GIS operators, will be needed annually. Currently, only 35,000 college students are graduating with degrees each year in agricultural fields, and these are not food studies majors (Gilpin, 2016).

Perhaps it's unavoidable that stereotypes should emerge from these two educational strategies. On the one hand, we can visualize the lab coat-wearing technician seated in the shiny corporate complex, bent over his laptop and within easy reach of the espresso machine. On the other hand, we see the scruffy, overall-wearing organic farmer loading bushel baskets of produce into the bed of his or her late-model pick-up truck for a drive to the farmers' market. There is much in those contrasting images that speaks, of course, to individual values and lifestyles, and as a member of the college class of 1972, I wish that I had a choice of curricula that would have resulted in either a lab coat or overalls. But like the other elements of the food system that I am attempting to define, the growth and diversification in food, agriculture, and dozens of related and interdisciplinary fields of study may breed a useful and necessary complementarity, or they may sow the seeds of a polarization that frustrates progress and unity.

In a later chapter, I will consider an example of how academic disciplines can break down their siloes in the interest of developing a common food system platform.

## Food Conferences

Let's close out this section with a look at one more popular information source that also serves as a networking and organizing vehicle—food and farm conferences. "Are you going to the National Hunger Conference?" and "Were you at the State Organic Conference? I probably didn't see you because there were so many people!" are examples of what passes for "water-cooler" chatter these days in food movement organizations. Making the scene at the right conference often means traveling a considerable distance and putting a crimp in a small organization's budget. But given the fact that the digital age has yet to find a suitable substitute for real human connectivity, people are more interested than ever in doing what they must to share their passions and learn directly from others "in the flesh."

I went to my first professional conference in 1979. It was held in un-air-conditioned classrooms at the University of Pittsburgh during a stiflingly hot week in August. Three hundred or so people had gathered to hear presenters on the general theme of alternative development strategies for socially and economically disadvantaged communities. Among the speakers were progressive economist Gar Alperovitz and food author and activist Francis

Moore Lappé. The topics covered the waterfront of self-help approaches for revitalizing lower-income neighborhoods including job programs, family health clinics, alternative energy projects, innovative home ownership models, and emerging food initiatives like coops, community gardens, and farmers' markets. The cross-sector interest was high and the enthusiasm for an all-encompassing approach to social and economic problems was intense. I returned home to Hartford with my head spinning from dozens of new ideas.

Not too many multisector conferences that attempted to find common ground followed in years to come. On the food side of the social action agenda, the coop movement would organize their own national conferences, so would community gardeners under the auspices of the National Community Gardening Association as would the farmers' marketers through various nationwide organizations that themselves would further subdivide into specialized interests. Later, as other major sectors emerged in response to the growing cracks in the country's social safety net, anti-hunger organizations and food banks would have their own conferences. The urge to gather face-to-face with one's own kind—to stay within a prescribed comfort zone—would trump any interest in meeting with others with whom you may have common goals but who pursued slightly different programs. Pretty soon every sector that had anything to do with food was hosting its own conference through its own national association: farm to school, nutrition and dietetics, school food service directors, food hubs, state agricultural marketing directors, WIC directors, sustainable agriculture and organic advocates, conventional farming organizations, and small farmers. From one or two cells, they would soon split in half, and those new cells would split again and again until the original cell was unrecognizable.

I have attended the conferences of nearly all of these subgroups, often on multiple occasions. I presented at many of them, and sometimes I was even a conference planner. Unless an emerging new cause had its own national conference and hopefully its own national association, it would develop a nasty inferiority complex. Like a private country club which sought to maintain its exclusivity by denying blacks and Jews membership (my parents belonged to one of those), single focus sectors like the ones I've identified don't want to dilute the conversation by designing their conferences with diverse sectors in mind.

As a member of the conference planning team for the 2004 Kellogg Foundation Food and Society Conference, a team largely made up of foundation staff and grantees, I was stunned to discover that they limited invitations to only those people who subscribed to a narrow agenda of smaller-scale, community-oriented food system principles. Apparently, these Kellogg-determined parameters excluded those who advocated for the tens of billions of dollars in federal food programs (e.g., SNAP, WIC, School Meals) and food banks. At that time, those people and organizations who did that work were the largest and most dominant force fighting food insecurity in the country. I argued that to keep them out of this conference would deny "us" and "them" each other's perspectives and a chance for cross-fertilization. In other words, both food system sectors would lose more than they would gain. The foundation staff relented and designated 10 conference slots (out of 500) for anti-hunger and food bank staff. A small victory though a step in the right direction.

To reinforce the notion that conference attendance is implicitly limited to a special club, participants will often adopt a certain tone, speak in catch phrases and shorthand, and accept basic assumptions as gospel. Much of this follows normal patterns of group behavior as well as the efficiencies necessary to manage any large group of people. But challenging certain group orthodoxies can be met with the same reaction one would get if he or she challenged the primacy of the Pope at a Catholic mass. At another Kellogg Foundation conference held in 2014, a workshop panel presenter made the claim that FPCs were dominated by chambers of commerce. Having worked with dozens of FPCs I knew the claim was patently false, but I also knew such an outrageous statement was countenanced by the listeners who uniformly held an anticorporate bias. When I attempted to challenge the speaker's remark during a break, she suddenly picked up her cell phone when she saw me approaching her. Knowing what my position was, she made it clear that a reasonable debate on the topic was out of the question.

In a similar vein, after I had been invited to speak at two separate anti-hunger conferences and one general statewide food conference, all of which I accepted, I was later "disinvited" after the respective organizations' CEOs had determined that my writings did not adequately support their party lines. By my rough count, I was simpatico with these groups on 80 percent of their substantive programs and policies, but had disagreements with the balance. As to style of presentation, I will say that every time I speak before a group my intention is to open lines of communication and, on some occasions, to promote a robust debate. If I offend people simply to vent my spleen, I know I have failed because they won't hear me, and the divides between us will only widen. My goal as an advocate for change is to find the "radical center" for two or more groups, a place that is a little bit outside each other's comfort zones but where we might both find some new and common ground.

The food movement has divided itself into very righteous and heavily defended compounds. Rob Wallbridge, an organic farmer who works with the Genetic Literacy Project, refers to this "them" and "us" syndrome as "sects and factions, driven apart by ideological dogmas that have nothing to do with reality." He cites the example of three leading food movement spokespersons—Marion Nestle, Michael Pollan, and Anna Lappé—who declined to participate in a food television series sponsored by Monsanto, which is generally regarded as the Darth Vader of the Big Food Corporate Empire. Wallbridge asks what is to be gained when each of us, attending and speaking to people who we already know are in our camp, is doing nothing more than preaching to the choir. Now I find many of Monsanto's actions reprehensible, often aspiring to a level of corporate arrogance heretofore unseen in modern times, but I would find it stirring to debate, argue, and even trade jabs with those whose values are diametrically opposed to my own. Without finding a common platform where dialogue can occur, there's little reason to be optimistic about food system change (Wallbridge, 2014).

The point is that what is said at conferences matters because not only can it define a submovement, it can unite or divide it from other submovements as well from those with whom you radically disagree. The obstacles to productive democratic processes and functional communication are many. They include an obsession with one's ideological beliefs, a need to claim superiority over another group's values or approaches, a lack of confidence in one's own position and beliefs such that the need exists to undermine the credibility of another group, and the competition for public recognition and funding. Assuming that "my way is the right way or the only way" doesn't just threaten the food movement, it is a universal obstacle to constructive human engagement from the interpersonal to the global.

Within the food movement, one great leap forward for unity was the emergence of the CFSC in the mid-1990s. Much more space will be devoted to this organization and the concept of community food security in later sections, but suffice it to say that the organization's bold experiment was to embrace all elements of the food movement by putting forward the broadest agenda possible. Its biggest success in this regard was its annual conference, which grew in attendance and popularity year after year. The last conference, held in 2011 (CFSC folded in 2012), drew 1,200 participants from across North America as well as contingents from Europe, Latin America, and Asia. The story of both CFSC and its conferences points the way to both the possibility for unity within the food movement as well as the enormous challenges that confront it. But conferences of the scope and inclusivity that CFSC attempted, and that other groups have sometimes succeeded in pulling off as well, make it abundantly clear that they have the power to promote unity. In that respect, multi-issue, multisector, and bridge-building conferences deserve more attention.

I've offered this summary review of the sources and venues that inform the U.S. food movement in order to demonstrate that food is not just a fact of life during our meal times but also a concept that consumes our attention in print, online, on screen, on college and university campuses, and in the workplace. Therefore, its influence extends far beyond meeting our basic need for survival. Those who comprise the food movement in ways that go beyond just eating have no uniform message nor do they espouse a one-size-fits-all approach, nor should they. A big, chaotic movement serves a larger purpose of making food issues an omnipresent part of our daily conversation and thought. But like many unchanneled streams meandering across a saturated landscape, the latent power of multiple submovements is never harnessed. As President Barack Obama told the *New York Times*, "You have to leverage different platforms because . . . people aren't part of one conversation; they're part of a million" (Galanes, 2016). How does one leverage those numerous platforms and thus gain the power of those disparate voices? Unless we find a way, we can only be certain that a million conversations will make a very loud noise. Without proper orchestration, however, the truth will be drowned by the din, and the noise will signify nothing.

# CHAPTER THREE

# Food Movement Divisions

Martin Bailkey is a close colleague of mine who has taught at the University of Wisconsin and held a senior staff role within the highly visible Growing Power food justice and farming organization. He once told me, "The food movement carries the essential necessity of its own goals." While I still ponder the exact meaning of that elegant statement, I've come to accept it as a simple recognition that people have organized themselves above and beyond the exigencies of the larger food marketplace. Food, in other words, is such a basic human need and connects so many points in our lives that we as a society cannot safely and reliably consign our provisioning to a single designated actor or set of actors. In some collective sense—as citizens, consumers, and stakeholders—we've chosen to accept responsibility for our food system apart from its nearly infinite number of commercial transactions.

Whether through distrust or the sheer vastness and complexity of the food system, the effort of taking responsibility has spawned many sectors, submovements, and enterprises, social as well as commercial. But given its "essential necessity"—that there is so much at stake—why haven't all these vectors coalesced around a common target, and more importantly, a common method? If we are in agreement about our shared need for food, why then is there no much disagreement over how to realize that need?

Part of the answer is suggested by the "vastness" of the food system, which one large team of academics has been trying to describe for the past six years. From 2011 to 2016, USDA Agriculture and Food Research Initiative made a multimillion-dollar grant to a consortium of 11 university and government agency partners for a project called Enhancing Food Security in the Northeast (EFSNE). The university partners used what they called a transdisciplinary approach involving no less than 16 academic disciplines from the social and natural sciences. Together they researched the depth and breadth of the 12-state (plus the District of Columbia) Northeast food system to learn as much as possible about the region's food production potential and assets. Their larger purpose was to determine what is required to ensure food self-reliance and access to healthy and affordable food for all of the Northeast's residents, seven million of which meet the definition of "food insecure" (Penn State College of Agricultural Sciences, 2017).

As of this writing, the data have been gathered and compiled, preliminary conclusions were drawn and presented to over 100 invited conference attendees in December 2015, and final reports are in the making. While I remain hopeful that the EFSNE project will produce a necessary road map for policy makers and practitioners, all of this work and brainpower may only provide partial answers. At the very least, we do know that it took dozens of highly skilled researchers and their graduate students six years and millions of dollars to get their arms around just one region's food system. Though considerably less epic in its purpose, the EFSNE endeavor invites comparison to the Manhattan Project.

At one level, EFSNE offers us a measure of hope that data—those ineffable particles of information we call facts—when carefully sorted and analyzed, can actually bring us together. Yes, people will argue over what constitutes a "fact," and how to interpret the collections of facts, but as objectively gathered and observed bits of information, they are generally regarded as neutral and as close to the truth as we humans can get. Science, when informed by the collective wisdom of many intersecting disciplines, can achieve a relatively high level of consensus as it seemingly has on the subject of climate change, and may be doing with food systems as well.

But even science runs into a brick wall, especially when the truth it reveals threatens to gore another's ox. This was the unfortunate outcome when a panel of 15 health and nutrition experts assembled at the behest of the U.S. Departments of Agriculture and Health and Human Services to recommend changes to the country's dietary guidelines. This is a process undertaken every five years, which requires the expert panel to review the most recent scientific research and to present their recommendations, based on that research, to the two department secretaries. The revised guidelines, in this case known as "The 2015 Dietary Guidelines for Americans," are finalized, written, and issued by the Secretaries, not the panel. They are the nation's most important health promotion tool since they constitute "official" advice for ordinary citizens on what and what not to eat. Just as important, they strongly influence food regulations and education related to all federal nutrition programs such as Women, Infant, and Children Program (WIC), Supplemental Nutrition Assistance Program (SNAP), and school meals (Department of Health and Human Services, 2015).

In the 2015 process, it became clear that politics had as much sway as science. As reported in *Time* (Heid, 2016), various food industry groups, especially those that represent livestock and meat, were able to dilute the recommendations after they were sent to the Secretaries, that would have advised Americans to eat less meat. The scientific panel also, for the first time in the history of the process, made an explicit link between what we eat and how it affects the environment and the sustainability of our food system. Again, these recommendations argued that more plant-based food and less meat consumption would reduce carbon emissions and conserve water, therefore benefiting the environment. Determining that sustainability—and agriculture's impact on climate change as well—was outside the scope of the panel's work, the secretaries ruled that any discussion of the connections between food choices and their impact on the environment were out of bounds. In other words, the scientific panel's recommendations, uninfluenced and unfettered by any outside interests including the food industry, were partially altered by the two cabinet secretaries once members of Congress, who *were* influenced by the food industry, protested to the secretaries.

There were some "wins" in the final 2015 Guidelines such as recommendations to further reduce sugar consumption, but clearly the power of the purse and politics prevailed in some cases over science. There is reason to believe, however, that the guidelines and the process by which recommendations are made and then accepted present a serious opportunity to promote food movement unity, and that a publicly transparent, evidence-based process can override self-interested industry groups. Over 30,000 people and organizations provided official comment on the recommendations, about 10 times more than for the 2010 version (Office of Disease Prevention and Health Promotion, 2015, personal communication with Angie Tagtow). While many of those comments passionately expressed opposition to the more far-reaching recommendations, for example, the meat and sugar industries, collectively, there was probably more participation from every segment of the food movement than at any other time in recent memory. The recommendations connected human health to diet, to the environment, to access to healthy and affordable food, and to food security. This was a rare moment of unplanned unity achieved through what, at least at the scientific level, was a powerful consensus about the validity of these connections. Though the results were far from successful once filtered through the political screen, the Dietary Guidelines give future food movement activists much to build on and common ground to till. Better organization, outreach, and planning may yield excellent long-term fruit during a future and less politically sensitive (or politically more emboldened) administration.

## Is the Food Movement Really a Movement?

As we'll see from the ensuing discussion, it takes more than science to bridge our differences. Until our knowledge base achieves a level of mastery sufficient to fully explain and manage communication and human behavior, the food movement will be bedeviled by differences in ideology and values, ethical struggles, and the cult of the "food hero." We butt heads over definitions of issues and unconnected public policies, programs, and projects. Funding sources as well as the language we choose to describe our cause drive us apart. A loyalty to one's organizational mission supersedes any attempt to create a shared vision for the movement as a whole. And if that list doesn't fill one with dread, the food movement also suffers from what can only be called an existential crisis, a dark night of the soul wherein its very existence is questioned.

Let's begin this review with that philosophical question: is the food movement indeed a movement, akin perhaps to the civil rights or environmental movements, which from all outward appearances have never suffered from such self-doubt. For Nick Saul, the Canadian food activist and founder of the Community Food Centre *movement*, there is no doubt that he and others like him are part of a movement. In his book *The Stop* (2013), Saul cites the many competing features of the food movement as evidence of its disunity. But he sees this disassemblage of groups more as a cause for celebration than concern, even quoting fellow Canadian food activist and writer Wayne Roberts who uses the term "fusion movement" to describe the movement's diffused but tacitly linked elements. Like some eclectic international buffet where each dish is uniquely different from the next, the perplexed but hungry visitor forfeits the search for any signs of culinary unity in return for the sheer glory of so much tantalizing diversity under one roof. Saul is simply grateful to be a part of the food movement, which he feels, "has become one of the most exciting social projects of our time" (p. 210).

In their book, *Food Policy* (2015), coauthors Janel Obenchain and Arlene Spark offer a slightly different perspective citing 250 years of food activism (starting with the Boston Tea Party of all things) and singling out notable food leaders such as Frances Moore Lappé and Michael Jacobson (founder of the Center for Science in the Public Interest) for their seminal contributions. But in spite of a brisk cataloguing of milestones and events that span from the 1968 CBS documentary *Hunger in America* to the recent state referenda and legislative battles over GMO labeling, Obenchain and Spark rein in their own fervor by saying, "There has not been a watershed moment when the influence of food activists has coalesced into an undeniable movement" (p. 123). In other words, the food movement doesn't have the equivalent of a March on Washington, an Earth Day, or a Selma. Perhaps if it had undertaken a symbolic purging of evil spirits from Monsanto's corporate headquarters, a la Abbie Hoffman and the Yippies' attempt to levitate the Pentagon during a 1960s anti–Vietnam War march, the food movement would not be suffering from philosophical dyspepsia.

Challenges to the food movement's identity and coherence often result from comparisons to other movements. The first is an obsession with the role of key individuals (the food movement doesn't have a Rev. Martin Luther King Jr. equivalent) as leaders with whom the food movement could supposedly not have advanced without. The second is the lack of "big wins" or momentous occasions that might have given the movement the dramatic tipping point it supposedly needs to take it to the World Series. Taking these two problems together, one can imagine a winning baseball team, which manages to stay solidly above .500 without the benefit of a home run hitter or two. Instead, it relies on a lot of singles hitters who manage to get on base regularly and stagger around the diamond enough times to score the necessary runs. Without a Babe Ruth or Hank Aaron, however, such a team gets little press, doesn't regularly sell out the ballpark nor secure big advertisers. But they do keep winning.

As previously mentioned, the food movement has many achievements under its belt in spite of falling short in fulfilling the much sought after goals of ending hunger, reducing unhealthy eating, and moving sustainable food production into a more dominant position. The achievements represent a whole lot of singles, but the inability to conquer our looming food problems isn't due to the lack of home run hitters, it's due to the lack of effective teamwork, that is, a creative application of collective impact. In fact, the role of leadership in the food movement is a bit of the two-edged sword. Yes, ideas and intellectual direction provide any movement with shared core concepts, but an overreliance on a few people—a reliance that sometimes rises to the level of deification—can be a distraction and even undermine the movement's ability to empower grass-roots leadership.

Contemporary movements like Occupy Wall Street and Black Lives Matter have spurned the need for one or even a few dominant leaders in favor of a democratized leadership style that takes its direction from within. Though their outward appearances suggest organizational anarchy, they are, perhaps by default, complex forms of organization that require considerably more group dynamic skills than traditional hierarchical, top-down organization management forms. They signal a generation's attitude toward the form and function of social movements that are not dependent on the charismatic leader or a close-knit cabal of insiders. As I reviewed articles on the food movement, a kind of schizophrenic approach to the topic of leadership emerged. On the one hand, there is the horde of creative cats running unherded and uncoordinated enjoying their freedom to pursue their own projects. On the other hand, there are many in the food movement who vest a significant amount of moral authority in a relatively small number of individuals. Let's take a look for a moment at what this latter trend might mean.

A sizeable furor arose when the *Washington Post* ran an op-ed by Michael Pollan, Ricardo Salvador, Mark Bittman, and Olivier De Schutter calling for a national food policy (of which the United States has none) that joins access for all to healthy food with food production practices that promote public health, a clean environment, and fair labor practices that include the payment of living wages (2014). All four contributors are well known in the food movement, with Pollan's food issue books remaining at the top of the charts longer than most Beatles' tunes.

The mantra generated by the op-ed, as well as many of Mark Bittman's *New York Times* columns and Ricardo Salvador's work at the Union of Concerned Scientists, was that the food system is broken and must be repaired. One thing interesting about this group, sometimes paired with chefs Alice Waters and Tom Colicchio and writer Eric Schlosser, is that they are largely journalists and/or chefs with the exception of Ricardo Salvador who comes out of agricultural academia and the foundation world, and Olivier De Schutter who possesses international and United Nations credentials. In spite of the fact that their investigations and research have been solid, their engagement with on-the-ground food programs and experience with public policy making was thin. Sam Kass, former executive director of Michele Obama's Let's Move! campaign and the White House's senior policy advisor for nutrition policy, criticized the original gang of four's op-ed, referring to their ideas as "lofty theories that set unrealistic expectations about what change should look like . . ." and fell short of what we need: "pragmatic, meaningful steps that reflect the political reality that we have to operate in" (Black, 2014).

In her piece reporting on the above, Jane Black summarized Kass's aggressive response as a call "for the food movement to grow up." His complaint was a bit of the age-old conflict between realism and idealism. Without detracting from the quality of their writing or the underlying correctness of their argument (or the deliciousness of the meals they prepare), many of the writers and personalities that the food movement has come to look up to lack an authoritative base, whether through scholarship or comprehensive experience with food system issues and politics. Though they have gained a multitude of adherents who often quote their writings, their leadership can be called into question, and hence the credibility of the food movement.

I was asked by a publisher to review a book proposal it had received that was titled "Fixing the Food System: Changing How We Produce and Consume Our Food" (the publisher could not reveal the author's name). The proposal set the opening scene this way: "On Nov. 18, 2013, four leaders of the emerging food movement met in the living room of Michael Pollan. . . . The opening question the food movement leaders asked one another was, 'Where to press?' It was clear to them that food issues weren't on the agenda of the nation's elected officials. . . . One year later, on Nov. 7, 2014, the four leaders published a widely circulated column in the *Washington Post*."

With this reverent, breathy tone and attempt to build dramatic tension, the writer may be trying to make this the milestone moment that the food movement supposedly craves, a setting of the stage for a drama equivalent to Martin Luther's nailing of the 95 theses to the cathedral door in Wittenberg. The mantra of the broken food system echoed by the title and the claim that "food issues weren't on the agenda of the nation's elected officials" are largely false, but it is common framing that plays well to a large segment of the food audience.

But the repeated use of "leaders," conferring a status not unlike that of the Three Wise Men, is equally problematic. In a movement that not only doesn't have a process by which to designate leadership, formal or otherwise, and in fact has traditionally used decentralized decision making (a de facto choice, not altogether a good thing), repeatedly asserting that a small group of relatively prominent people are "the leaders" leads to conflicts and divisiveness.

Backlash is one tangible result of placing a few people on a pedestal, especially when they are associated with a movement that maligns major segments of the food system, particularly its large corporate sectors. Often the backlash comes in the form of ad hominem attacks that are also used to paint the whole movement as uninformed, naïve, elitist, and ineffective. In a *New Republic* article by Phoebe Maltz Bovy (2015) titled "Food Snobs Like Mark Bittman Aren't Even Hiding Their Elitism Anymore" (a title that largely makes it unnecessary to read the rest of the article), the "leaders" (in this case, in addition to Bittman, are Michael Pollan and Alice Waters who were all inhabiting the same Berkeley kitchen at the time) are singled out for their pretentious food ways, which presumably dismiss how the other 99 percent eat. While these three have probably developed thick enough skins at this point to let charges of elitism slide like fried eggs from a well-seasoned pan, the rest of the movement is dragged into the heat of the kitchen. "The food movement has officially stopped pretending it has anything useful to offer to anyone with ordinary, or even better-than-ordinary, grocery options," writes Maltz Bovy as if a few well-known chefs and food writers *are* the food movement.

Places like Berkeley often become collateral damage in these attacks. Even though Pollan and Waters reside there, and Bittman was sojourning there at the time the article appeared, "Berkeley" had already become synonymous with food elitism. In spite of the fact that many a cutting-edge food project or policy was incubated there, for example, The Edible Schoolyard, a "sugar tax" on soft drinks, this particular clustering of "food leaders" only made it a little easier to find the artillery fire coordinates. (Author's confession: I have learned over the course of providing food system and food policy consultations to so-called ordinary communities around the country to never cite Berkeley as a model food city. It was considered an immediate "turn off" to an audience.)

Branding various people and elements of the food movement "elitist" is taken to a new high, however, by Julie Guthman, who, in her book *Weighing*

*In* (2011), unleashes an assault on many of the dearly held assumptions of the food movement. Replenish "food deserts" (communities underserved by supermarkets) with gardens and farmers' markets and fill our schools with tons of fresh fruits and vegetables? No, says Guthman, who believes that "the alternative food movement is the problem [due to its] inability to seriously challenge the cheap food movement, but also in its production of self-satisfied customers who believe that . . . good food is enough." Eliminate the commodity crop subsidies that have made us sick? Our long and complicated farm policy history, contends Guthman, has many causes and alternative explanations that have more merit than the carefully laid out logic in Michael Pollan's *Omnivore's Dilemma* (2006) that connects high fructose corn syrup, "cheap" calories, and federal farm policies. We should encourage more physical activity? Guthman retaliates against America's obsession with working out and thin bodies by labeling it "healthism." Under her peevish academic glare, she makes physical activity an illness rather than a healthy behavior. Not only does healthism reek of "self-absorption," says Guthman, it leads to attitudes that discriminate against fat people.

After skewering most of the food movement's most dearly held assumptions, she declares that our health and diet issues can be laid at the feet of cheap food, low wages, and degraded working conditions. Walmart, in her mind, not only causes obesity but also profits from it.

I call it "Mark's First Law of Social Movements," that for every reasonably well-organized action designed to develop a substantive alternative to the status quo, there will be an equal and opposite reaction designed to discredit the alternative. In the case of the food movement, given the David and Goliath relationship between the insurgents and the entrenched forces of Big Food, the reaction is disproportionately greater—one can expect large food corporations, for instance, to counterattack against those who attack them, especially if their bottom lines are threatened. It's a little less clear as to what the motive is when ideas and philosophies are at stake. It may be egos, it may be recognition, or may it be as honest as the pure pursuit of truth. Whatever the cause, certain methods do more to divide the movement than to invite those who disagree to "reason together." It's not that the food movement should avoid robust debate—that's not possible nor desirable—it's just that it needs to learn how to manage the exchanges more tactically and tactfully.

Another proxy target for these counterattacks is the widely used term "local food." The oppositional strategy here is to say such things as local food will not feed a hungry planet; local food is more expensive than food sourced from the chain supermarket; and local food is just one other way that elitist parvenus accessorize themselves. Granted, local food advocates do have a habit of cloaking themselves in multiple layers of virtue. A 2016 *New Yorker* cartoon captured this annoying tendency to perfection depicting a middle-aged couple having dinner together, and the husband asks his wife about the meal: "Is this food from the community garden? It tastes sanctimonious."

While anti–local food framing directed at people who wear their food preferences on their sleeves is not always undeserved, the main flaw in the attack—one that promotes disunity—is that there is in fact no single solution to the dilemmas facing our food system. Local food is no more the answer to the health and well-being of our planet than are food coops, supermarkets, farmers' markets, GMOs, or SNAP. Multiple interventions, including ones that strengthen and draw on local and regional food production and are based on collaboration between all the actors, will give the movement its strongest hand. Looking for a little bit of virtue in all approaches, while considering their limitations and downsides as well, is what's called for.

No doubt, local food is not only a big trend, it's also big business, and the more "local," the better for business. The 2015 A.T. Kearney survey of U.S. shopper habits found that 96 percent of shoppers define local produce as grown within 100 miles of the point of sale. Seventy-eight percent of respondents said they would also pay a 10 percent premium for local food. The same survey conducted in 2014 found that only 58 percent thought local food should be no more than 100 miles from point of sale and that only 70 percent would pay a premium (Burt et al., 2015).

Even though more Americans are joining the locavore church, the relative importance of local food and the reasons for purchasing it can be quite different. A 2015 Harris Poll found shoppers are divided with half of the respondents saying that buying local is an important consideration for them while half say it is not. But the poll also suggests that the tenets of the "buy local" religion are not as strong as other more basic dietary concerns. In fact, local trails in importance when shoppers consider a food item's sugar, sodium, and calorie content, and is at the same level of interest when it comes to buying antibiotic/hormone free food. Interestingly, the top reason for buying local is not its quality and content attributes, it's simply to support the local economy (Harris Poll, 2015).

Amidst the consumer trends and buyer choices that investors want to understand with as much precision as possible are certain values and lifestyle choices that drive most shoppers. Ion Vasi, an associate professor in University of Iowa Sociology Department, describes the local food market as a "moralized market" that combines economic interests with social values (Diedrich, 2015). Yet interest in farmers' markets, still viewed as the mother church of local food, is not necessarily being reflected in growing sales. As reported in the *Washington Post* farmers acknowledge lagging sales since "a new generation of shoppers . . . view these outdoor markets as more a lifestyle choice than an opportunity to support local agriculture" (Carman, 2016).

The winds keep shifting even though they blow with more gusto than ever. The early local food pioneers brought a certain level of purity and authenticity to their enterprise. Portions of those values have been transmitted to newer generations of shoppers, but some have been reinterpreted by Millennials and newer generations as lifestyle preferences—ones that bring benefits to their health and that of the planet but not necessarily speaking to the hard-fought battles over what's being sold by a *real farmer* versus what's being sold by a "middle-man" or "jobber." In a *New York Times* article, the multiple challenges coming to farmers' markets and Community Supported Agriculture (CSAs) farms from well-financed businesses that purport to sell local are highlighted (Moskin, 2016). The entry of Peapod, the online shopping service owned by grocery giant Ahold, and FreshDirect, both of which offer farm-sourced items, are cutting into the more traditional CSA farm businesses. Paula Lukats, a local farmer advocate and program director at the nonprofit organization Just Food, points out that 2010 was probably the peak for CSA memberships, which have been going down since (Ibid.). The inevitable conclusion seems to be that local is big and getting bigger, but having the most authentic connection to the farmer possible is a declining motivator.

Much of this pales, of course, in comparison to the size of the local food footprint being made by corporate giants like Walmart. Though big-box stores are giving more shelf space to their local and organic sections, millions of local food loyalists would no more buy local/organic food at Walmart than would a Baptist kneel in a Catholic pew.

Arguments abound on both sides, but what is clear is that the clarity of vision and the sturdiness of purpose that characterized the heady days of the early local food movement have been disrupted by expanding consumer demands—ones that the local food movement created in the first place—and newly evolving business models that are responding to those demands. As with most aspects of the food movement, local food often finds itself at a crossroads as well as at cross purposes. And the prospects of winners and losers don't make for a happy encounter.

## Attacks from the Perimeter

When not struggling from the inside, the food movement is always taking hits from the outside. In a *Wall Street Journal* article (2015), Todd Myers and Steven Sexton argue that "the local-foods movement could actually threaten the environmental and human health objectives that inspired it." Their case is supported by the comparable agricultural benefits of one state or region over another. California, for instance, is far better suited to growing strawberries than Michigan, which, in turn, is better suited for growing squash.

The additional inputs required for states to achieve the same yield as other states better suited to grow a certain crop would require more inputs such as fuel, fertilizer, and pesticides. All in all, a more locally distributed food production plan across the United States would require up to 60 million more acres of farmland—an area the size of Oregon—to achieve the same total crop yields (Ibid.).

A similar line of attack is used to discredit urban agriculture, including community gardening and small-scale food production in unconventional areas, for example, city rooftops or old factory buildings. In *Demystifying Food from Farm to Fork* (2012), author Maurice Hladik disparaged urban farming as no more than a hobby that does not offer a solution to hunger. While urban agriculture advocates have brought on some of this opprobrium themselves with exaggerated claims of economically feasible food production methods as well as unsupported claims of creating many new jobs, the criticism only addresses urban farming's obvious disadvantage. In a literature review conducted by the Johns Hopkins Center for a Livable Future, urban agriculture's food production and job creation limitations were generally acknowledged. However, a slew of other benefits—quality of living, environmental and open space, recreational, therapeutic, aesthetic, education and vocational training, and even an increase in nearby property values—were found to be quite real and important (Santo et al., 2016). When taken together and added to the food that is produced, urban agriculture can add considerable value to life in the built environment. Like nonurban agriculture's ability to preserve open space, promote a measure of local food security, maintain diverse communities and economies, and keep a town's cost of services lower than fully built-out areas, urban farming and gardening are multifunctional and should be regarded as one of many interventions that strengthen a region's food system.

And if local food enthusiasts are not dazed and confused enough by incoming fire, try hitting them with the ethical arguments as well. Many of these challenges come down to claims that the food movement is not inclusive enough of social and economically disadvantaged people, people of color, or the workers who produce, process, and prepare food. I started throwing those same rocks in my 2008 book *Closing the Food Gap*, which, among other things, took the local (and organic) movement to task for seeking the best food available for its faithful disciples but disregarding those who have no choice but to shop at Walmart (which many claim houses only cheap, industrial food) or use food banks (free, frequently unhealthy food).

That challenge has woven itself into the fabric of the food movement. In an article that appeared in the Yale Divinity School journal, *Reflections* (2016), author Willis Jenkins asks, "Has the food movement allowed us to think that we can eat our way to justice? That perhaps the best thing we can do about malnourishment . . . is enjoy some local heirloom tomatoes?" No small measure of guilt is spared for those who have gained a modicum of happiness from the increased availability of locally produced food. He takes a shot at those who supposedly think that food deserts will turn to oases simply by developing farmers' markets and community gardens, and suggests that our priorities are morally skewed when "vineyards cover the earth when there are malnourished children on every continent." Guess I won't be enjoying that glass of Merlot tonight.

Hurdles, litmus tests, and finely ground lenses are constantly applied to every food project and initiative to determine how many social, racial, and economic criteria are met. It can be a perilous run through the gauntlet of political correctness for one who dares to appease the self-appointed jury.

Some initiatives simply ignore the moral and ethical caterwauling. The *Edible* magazines keep their eye on their marketplace and mission by unabashedly celebrating their respective city's and region's local food scene and the simple joy of its food and beverages. Others embrace and attempt to "fix" the dualities and exclusions that naturally arise when an approach is conceived of that meets the needs of one group without being mindful of the needs of other groups. In these cases, such as making farmers' markets more "low-income shopper friendly," a policy-based resolution is sought to address the imbalance. This is why federally funded programs such as the WIC-Farmers Market Nutrition Program or the Food Insecurity Nutrition Initiative (FINI) were developed. Like a carbon offset for those who fly frequently, such public policy interventions represent a moral offset to a marketplace that is driven by demand for local and sustainably produced food.

Some elements of the food movement simply select terms that employ their own idiosyncratic definitions and histories. In the book *Food Movements Unite!* (Amin et al., 2011), the editors draw on a revolutionary fervor and language that incorporates the concepts of food sovereignty, peasant struggles in developing nations, and the Black Panthers. Though books like these bring to mind the Beatles' song "Revolution" ("If you go carrying pictures of Chairman Mao/You ain't gonna make it with anyone anyhow!"), they do attempt to describe a "big tent" approach that claims to cover most everyone in the food movement.

Upon closer examination, however, *Food Movements Unite!* makes it clear that you must have an anti–industrial-corporate food outlook and subscribe to something approaching a Marxian class-analysis to gain entry to the tent. The collected articles delineate components of the food movement with a typology that includes most of the major grassroots food actors but completely leaves out the larger institutional sectors such as the anti-hunger, food banks, obesity reduction, and nutrition. In his book *Big Hunger* (2017), Andy Fisher states that 79 percent of all Americans donate at least once annually to some kind of emergency food provider (e.g., food bank, food pantry, soup kitchen). For good or for bad emergency food is how most Americans relate to the food movement. To leave them out of the struggle is to undercut your own cause. To gain access to the *Food Movements Unite!* tent you must be small, loud, and toe the revolutionary party line. Targeted for exclusion are the big and bureaucratic. Call it the elevation of the fist pumpers over the PowerPoint pushers.

Unfortunately, leaving the tent's flaps open to a select few is not limited to any one sector of the food movement. As also noted in Fisher's book, the anti-hunger movement isn't any better at embracing a larger agenda than those who limit their field of interest to food sovereignty. The Food Research Action Center (FRAC), the nation's primary anti-hunger advocacy organization, doesn't care where the food comes from that lower-income people buy with their food stamps. It simply doesn't matter to FRAC if the food is produced by local farmers and purchased at a farmers' market, or produced on a factory farm with a history of labor and environmental violations. And given its opposition to efforts to eliminate sugar-sweetened beverages as an allowable SNAP purchase, it has made a de facto choice to place food's nutritional value at a lower level than its caloric value.

Simply put, the more radicalized elements of the food movement don't acknowledge the mainline anti-hunger programs and policies like food banks and SNAP, while anti-hunger elements give short shrift to the source and nutritional quality of food.

Everybody has their pet peeve, farmers especially. At a meeting of the Rocky Mountain Farmers Union (January 26, 2016; Santa Fe, New Mexico) representatives of what is considered one of the more liberal farmer organizations complained that "food is too cheap" and mocked consumers who supposedly want to "get closer to farmers" and "learn more about where their food comes from" but balk when asked to pay what a farmer feels is a fair price. Most commercial elements of the food movement see things in black or white terms, not through the rose-colored glasses of advocates and local food enthusiasts. Besides farmers, those elements can include supermarket managers, chefs, and school food service directors whose mandatory adherence to the bottom line can rarely be budged, and whose anger toward federal regulations is hot enough to brown a chicken nugget without a broiler.

In spite of the "group-hug" rhetoric that envelopes local food advocates, there are important gaps between the farm and consumer sectors. Again, looking at New Mexico, which has large and diverse agriculture communities as well as high rates of poverty and food insecurity, one defining conflict has been agriculture's lack of sympathy for issues facing lower-income consumers. At one meeting of the New Mexico Food and Agriculture Policy Council in 2015, the state's Secretary of Agriculture Jeff Witte gave a presentation in which he said SNAP recipients would be able to afford more locally produced food "if they didn't spend their food stamps on frivolous things like cable-TV."

In another indicator of agriculture's anti-poor attitudes, stubborn resistance to paying workmen's compensation insurance for its farm and ranch workers persisted for a very long time in New Mexico. It is only one of six states that managed to preserve this exemption for farming and ranching as a form of "agricultural exceptionalism." The losers in this arrangement, of course, have been low-paid farm and ranch workers who are at high risk for serious on-farm injuries, but receive no health care coverage for medical expenses or compensation for missed work because of those injuries (see my second book *Food Rebels, Guerrilla Gardeners, and Smart-Cookin' Mamas*). It took several years of persistent action by groups like the New Mexico Poverty and Law Center to finally roll back this exemption, work that was first frustrated by a state legislature that, in spite of its overall liberal leanings, remains pro-agriculture. The work wasn't fully completed until the Center received a ruling from the New Mexico Supreme Court in 2016 declaring the agricultural exemption unconstitutional.

At the meeting mentioned earlier of the Rocky Mountain Farmers Union, the court's ruling was angrily denounced as antithetical to the interests of the West's farm and ranching communities. Part of what is dismaying about this position is that a New Mexico legislator attending this meeting, who was most critical of the court's ruling, is from the county with the highest rate of SNAP users—fully 44 percent of the county's population, twice that of New Mexico's average. It is a high-poverty county as well as a county with a very high percentage of farmworkers due to the large concentration of factory dairy farms—in other words an area whose farmers are anti-workmen's compensation. During the same Rocky Mountain Farmers meeting, a report was also presented noting how the state's "Double Up Food Bucks" program for SNAP recipients was bringing additional income to the farmers and healthy food to low-income households in this legislator's district. The same legislator didn't even acknowledge it. Needless to say, the attempt to bring traditional rural farm interests together with low-income food and labor interests has a long way to go. Building a shared concept of prosperity—let's all try to win and let's distribute the accrued benefits equitably—is too often undermined by politicians who rub salt in the wounds of those who feel they've been wronged by government. Their success in pitting one group against another often rests on their ability to convince farmers that someone—government, immigrants, or the poor—is taking something away from them. To put it another way, fairness is a concept not fully embraced by those who are currently paying less than their fair share for it.

# CHAPTER FOUR

# Communication

As can be seen from the previous discussion of the food movement's divisions, some of its causes can be attributed to poor communication practices, as in the *Cool Hand Luke* film's infamous line, "What we have here is a failure to communicate." I'm referring to communication problems between food movement groups and sectors as well as communication designed to inform the general public or key constituent groups.

Some communications gaps, of course, can be described as both intentional and negligent actions on the part of one or more parties. For many in the food movement (as elsewhere) information is power and can be "owned" and used to gain maximum power over others with whom I may be competing in the same marketplace. Sharing information and being fully transparent in one's exchanges are generally admired virtues in the food movement, but that doesn't mean they are always adhered to. Negligence can be a factor as well. The case in New Brunswick, New Jersey, cited elsewhere in this book where a major foundation didn't tell all coalition parties that they were funding different members of the coalition for similar work is an act of negligence. The fault can be attributed to an unexpected shifting of foundation staff; nevertheless, a tremendous amount of confusion resulted.

Though a host of personal and interpersonal issues as well as a hypercontrolling form of message management—we'll tell you the party line, but we won't tell you what we actually think—can be blamed for numerous "failures to communicate," it is in our choice of language and the way we frame problems and solutions that we find the greatest challenges to building a unified food movement. Language is a powerful force that when used thoughtfully can promote collaboration. When used carelessly or in service to a very narrow range of interests, it defines a posted turf whose signs say, "Keep Out (unless you see things my way)!"

"Framing" is a term that has, since its inception by those who study the art and science of communication, been used so often that it can sometimes mean everything and sometime nothing. But when understood and applied correctly, framing can be an immensely valuable tool for activists of all stripes. Let's take a little time to review its meaning and see how it might be more effectively used to promote a better, and perhaps a more universal, understanding of our food system.

Frames are "organizing principles that are socially shared and persistent over time, that work symbolically to meaningfully structure the social world" (Reese et al., 2001). In other words, frames give us a picture, and ultimately an understanding, of issues and events that we aren't likely to have any direct experience of. If we don't understand a communication from someone or somewhere, we still have an image or picture of those events in our head, whether it's objectively correct or not. If these things are explained in a way that helps me understand their relationship between events differently, that is, "reframed," I generate a new image in my head that corresponds to a closer perception of the facts.

In food system work, the food movement's many parts don't share a common frame. If I work at a food bank, I understand the problem to be that people simply don't have enough food, and therefore, my job is to secure and distribute food to needy people. If I work with local farmers and farmers' markets, I understand my part of the food system as about assisting farmers become more economically successful by selling at a farmers' market and other direct purchasing outlets. Our respective measures of success reinforce our understanding of our work. As a food banker, I count the pounds of food I distribute each year as well as the number of people who have received that food. Farmers' market advocates count the number of farmers who sell at the market, the variety of goods they have available, and their sales (e.g., how often they sell out, the size of the crowds, etc.). It's not that one actor in the food system doesn't care about the mission or the measurements of other actors; it's just that no one ever helped them understand why it's important. One could say that intersectoral food system empathy is low—it's hard for the actors who do one kind of work to "feel" for actors in another sector because they've never walked in their shoes before.

Let's dig a little deeper into framing by looking at one fairly significant source of conflict within a major portion of the local food movement. Michael Rozyne is another one of those people whose food system rap sheet goes on for miles. He has worked on farms, worked in India on hunger, was a leader in the fair-trade movement as cofounder of Equal Exchange, and later shifted into supporting the marketing efforts of the Northeast region's farmers. As the founder of Red Tomato, a farmer-oriented food distribution nonprofit, he has worked harder than most people I know to bridge the divide between consumers who want it all—fresh, local, organic—and farmers who want to produce a healthy product for regional markets but also want to make a decent (middle-class) living.

The frustration, as Rozyne sees it, is that consumers make what they believe to be reasonable food demands without having any understanding (empathy) for the challenges that farmers face. From the relatively limited and selective information they've gleaned from the media and friends, they expect their food to be GMO-free, locally produced (very few "food miles" between the producer and them), and of course grown in a certifiably organic way (many other "consumer wants" may be tacked on as different food, health, and diet trends ebb and flow in the media). There is a "hyper-curated approach to food selection," as Rozyne puts it, "that is not based on cognitive science." But he appreciates the anxiety that consumers feel, given the bombardment of information and the simple fact that, "the human species is incapable of absorbing anymore data or qualitative information about food." Effectively, so much information about the environmental, human, and animal health consequences of our diets is thrown at us, and that dozens of more studies are required to sort out the hundreds of previous studies only adds to our confusion.

Associated with this disconnect, Rozyne sees a kind of reductionism creeping into our institutions, language, and decision making that narrows the range of choices we make. "The food movement is becoming more sanctimonious with growing categories of what's 'good' and what's 'evil.'" Reductionism is reinforced by the singular category of issues that suddenly trend upward in the public consciousness. These may include the plight of farmworkers, the growth in food banks, and more recently, the way the bright light has been turned on food waste. All of these are important issues, he concedes, that need to be included in our larger understanding of our food system, but rather than striving for inclusivity—a rational organization and understanding of how these things can fit and work together—our narrowing frames of reference are achieving a kind of exclusivity.

To reduce the gaps in people's understanding of how the food system works, Rozyne has joined forces with a new collaboration known as The Food Narrative Project. In addition to Rozyne's organization, Red Tomato, the collaboration includes IPM Voice, a nonprofit that educates the public about integrated pest management, and FrameWorks Institute, a communications research think tank. Together, they hope to achieve a much broader understanding among consumers of how our nation's farming and food supply system function so that their food choices are informed by science and are not narrower, often inaccurate vectors of information. Their work is inspired by a two-point diagnosis of the general public's food limitations (Frameworks Institute, IPM Voice, and Red Tomato, 2016; personal communication with Michael Rozyne, 2015).

The first point is the existence of a high rate of agricultural illiteracy. Most Americans know so little about how food is raised (less than 2% of us make any kind of living from agriculture), they are ill equipped to understand different farming practices and policies or make food choices that serve their own best interest, let alone that of a sustainable food system.

The second point is called *polarized simplicity*. The public conversation about food and farming has turned into a debate in which complicated science and sophisticated growing practices are reduced to oversimplified versions of good versus bad, either/or, all or nothing. When people lack personal experience, they sometimes compensate by taking a mental shortcut in which they form opinions based on whatever they can easily recall about a subject, from whatever source is readily available.

One example that I've used before in this book is the debate (more of a screaming match) over GMOs. The Food Narrative Project describes the problem so well that I will quote a large section in whole from their proposal:

> The debate over GMO technology provides another window into polarized simplicity. The pro-GMO voices argue that technology (i.e. GMOs) is essential to feed a growing population. They ignore or downplay concerns about environmental health, including resistance, the need for more research, or issues of patenting and control over seeds. The anti-GMO voices treat all forms of GMOs as monolithic, and treat the technology itself as the problem, ignoring the potential to reduce insecticide and fungicide use, help provide greater nutrition, or cure plant diseases such as citrus greening or apple scab. The debate seems to have no middle ground. Journalists who have tried to carve out a middle ground with research into the science on both sides are dismissed by the anti-GMO side as having "vested interests" and by the pro-GMO side as "anti-technology. . . ." As a result, solutions to real issues are not addressed, and positive uses of the technology are left unexplored. (Ibid.)

With the hope of finding a way forward that might salvage the benefits that science and technology can bring to the world and to avoid the harm that their overzealous application might cause, the project is suggesting a number of directions. One is the recognition that there is already a substantial amount of agreement about certain elements of the food system. For instance, the large, industrial agriculture world generally recognizes organic as here to stay and sees scientific validity in the basic agronomic claims that lie at the heart of organic farming. The medical establishment recognizes that exercise and good nutrition reduce disease and increase health. The marketplace recognizes local as a growing consumer value they must deliver on. Nonprofits and policy makers alike have elevated the legitimate demand of low-income citizens for healthy, affordable food.

The project plans to build on this rough consensus that some kind common ground exists through better application of communication strategies. Again, I quote a large section from the proposal:

> There is an opportunity to rewrite the food narrative so that it guides our nation in moving steadily in the direction of a sustainable food system that can provide healthy, safe, affordable food for all its citizens, while improving its soils, protecting its environment, and enabling profitable farms, small, medium and large. . . . The purpose is to broaden the national food and ag conversation, to motivate education and change, and to diversify the field of players who collaborate to do the necessary work. . . . If we are to increase the public's engagement around food and farming as allies for positive change, we must start with a more sophisticated knowledge of effective communications, including framing and the science behind how people form their worldviews and day-to-day opinions. . . . Many organizational leaders still associate effective communication with writing a better slogan or spending more on communications. The more the leaders of food and farm organizations understand about framing and the science behind effective communications, the more strategic and collaborative they will be in their efforts to engage the public, and the more they will be able to help people see the connections between how we eat, how we farm, and how this impacts our communities, our health, and our planet (Ibid.).

What is hoped for in the Food Narrative Project is perhaps a grand meeting of the minds—that there can be a kind of coming together within one large communal frame. At its most idealistic, one can imagine a national group portrait along the lines of be-wigged men, quill pens in hand, affixing their now-famous signatures to the Declaration of Independence or the Constitution. This time, of course, the portrait would include women, African Americans, Asians, Native Americans, and Hispanics, an assemblage which would forever cement the momentousness and authenticity of the occasion. They would be dressed differently, of course, from Brooks Brothers suits and Florsheims to stained overalls and Birkenstocks. But I'm sure portraitists are not waiting in line for the commission—decades may pass before such a gathering would even be proposed. But if the food movement is to make any kind of progress toward that vision, it might very well require that we go down a path not unlike what The Food Narrative Project proposes.

I'll close out this discussion of food movement communication with what I consider to be the hardest, easiest thing we can do to increase the likelihood of intersectoral food movement empathy: *relationship building.* While this basic outcome of everyday human interaction may not rise to the level of applying cognitive science to the powerful concept of framing, it is a much-overlooked tool that is readily available to anyone. I'll illustrate my point with a true story from my days in Connecticut, one that I've told often at training workshops. I call it the "Story of Ralph."

Shortly after organizing the Connecticut Food Policy Council in the late 1990s, I was trying to facilitate communication and decision making among the members who had been appointed to what was then the first of its kind state council in the country. The state statute that created the body mandated participation by representatives of six different private food and farm sector interests and representatives from six different Connecticut government departments. It took us at least a year before we arrived at a mission statement, but we continued to struggle with how to work together. The biggest challenge was that each member's frame of reference was not supposed to be limited to only one food system sector, for example, agriculture. Though they came from only one department or sector, the hope was that they would be able to understand and represent the state's entire food system.

This idealistic assumption was a challenge for all the members, but the person for whom it was certainly the most opaque was Ralph, the representative from the Connecticut Department of Transportation. Admittedly, ConnDOT, as it was affectionately known, was a harder piece to fit into the food system puzzle than departments like agriculture, social services (food stamps), and health (nutrition, WIC), but Ralph seemed to go out of his way to *not* fit in. During one meeting, he vented his frustration by proclaiming, "I don't get it! What's this food system stuff? Transportation has nothing to do with food." He crossed his arms over his chest, pouted, and refused to communicate.

As the meeting was breaking up, I caught up with Ralph as he was heading down the hallway. I asked him if something was wrong and offered to try to clarify things. He wasn't interested and brushed off my offer by saying that he had to get to a retirement party for one of his ConnDOT employees. But then he stopped in his tracks, turned to me, and asked if I'd like to go to the party. I was stunned, especially after he told me what bar they were meeting in, a sketchy place as best. But a little voice inside of me said, "Go, Mark!"

The cigarette smoke was so heavy you couldn't see clearly across the room; the food was so greasy it slid off your plate; and the beer came in two types: bad and worse. But I found myself sitting in a beat up old booth with ripped seat covers talking to Ralph about stuff—family, baseball, what town he was from, and so on. Not a word was uttered about the food policy council or food systems. After I met some of his colleagues and pals, inhaled polluted air, and ate bad food for nearly two hours, I decided I had enough. When I arrived home, my wife told me I smelled like an ashtray and didn't look well. I lay on the couch wondering what I had just done.

A few days later I had an excited call from Ralph. He told me he'd been looking at some of the work of ConnDOT and wondered if he could talk about them at the next Food Policy Council meeting. I said sure not knowing what to expect. Three weeks later Ralph walked into the meeting with a pile of folders and, like a kid who had just discovered a treasure trove, began to tick off a list of goodies. He told us that his department had a special fund that could be used to provide grocery shuttle services to senior citizens who lived off public transit lines and far from supermarkets. He also explained how new public bus routes could be established to connect residents in low-income city neighborhoods to suburban supermarkets (which had all moved out of the city), and how every other year, the ConnDOT, which was responsible for producing the state's official road map, could produce a "specialty" road map. "Why not produce a Connecticut Farm Map?" Ralph eagerly asked with a big grin on his face. Every jaw around the table hung agape; every set of eyes was wide open. Ralph had apparently been reborn as a food system evangelist. Over the next year or so every one of his ideas would be implemented. Was it the "relationship" we had developed in that smoky bar that had "lit him up?" I can't say for sure, but I'm convinced that some of that "off-work" time we spent together had at least provided some kindling for Ralph's ignition.

# CHAPTER FIVE

# Funding the Food Movement

Somebody has to bankroll the food movement. When the marketplace has failed to make healthy and affordable food accessible to all; when it forces farmers to produce as much food as possible at the lowest cost regardless of the consequences for human, animal, and environmental health; and when the overwhelming presence of unhealthy food options and advertising messages erode our will power, then someone has to write the checks to right the wrongs. As Nick Saul said in *The Stop*, "the revolution must be funded."

Nonprofit organizations have typically been the shock-troops in efforts to develop and operate services or advocate for change. Because they have limited capacity to earn income from their activities (Internal Revenue Service restrictions on nonprofits' revenue sources as well as their lack of for-profit business acumen being the chief obstacles), nonprofits generally turn to the philanthropic world and government for funding. Even though food-related foundation philanthropy was nearly $500 million in 2012—a threefold growth since 2002—funding is a never-ending source of disunity in the movement (Stiffman, 2015).

Fund-raising for food work is hard work. Those who have never done it tend to think that securing money for charity, any charity, is inferior to the rough and tumble world of raising capital in the debt and equity markets, or running a profitable business that pays its bills by selling goods and services. Indeed, I was inclined to think that myself after my very first fund-raising experience at the ripe age of 20. I and a few college friends had decided to start a drop-in center to provide peer counseling and a few basic services to the lower income young people who made up a large portion of our college town. We had heard that the local catholic archdiocese made small grants for projects like the one we envisioned, so myself and an equally scruffy 20-year-old college pal made an appointment to visit the archdiocese's office. Having never asked anyone for money before, except my parents, I was feeling very nervous. But we made our pitch, crude as it was to a kindly gentleman who promptly gave us a check for $300! Safely out of sight of the office, my pal and I high-fived each other saying, "that was easy!"

Like a would-be junkie who just got his first fix for free, I was hooked. Fired up by my early success, I proceeded under the assumption that securing donations for good causes would be like taking candy from a baby. How wrong I was! As I moved on to progressively larger and more complex nonprofit organizations, the programs grew requiring more staff that in turn swelled the budgets. With an ever-expanding nest of hungry baby birds to feed, I was forced to devote more and more time to raising money to keep them from starving. Looking back at the 25 years I ran the Hartford Food System, I estimate with reasonable certainty that I devoted a significant portion of every weekday, often extending into weekends and holidays, to fundraising. That "easy money" of my early twenties gradually became harder and harder to obtain because now I needed more of it. And the stress and pressure associated with raising hundreds of thousands of dollars every year drove me into making some hard choices, the kinds of choices that have proven divisive to the movement.

But raising enough money to support the initiatives capable of meeting human needs and securing necessary system change is not the only financial challenge. Two additional funding factors have contributed to disunity in the food movement: (1) the source of the funding and (2) how funders want you to use their money.

When it comes to the question of who is doling out the money, the ethical quandaries persist and have led to the erection of severe philosophical barriers between groups. Perhaps it is unique to the food movement—compared to other social and economic fund-raising concerns such as housing and education—but if a "Big Food" or "Big Ag" donor produces products or services that some deem harmful, or engage in labor or business practices that are regarded as exploitative, the prevailing attitude of many food organizations is to not take their money. Why? Because that corporation's harm undermines the mission of the food organization.

The second factor is decidedly subtler and does not provoke the same angst that the first factor does but is just as important. While usually making rational choices about where to put their money, the simple necessity for a foundation to choose one type of food organization recipient over another evokes jealously, envy, and sometimes scorn from the so-called losers. In what can only be considered a case of the tail wagging the dog, many a nonprofit organization has shifted its mission in response to the signals it perceives from the foundation community.

But where the food movement and foundation world face the biggest challenge is with the matter of encouraging, discouraging, or simply ignoring the need for cooperation and collaboration between food organizations. Whether it is at the local, state, or national levels, funders have rarely incentivized or set conditions on their grants with the intent of promoting partnerships or more ambitious forms of collective impact. But let's begin with the philosophical quandaries.

## Running with the Devil

The view from the 21st floor into mid-town Manhattan was breathtaking. Shapes that Walt Whitman never imagined arose with asymmetrical splendor before my eyes. The late afternoon sun on a near-perfect New York day splashed golden patterns across soaring plate glass canvasses, shifting rapidly from bursts of blinding reflected light to the deepest shadows kidnapped by hundreds of masonry troughs. Grand Central Station's iconic façade was to my left, while Park Avenue's trillion-dollar mile stretched to my right. What more could there be in life to increase my astonishment?

The well-appointed conference room where I stood, gazing at the floor-to-ceiling windows and sipping a yummy Chardonnay, was aglow with pleasant smiles and the soothing burble of cocktail chatter. Waiters in white tunics moved unobtrusively among the noshing clusters to refill glasses and pass trays of caviar-stacked toast squares. A beautiful blond woman dressed in an elegant floor-length gown was tucked discreetly into one of the room's corners where she strummed a harp. Her heavenly notes filled our little empyrean, taking the room's habitants a story or two higher.

Though professionally dressed, the drinkers and gobblers were not attired in the requisite button down, business wear that was mandatory for the regular occupants of this and adjoining New York office buildings. The men—some with ties and most without—wore sports jackets, and the women were dressed in casual business skirts and pant suits—more J.C. Penny than Nordstrom's. But that was as it should be, because after all, these were nonprofit people—folks who earned their livings doing work that was primarily for the benefit of others. They served the public interest or a charitable purpose through their respective organizations—some with no more than one or two employees—for no other reason than some larger good might be rendered unto humankind. Their bottom line was distinctly different from that of corporate America's where the financial return to the shareholder was the highest (and sometimes the only) good. For those like myself, now temporarily suspended within the city's opulence, the bottom line was the social return to our communities, constituents, and clients.

Though driven by mission, they weren't driven solely by altruism. They worked hard not only to serve others but also to cobble together a middle-class lifestyle for themselves from their nonprofit organization salaries. For even the best paid among them—executive directors, program heads, fund-raising experts—earned a salary barely on par with the receptionists, secretaries, and entry-level professionals who scurried about the floors just above and below this humble gathering.

Though driven by their respective organization's mission, they were definitely not driven by a vision that was commonly shared by those in the room. They may have been genuinely sympathetic to each other's endeavors, willing on some occasions to help each other out or even collaborate if there was money to do so, but those enjoying this glamorous moment were not known to regularly communicate with one another nor support each other's various projects and initiatives. If one of the organizations in that room went out of business due to lack of funding, there would barely be a murmur of condolence. Silently, even darkly, they would say to themselves, "It's a shame but I'm glad it wasn't me." The more ruthless among them would even be saying, "Hmmm, that might mean a little more money for me!" Social Darwinism was more prevalent than social solidarity.

Such morbid speculation didn't matter right now. The people present were the survivors, the chosen few. Their long hours, their efforts to keep their agencies' doors open, and their weekly struggle to make payroll were all forgotten for the moment in the rarefied air of a Manhattan office tower. It wasn't just that second glass of wine that relieved the sore muscles of nonprofit work; it was the fact that the people who walked out of that room and entered the elevator for the descent to Park Avenue would have a very fat check tucked into their suit jacket or purse, courtesy of the Philip Morris corporation, formally known as Philip Morris USA, and now known as Altria. Yes, the tobacco corporation that had been manufacturing and selling tobacco products since 1847, and since 1983, was the largest cigarette manufacturer in the United States. According to their 2011 annual corporation report, the company had the largest share (49%) of the retail cigarette industry. The iconic Marlboro brand itself, which is the leading seller in every state in the United States and controls a 42 percent retail share, is purchased more than the next 13 tobacco brands combined (Phillip Morris International, 2011). There could be little doubt that the room's merrymakers were unaware of tobacco's impact on human health or its ranking as the nation's number one public health problem. It had been a well-established medical fact for decades that cigarettes can kill you, and not just here and there like a stray bullet or car accident but in numbers that make our world wars look like an occasional gangland shootout. The World Health Organization's 2008 report starkly summed up the body count: 100 million people dead from tobacco-related diseases in the 20th century alone; currently, 5.4 million die every year; and tobacco increases the likelihood of contracting six of the eight leading causes of death such as heart disease, stroke, and cancer. Bodies stacked up like cordwood across the world, or maybe more appropriately like cigarettes tucked snugly into their cartons (World Health Organization, 2008).

Yet the tinkling of wine glasses, the ethereal sound of the harp, the suffused laughter, and the all-round gaiety of the moment would not be overshadowed by these grim statistics. Maybe all of us, the soon-to-be-a-little-richer, had been reassured by the "No Smoking" signs discreetly placed in the event room and the building's corridors and restrooms. Contrary to my expectations, my stroll down the well-lit hallways whose walls were tastefully adorned with an enviable collection of artwork didn't yield clouds of cigarette smoke belching from open offices. Like all the other "progressive" NYC-based corporations, Philip Morris had largely banned smoking from the building's public areas. Its remaining puffers and hackers were relegated, like the remnants of a defeated army, to nearby windy sidewalks.

One woman in her fifties with whom I conversed seemed to express the crowd's prevailing sentiment. She ran a Meals-on-Wheels program that delivered prepared meals to "shut-in" senior citizens and other disabled people. She told me that she currently could only serve a fraction of her community's need because of funding limitations, and that the Philip Morris grant would enable her to reach another 1,000 needy elderly. When I asked her if she had any qualms about taking tobacco money, she cringed a bit, acknowledging the ill-effects of tobacco, but said without embarrassment that her agency desperately needed the money. If she had taken a conscientious stand and rejected the funding, she said, "my board of directors would kill me!"

Of course, I had to answer my own question. Having been less than candid with my staff about why I was leaving the office early that day, I mumbled something about meeting with a foundation in New York. As a person who spoke often and loudly about the need to promote healthy eating and lifestyles for everyone, especially the poor, it was more than a bit ironic that I was now guzzling the Devil's booze and taking his bucks. I was that very same person, for whom "doing good" was not just a personal preference but a self-imposed life sentence, now making obsequious chatter with the corporation's staff, and, like a thirsty dog with his tongue dangling obscenely, waiting for his share of Killer Tobacco's loot.

My thoughts on the train back to Hartford were a case study in situational ethics. As if Socrates was sharing the seat next to me on the 8:37 P.M. Metro-North, I carried on a "yes, but" conversation in my head that drew more than one worried stare from neighboring riders. In one ear, I could hear Gunter Grass saying "something that's morally wrong must be opposed regardless of personal consequence." In the other ear, I could hear countless community voices telling me what Philip Morris' money will buy—lots of organic, locally grown fruits and vegetables for low-income families; lots of additional income for hardworking farmers. I was bringing home the bacon for my people, I told myself; I was only doing my job. One colleague would later try to lift my spirits by explaining that if government had made more money available in the first place, nonprofits like mine would not have to stoop so low in order to meet their budgets. I asked myself what would Gandhi do (the Mahatma's life being my college thesis topic); what would the Reverend Martin Luther King Jr. do; what would Ralph Waldo Emerson do? All three of my beloved heroes were sitting in the seat across from me just shaking their heads. When I offered them each a cut of the check I held inside my coat pocket in hopes that I could win them over, they all got off at the next stop.

The above is not just an account of how I've wrestled with the Devil for my soul. Who you take money from and what fund-raising practices you employ really do matter in the food movement. For instance, the Center for Science in the Public Interest, a long-standing dietary-health advocacy organization that has taken very strong positions against the food industry, doesn't take money from government or foundations in order to protect its independence.

A typical food movement argument about the corrupting influence of Big Food's money was presented in an essay by Andy Fisher and Robert Gottlieb that appeared in *Civil Eats* in December 2014. The following excerpt from that posting defines the issue well.

> In a disturbing trend, an increasing number of food and farming nonprofits are relying on the Walmart Foundation to fund their programs. The Milwaukee–based urban agriculture leader Growing Power paved the way when it accepted a seven-figure grant from the Foundation in 2011. Since then, Food Corps, a service corps program focused on educating kids about healthy food, and the food hub pioneer National Good Food Network (NGFN) have both followed suit.
>
> Neither Food Corps nor NGFN staff responded to our request for comment on their rationales for accepting Walmart funding. In Growing Power's blog from 2011, however, Will Allen argues: 'We can no longer be so idealistic that we hurt the very people we're trying to help. Keeping groups that have the money and the power to be a significant part of the solution away from the Good Food Revolution will not serve us.'
>
> We've been party to discussions within one unnamed national organization as it decides whether to apply for a $1.5 million grant from Walmart Foundation. In those considerations, we've heard crop up one common misconception. Those in favor of accepting Walmart's money rationalize that the Walmart Foundation and Walmart, Inc. are separate entities. They believe that accepting Walmart Foundation money is not akin to aiding and abetting Walmart . . .
>
> . . . Yet, we encourage food and farm groups to weigh the political implications of their fundraising practices. It is not enough to consider how a grant benefits a single organization's programs, no matter how valuable that work may be. What is good for one organization may not be good for the food movement as a whole. We must all start acting as a coherent social movement if we are to ever have a chance of reaching our common goals of creating a sustainable, just, and healthy food system.

Groups like Growing Power and the National Good Food Network take a practical view of what's good for the movement by accepting money to support their work regardless of where it comes from. Their work is good because it benefits many, they argue, and that there's not enough evidence that those who give them money are harmful to their constituents. Fisher and Gottlieb, on the other hand, introduce a moral dimension to those choices by suggesting that a big part of the food problem is caused by those corporations who are "buying you off." Their definition of what's good takes the movement to a loftier plain where solidarity is required among food organizations to defeat or, at the very least, not aid and abet those corporations whose products and practices are part of the problem.

The purpose of this book is not to resolve these sticky philosophical problems but to identify the causes of strife and disunity within the food movement. However, I will offer this limited form of moral guidance, derived in part from a lot of painful reflection from the Philip Morris experience recounted earlier. In the matter of deciding whether to take money from a dubious source, I found the need to serve two masters. The first master is presumably a rational process that relies on the application of an imprecise kind of math. Can I calculate, qualitatively or quantitatively, that the pain a company may cause, such as treating its workers badly or causing harm to the environment, is greater than the benefit derived from the good I might do for those same people or place by taking that company's money? If I determine that the pain is greater, then it seems that at the very least I'd be wasting my time by taking the money of those companies, or worse, I'd be shamelessly serving my own interests, knowing very well that my work is a lost cause.

A case in point is Walmart. With its low-wage structure, many workers for America's largest employer qualify for Supplemental Nutrition Assistance Program (SNAP) and other federal food programs and nonfood benefits. The estimate of the value of these public benefits by some worker organizations was $6.2 billion in 2014 (O'Connor, 2014). In the same year, the Walmart foundation gave away about $1.4 billion in donations, much of it in the form of goods like food, to nonprofit organizations. I'd much rather not let Walmart off the hook by seeing them pay their workers enough so that we, the taxpayers, didn't have to subsidize their workers or their bottom-line.

The second master is far crueler than the first, because it comes from my parents who hammered home the simple notion that if something you're doing feels wrong, then it probably is. When that happens and the gnawing ache of guilt robs your sleep and twists your stomach into knots, well, self-interest dictates that I do not take the money. In retrospect, applying these two criteria, I should have refused the Philip Morris grant, or more precisely, never applied in the first place.

## Funders: Friends or Foes?

The rise in the number of food organizations, fueled in part by the rise in food problem awareness, has been accompanied by a rise in funding support by both the private foundation community and the federal government. As referenced earlier, the private sector, which also includes individual donors, has put its money where its mouth gets its food. "I don't see anything philanthropic that's been on a similar trajectory or anything even close to this," was how the *Chronicle of Philanthropy* quoted Scott Cullen, the head of the Grace Communications Foundation, which funds food, water, and energy organizations (Stiffman, 2015). But the dramatic escalation in funding for food—when we think "food systems," has multiple dimensions—hasn't necessarily led to better results. "So many funders are working in programmatic silos, and that makes it difficult to understand the broader food-funding landscape, how it fits together, and where opportunities exist for collaboration," was how Carra Cotte-Ackah, a high-ranking staffer at the University of Pennsylvania's Center for High Impact Philanthropy explained the problem to the *Chronicle of Philanthropy* (Ibid.).

Part of the problem comes in the way that specific food issues will suddenly soar to stratospheric heights in philanthropic galaxies. Take the challenge of reducing food waste as an example. Given that Americans supposedly do not consume at least 30 percent of the food that is produced in our food system—losing it along a food chain that stretches from unharvested field crops to household plate waste—multiple spotlights have been turned on the issue. Presumably this is because reducing food waste has the potential of addressing multiple problems, among them reducing greenhouse gas emissions, feeding the hungry, and responding to American's innate sense of frugality ("We have a 'clean plate policy' around here," is how my Depression-era mother motivated me to eat my vegetables, that is when she wasn't threatening to send my uneaten food to "starving Europeans"—this was the mid-1950s).

While the issue has merit, it's hard to make a convincing case as to why it should suddenly rise to the top of the philanthropic charts. Ferd Hoefner, the former policy director of the National Sustainable Agriculture Coalition (NSAC), a Washington-based food and farm advocacy group, told me in July 2016 that every major national environmental organization, for example, the Natural Resource Defense Council, have multiple staff (and sometimes whole divisions) working on the food waste issue. "There are so many more important issues than food waste that are under-resourced now," said Hoefner, who is a 25-year-old veteran of national food and farm policy.

The *Chronicle of Philanthropy* article that I continue to reference lists three top food issues: Food insecurity, obesity, and *food waste*. In spite of the fact that the nation's 206 very large food banks and the 60,000-plus soup kitchens and food pantries have relied on and refined the art of managing the receipt and redistribution of hundreds of millions of tons of uneaten food every year—from farm field gleaners to tractor-trailer loads of unsaleable processed food to restaurant and cafeteria food recovery programs—there seems to be a new-found urgency to make food waste a national issue. If there was more than anecdotal evidence that more robust food waste reduction efforts would reduce hunger, then perhaps the emphasis is warranted. However, as we have seen from previous discussions, domestic food insecurity has continued to increase even though the food banking system has grown larger and more efficient over the past 20 years.

In a phenomenon that I call "mobbing the issue," foundations, other well-intentioned donors, and social entrepreneurs are stampeding to food waste (as they have to other issues in the past). I first observed this characteristic, when I, like thousands of parents, put in my time as an assistant soccer coach. About the only thing that we amateurs hoped to teach our 10-year-old children was to spread out and play their positions. Short of nailing their little feet to the turf, however, there was virtually nothing we could do to keep them from "mobbing" the ball. The result was a giant, 44-legged insect crawling up and down the field pursuing the ball until by some freak of nature, it landed in one team's net. Until there is a process by which funders, policy leaders, academics, and organization directors can rationally evaluate needs and coordinate appropriate responses—preferably within a food system's and collective impact context—"mobbing the issue" will remain a problem.

Losing sight of the bigger vision, of the need to develop comprehensive solutions, Americans are in thrall to the "cult of the entrepreneur." As a society, we *just love* innovators, disruptors, inventors, and anyone who builds the so-called better mousetrap. From Thomas Edison to Henry Ford to Bill Gates, we celebrate the genius of the inventor even more than the utility of the invention. Part of my own family's lore is a great-grandfather who earned a U.S. patent by inventing some small device that did something to fountain pens to make them more, well, "fountainy." Whether his invention did anything to appreciably advance civilization is an open question, but in our family's circle it earned him enough distinction so that we overlooked his not inconsiderable other failings.

When it comes to entrepreneurship, the food world is no different. Though food movement adherents tend to label the development of new ideas and applications "social entrepreneurship," new strategies, projects, and models are widely praised and often eagerly supported by foundations—long before they have proven their efficacy. The result is that the new supplants the old only because the new is supposedly better than the old. We proceed to implement the new without careful coordination with what's already there. We don't conduct impact studies or comprehensive community need assessments. There is rarely a consensus that the new is needed or adds value to what's already working. The urge to get on the train before we know where it's going becomes an irresistible force.

## The Daily Table

A case in point as to how an entrepreneur may have a good idea but doesn't consider the big picture is the Daily Table, the brainchild of Doug Rauch, former president of the much beloved Trader Joe's. Daily Table is a nonprofit grocery store that opened in Dorchester, Massachusetts in June of 2015. It's located in a low-to-middle-income area, which has not enjoyed much success attracting conventional supermarkets. Relying largely on the donation of "seconds"—food that is edible and safe, but just beyond its expiration date or a few days shy of the compost pile—Daily Table is, according to CBS News, "on a mission to solve two problems: preventing tons of food from going to waste and offering healthy alternatives to families who may not be able to afford traditional stores" (CBS News, 2015).

The food, befitting its less than top-quality condition, is sold—packaged and fresh, as well as in the form of prepared meals—at prices that are often one-third of those found at conventional retail food outlets. Daily Table sources its merchandise from places as diverse as the Food Project, a nearby nonprofit community farm, Whole Foods, and the Greater Boston Area Food Bank. When food isn't available pro bono, Daily Table will occasionally resort to making cash purchases. And based on the comments of the people I talked to, consumer response has been over the top, leaving Daily Table's shelves virtually bare at the end of its first opening days.

Some sustainability and waste-reduction advocates are ecstatic, drooling over all that methane-churning matter that might *not* find its way into metro-Boston landfills. Rauch, who likes to use social math to describe the gulf he's trying to bridge, says that the U.S. food system is wasting enough food every day to fill the Rose Bowl (Ibid). The U.S. Department of Agriculture (USDA), which favors the old math, reports that about 31 percent of all food produced in the United States is wasted (USDA, 2015). This amounts to about 133 billion pounds per year. With respect to what that might mean for the nation's food-insecure households, Ben Simon of the Food Recovery Network (2015) estimates that we could cut hunger in half with just 15 percent of our food waste. I've always been more than a little perplexed by our penchant to link waste reduction to food security. Though I'm an ardent composter, the waste diversion fervor associated with feeding the hungry seems at times like a distraction from the more critical task of a moral society: ending hunger. With an industrial food system that overproduces by a gigantic proportion, and a food-marketing machine that spends billions to convince us to consume more calories than we need (65% of Americans are obese or overweight), it seems like the more sensible waste reduction plan would be to tackle the problem at its source. Since the USDA tells us that only 10 percent of our waste can be traced to the retail and restaurant segments of our food system, logic tells me to reduce the flow at the spigot rather than catch the spillage over the rim of the bucket (Ibid.).

In one sense, Mr. Rauch is already late to the waste reduction/food recovery game. Boston's renowned Haymarket has been offering some of the biggest fresh produce bargains in the region since 1830. The greater Boston area already has a robust network of food rescue organizations and schemes. "Food for Free" in Cambridge, for instance, is picking up prepared food from Harvard University's dining services and working on ways to safely distribute it in portion sizes and forms that will be usable by their clients.

Several area food advocates that I spoke with worried that the Daily Table will only exacerbate the competition for "seconds" and further threaten the sustainability of the area's emergency food system. And since Mr. Rauch has already announced his intentions to open at least two more Daily Tables in Boston, these fears may very well be justified.

In *Closing the Food Gap*, I deferred to Janet Poppendieck's (http://www .janetpoppendieck.com/about.html) summary of the odd bedfellows that our system of *not* ending hunger has bred. In her important work, *Sweet Charity?: Emergency Food and the End of Entitlement* (1999), she wrote:

> The emergency food system has become very useful indeed . . . The United States Department of Agriculture uses it to reduce the accumulation of . . . agricultural surpluses. Business uses it to dispose of unwanted product [and] to avoid dump fees. . . . Environmentalists use it to reduce the solid waste stream. A wide array of groups, organizations and institutions benefits from the halo effect of "feeding the hungry." If we didn't have hunger, we'd have to invent it.

Sadly, we do have hunger, and based on the USDA's data, food insecurity in the U.S. has actually increased over the past ten years. Food banks have grown significantly in both numbers and size. In other words, we are either losing the war on hunger in America or at best, we've reached a stalemate. While the new merchandising strategies of projects like The Daily Table and the fervor of the massed troops of waste recovery armies may mitigate the effects of food insecurity, they'll never resolve it. After all, hunger is a function of poverty and our nation's grotesque income inequality.

But in the complex world of attacking devilishly difficult socioeconomic problems, it's not always what you do, but how you do it that counts. In the case of Daily Table and Mr. Rauch's earnest, hard-driving entrepreneurism, it might have been more useful if he had turned his prodigious talents on devising long-term systemic solutions rather than another variation on a short-term mitigation strategy. Systemic solutions fueled by public policy and private partners are what's called for.

For instance, just down the road apiece from Daily Table sits the future home of the still-in-development Dorchester Community Food Coop. Several years in the making, the Coop intends to provide a full range of healthy and affordable food in a community that is sorely in need of both. Moreover, the Coop will, according to Darnell Adams, the project manager, "build community wealth and ownership." Like any other business, it will also pay taxes, which the nonprofit Daily Table will not, a point that prompted one community member to note that Dorchester "is saturated with non-profits that don't pay taxes."

Jennie Msall, a member of the Coop's board of directors told me, "People in Dorchester are not poor because they're spending too much money on food; people are poor because there aren't good jobs, while at the same time social services are being cut." While she and other Coop members I spoke to did not object to Daily Table—they saw it as one of many options to increasing access to healthy food—they felt that Dorchester, like many economically challenged communities, needed numerous connected projects that would empower their residents, bring lasting economic benefits and system-wide change, and meet basic community needs.

That's a tall order, especially in a country that can't seem to raise its minimum wage above that of Burundi's. But the fervent hope that better coordination, a vibrant food economy, and a shared vision for ending hunger may be in the works. Labeled the Massachusetts Food System Plan, contractors working under the auspices of the Massachusetts Food Policy Council have developed a comprehensive framework to create jobs, reduce hunger, and increase the availability of fresh, healthy food to all residents, and also *reduce waste*.

In speaking with Jessica del Rosario, who heads up the Food System Plan's Food Access, Food Security and Health Work Group, I was told, "The Daily Table is a niche within a broader frame of what a food-secure community can look like." Acknowledging that she was generally biased against "seconds" as a food source, especially for lower-income people, she noted that "people I know who are food insecure want to buy food from a regular market." As such, she and other members of the planning team strongly favor the development of high-quality affordable food outlets in the state's so-called food deserts, more food and nutrition education opportunities for consumers, and, ultimately, measures that will increase income of everyone to purchase healthy and local food.

But getting all the players who need to be on the same team to "own" this plan and take responsibility for it will take wisdom, leadership, and, yes, sacrifice. As del Rosario pointed out, the Food Plan recommends a mechanism, that is, an organizational structure, to "increase communication, foster food-related, cross-sector networks, and maximize existing and future resources." In other words, a really big sandbox where grown-up, interactive play is the law of the land.

Until all eyes are on the same ball, any community's collection of food projects, agencies, and businesses will be nothing more than a bunch of singles hitters scattering their shots all over the field, but never scoring enough runs to win the game. Absent a shared vision, shared goals and a common mechanism to work together, the field will be open to the next entrepreneur or food issue that manages to float to the top.

## But There's Never Enough

In 2015, the Michigan-based Kresge Foundation sent out a request for proposals for organizations to develop comprehensive food plans for their neighborhoods and communities. Much to the surprise of their staff, they received over 500 applications of which they were only able to fund 26 at about $75,000 each. The foundation had read the landscape correctly—communities wanted to do longer term, integrated planning with numerous partners—but the demand for that kind of funding far exceeded supply—by a ratio of nearly 20:1 (Williams, 2016). As Tufts University nutrition professor and 40-year food activist Hugh Joseph defined the funding problem, "We all get a pittance because there are too many food organizations and not enough money." Joseph is also a grant writer par excellence. Joseph's "batting average" for writing successful grant applications would place him on the Grant Writers Hall of Fame All-Star team. But his success comes indirectly at the price of so many food groups who then don't receive the funds they desperately need. He cites the fact that his home state Massachusetts has 260 farmers' markets, which, he feels, are far too many. Similarly, he notes that the state is "too rich with competent non-profits and academic institutions" who are highly capable but constantly competing with one another for funding.

Funding levels, the length of a funding term, and funder priorities are the shifting sands upon which organizations try to build their action plans. Reading the changing winds is the art required of any good executive director and fund-raiser. But even the most artful among them is often baffled. Ferd Hoefner speaks of the frustration of dealing with big issues, such as the farm to school movement and the Food Safety Modernization Act (FSMA) without adequate foundation funding. He says that foundations put considerable pressure on the National Sustainable Agriculture Coalition to adopt the budding farm to school public policy work with an expectation that they do the work virtually for free.

FSMA is imposing an array of food safety regulations on agriculture, which, as many experts say, threatens to drive small farmers out of business due to higher costs associated with rule compliance. Given that the Congressional law making system and the USDA's rule making process take years to complete, it's necessary for national advocates, especially those who represent vulnerable groups like small farmers, to be engaged in the process for the long haul. For instance, the proposed FSMA rules are now up to 1,000 pages. Hoefner says he has difficulty convincing foundations to commit the long-term funding required to do the painful work of making sure the rules don't adversely affect smaller, sustainably operating farmers.

Foundations are often possessed by the venture capitalist spirit. Though they are not looking for the financial return that traditional investors want, foundations are expecting a demonstrated "social pay-out"—that society is better off because of their intervention. The problem is that changing society generally requires more time than the development and commercialization of the latest digitalized widget gizmo does. When foundations only make one-year grants, change their priorities frequently, and even decide that they know how to change society better than the groups that have been working on it a long time, then groups have little or no incentive to work together and build long-term collaborations.

As a counterpoint to this all-too-common "we want results now!" approach to foundation giving, Valentine Doyle, the head of the Lawson Valentine Foundation, based in Hartford, Connecticut, sees long-term commitments to nonprofits with proven effectiveness as the key to success. "My drug of choice, the cherry on the cake's icing" as she puts it, is to connect groups that are doing similar work. She's noticed, for instance, that there are numerous urban agriculture youth projects throughout New England. By playing "matchmaker" Valentine has been able to encourage these agriculture and youth organizations scattered across multiple cities to do some joint problem solving and even consider what their collective advocacy potential might be. It seems like an easy thing for a grant maker to do—"since I'm giving you money, I want you to spend a little time working with others doing the same thing"—but I have found that attitude is rare in the foundation world.

The Lawson Valentine Foundation thinks it's important to the process of food system change to promote networking between new and emerging food system sectors. One such "emerging" sector is farm workers and food chain workers who generally subsist on wages at or just above the minimum wage. Organizations, such as the Coalition of Immokalee Workers (harvesters in Florida's agricultural areas) and Food Chain Workers Alliance, are bringing to the attention of the larger food movement the critical needs of those who pick, process, and serve us our food. Valentine has been active in ensuring that long-standing food organizations, particularly the ones that her founda-tion funds, are paying attention to these groups and needs.

The Jessie Smith Noyes Foundation based in New York City has been a food system funder for at least 20 years. They have funded comprehensive food system-focused organizations like the one I ran in Hartford, and more recently they have been an active supporter of grassroots organizations often led by people of color. According to Kolu Zigbe, Noyes's Food System Pro-gram Officer, they want to empower local leadership with the intent of increasing community control of the food system, a process that sometimes starts with the development of alternative food enterprises. Kolu acknowledges that her foundation is atypical because of its system's orientation and a board of directors made up of many community organizers. "There is a culture in philanthropy that is atomistic," she says. "They don't know whether they are funding a network or something else, like a single project." She also echoes a theme heard often in philanthropic circles that foundation boards often lag behind their staff who tend to be more progressive in outlook and closer to the problems and issues. For that reason, foundation policies, including who and what they fund, are slow to catch up with changing needs.

Oran Hesterman, a former program officer with the Kellogg Foundation and the CEO of Fair Food Network, describes in his book *Fair Food* [2011] the slow, sometimes torturous route that foundation boards take to finally embrace new ideas. When he began work at the foundation in the early 1990s, he says "we were not allowed to use the words 'sustainable,' 'environment,' or 'policy'" (p. 156). Through an active process of internal education, largely led by a progressive team of staff, the Kellogg board began to shift its understanding of these issues during the early to mid-2000s. Of course, this was probably a good thing 20 years after the food movement had been using those words and engaging in that work. Since I and organizations I worked for received Kellogg funding during that time frame, I can remember hearing from foundation staff how sensitive the issue of policy funding was, for example, funding that would support efforts to change federal food and agriculture policy. I have it on good authority that teams of lawyers were kept well employed coming up with definitions, guidelines, and do-or-die restrictions on exactly how the foundation's money could be used when it finally crossed into a kind of food policy Demilitarized Zone (DMZ)—a place in the Vietnam War where combat was supposedly forbidden but took place anyway.

But as Hesterman makes clear, the breakthrough in the foundation world's embrace of sustainability and public policy gradually picked up speed during the 21st century's first decade and became a fast train over the last few years. Today, there are about 100 foundations that make up the Sustainable Agriculture and Food System Funders network, many of whose members support policy work. But what's important in understanding this growth is that while it represents a philosophical sea change, it still does not support the kind of collaboration among grant recipients and others that is necessary for transformative change.

One notable exception to the collaboration challenge was instigated by the Kellogg Foundation in response to the 2002 Farm Bill. As reported by Hesterman, Kellogg had become comfortable enough with supporting organizations to do education and outreach work that was related to public policy (dire threats were still issued to grantees that invoked Hammurabi's Code if they dared to cross the line into lobbying). Though $2 million was distributed to eight organizations to work on their 2002 Farm Bill priorities, there was no explicit attempt made to forge a coalition or any other collaborative mechanism between them. Some of the grantees secured modest policy successes such as the authorization of the Farmers' Market Promotion Program and additional funding for conservation programs. However, as Hesterman makes clear, the hoped-for collaboration never occurred: "My biggest revelation . . . was that non-profit organizations couldn't be expected to behave in mutually supportive ways. . . . Because the grantees . . . were never funded as a coalition or collaboration . . . when one organization . . . decided to leave the coalition [the loosely connected eight grantees] . . . because it was offered a deal, the support for a major reform bill fell short of what was needed to pass" (p. 202).

Having learned its lesson, Kellogg altered its path in preparation for what would become the 2008 Farm Bill. In hopes of achieving more food and farm policy victories, the foundation funded five "core organizations" with $6 million over a three-year period (at the time, I worked for the Community Food Security Coalition, one of the five funded organizations). The difference was that the organizations formed a collaborative called the Food and Farm Policy Project that was guided by a secretariat or "hub" known as the Northeast/Midwest Institute, which itself did not have a specific policy agenda. Under Kellogg's watchful eye, the Farm and Food Policy Project (FFPP) forged a vision and a set of policy goals that provided the initiative with a reasonably strong organizational framework.

Ultimately, the policy outcomes that occurred in a difficult political and economic environment—a Republican administration that was not keen on establishing and funding more government programs, and the beginning of the Great Recession—were substantial. They included continued funding for the Community Food Project Grant program, funding under the previously authorized Farmers' Market Promotion Program for electronic benefit transfer (EBT) technology to enable farmers' markets to accept food stamps, a USDA food desert study, geographic preference for local food purchased by schools, specialty crop block grants for states, and the Healthy Urban Food Enterprise Development Program to create healthier food access in underserved communities. Along with other programs that were also priorities of FFPP team members, these constituted a much better "won-loss" record than six years earlier. According to an estimate by Alan Hunt, a key member of the team and staff person for the NE/MW Institute, the five-year value of the programs that the FFPP addressed came to $5 billion (2015, p. 163). Though many factors outside of the collaboration contributed to this success, it's clear that the $6 million of Kellogg funding leveraged an enormous return.

Though most of the collaboration's members stayed through to the end, there were clearly fault lines that, in one case, led to the abandonment of the collaboration by one of its biggest partners. There will be much more discussion about the group dynamics and structural issues that the FFPP struggled with in later chapters, but suffice it to say that Kellogg's commitment to insisting on collaboration between grant recipients, in fact funding the collaboration rather than just the individual organizations, had an impressive pay off.

## Federal Funding

Let's use this point to transition from private funders to federal funding. I will say from the outset that it is through the development, funding, and support of numerous federal food and agriculture programs over the last 40 years that one can track the movement's evolution. Like a long-distance traveler trekking across an ever-changing landscape, the food movement historian would witness a complex evolution of public interests, consumer values, and the exercise of market power gradually revealing themselves through federal policy. While from a distance that landscape may appear to a sensible hiker as too rugged to traverse, it may also be the place where, with the benefit of a good GPS device, people can navigate their way to greater unity.

As an emerging student and practitioner of Washington, D.C., politics and policy making, I learned in the mid-1980s that establishing a federal food program, usually within the USDA, was not as hard as you'd think. Sustaining that program, however, with regular Congressional appropriations and ensuring that the federal bureaucracies make good on their responsibility for implementing those programs is actually harder than gaining the initial Congressional authorization. Both the policy formulation and its implementation require well-organized nongovernment groups and constituencies to advocate in Washington, D.C. Such groups require "inside the Beltway" policy offices either staffed with lobbyists and analysts or, at the very least, policy experts hired as private contractors.

When the USDA prepares and recommends rules and regulations, as they generally do for programs newly authorized by Congress, an even more intense and technically sophisticated engagement is necessary (see the discussion of NSAC's role and FSMA rule-making) to ensure that the final programs conform to the wishes of Congress, but more importantly, the wishes of the interest groups that "own" that program. And "own" is not too strong a word because it's within this elongated policy making and implementation process, which sometimes stretches over many years, that the policy turf is carefully divided and controlled, and where the landscape requires increasingly specialized navigation.

In the review of my early days in Hartford, I described how one Connecticut organization willingly shared a federal grant with my organization to develop Connecticut's farmers' market nutrition program. The funds came from a small federal program, now extinct, called the Community Food and Nutrition Program (CFNP). CFNP gave out grants of only $50,000 from a small pool of a few million dollars each year. Now even in the 1980s, $50,000 was a modest sum of money and, if you had to apply for it every year, it sometimes felt like it was more trouble than it was worth. But I learned two things from CFNP. The first was that the grant allowed you to be innovative, which gave you enormous flexibility to try out new community nutrition ideas, for example, the Farmers Market Nutrition Program. And second, and I think more important, by giving out small grants all over the country on an annual basis, CFNP developed a significant and potent number of supporters. This constituency would fight very hard from year to year to defend the program in Congress, largely to ensure a steady flow of funds, even if they were a mere pittance in comparison to programs like food stamps and Women, Infant, and Children Program (WIC). Many grants spread across many states and congressional districts translated into more supporters in Congress.

While not exactly a formula, this process for developing and sustaining "small" federal food programs would become a common practice. I became involved in a similar effort in the late 1980s to start what would become USDA's WIC/Farmers Market Nutrition Program, then, about 10 years later, the Senior/Farmers Market Nutrition Program, and in 1994, the Community Food Projects (CFPs) grant program. All three programs did something that previous federal programs didn't; they were designed to connect at least two different constituent groups—WIC participants (later, lower income seniors) and farmers, and in the case of CFP, to connect as many local food interests as possible in a single project (CFP's role and its attempt to transcend single project, nonfood system thinking will be discussed later).

As I was celebrating the creation of all of these innovative and dynamic new federal food programs, which I frankly regarded as a huge affirmation of my life's work, I heard that questioning voice in my head that has plagued me throughout my career. It was asking if this was the right way to transform the nation's food system. How many of these little programs, each with their own supporting associations, networks, funding streams, Congressional and USDA champions, conferences, and local and state supporters, would it take to fulfill a much larger vision?

The "aha" moment would come for me in 1991. The association that we had formed to advance the WIC/FMNP in Congress was called the National Association of Farmers Market Nutrition Programs. Up until that point we had only been successful in getting Congress to approve a three-year pilot for $2 million each year. Following a great deal of education, lobbying, and organizing work, we finally convinced Congress to make WIC/FMNP a permanent USDA food and nutrition program. Our leader, who was a seasoned policy hand in his home state of Pennsylvania as well as in Washington, D.C., came on to our association's conference call and said, "Congratulations everyone! We have just received approval from Congress to start USDA's 13th food and nutrition program!" Thirteen, I gasped to myself! Why do we need 13 separate federal programs to address hunger, poor nutrition, and the survival of our local and regional farms? As it turns out, my confusion was premature, because today we have 16 USDA programs and I've played at least a small part in starting numbers 13–16.

## So, What's the Problem?

Shouldn't we echo Spike Lee by saying "the mo' federal food programs, the mo' better?" We all take great pride in the creation of a program, policy, or project. Its birth is a validation of our work, our progeny, and our legacy. Like our children, we're willing to do almost anything for them. We nurture them, keep them from threat or harm, and seek to maximize their potential. We may be constructively critical of them, but we never objectively evaluate them to determine their strength and weaknesses, how they might perform substantially better, possibly merge them with other programs, or God forbid, consider their elimination due to low performance, redundancy, or the emergence of more effective strategies. Such rational approaches to program development and evaluation are tantamount to surrender.

While this may be viewed as heresy by some, federal food programs are not children nor are they humans of any kind. They are of course created by humans, managed and even nurtured by humans, but they deserve a much sharper scrutiny than we could ever imagine giving our children. Unfortunately, they are only criticized by those who have a political axe to grind or an ideological position to stake out, for example, "government is too big." Rarely is opposition to a federal program based on a thorough review of its merits. The defense of these same programs, with equal avoidance of the data, comes from their staunch guardians who often act like parents who think their children walk on water, for example, "don't dare touch my program, it feeds hungry people!"

This pattern of program protectionism—"it's sacred, don't touch it"—has historically extended to the way veteran program advocates treat the new kid on the block and their upstart programs. In the early 1990s, the Center for Budget and Policy Priorities, a staunch defender of the WIC program, tried very hard to stifle the development of the WIC/Farmers Market Nutrition Program. Starting in 1995 and continuing up until the 2008 Farm Bill, the Food Research Action Center tried to slow down or derail the development of the Community Food Project Grants program. In 2008, the National Alliance for Nutrition and Activity (NANA) and the Child Nutrition Forum both opposed support for the Community Food Security Coalition and the National Farm to School Network's effort to create a federal farm-to-school program (Ibid., p. 40).

The arguments were always the same: We don't want a new program with separate funding authority until we fully fund our existing program, even though the existing programs, for example, WIC that was funded at $5 billion compared to about $10 million for the FMNP, were vast multiples more than the new one. They also had no interest in connecting multiple food system dots, for example, local farmers to child nutrition. As Andy Fisher makes clear in *Big Hunger*, the advocacy organizations that defend SNAP, WIC, and all the school meal programs have at best a limited interest in expanding the impact of their somewhat narrowly defined programs. In the case of SNAP (formerly food stamps) this has led to serious criticism of the $75 billion food program's lack of focus on the nutrition and health impacts of the foods purchased by its recipients.

The squabbling in the food movement community is of course music to the ears of antagonistic members of Congress. When budgets are tight (and when are they not) and ideological tensions running high, it is easy for powerful committee chairs to play one group off against another (Hunt, pp. 53, 54). Cuts in the always vulnerable SNAP program are threatened or imposed with the "savings" supposedly directed to other government priorities including a favorite new food program of another Congressional member. The lack of a unified food movement voice in Washington can leave even supportive Congresspersons perplexed as they are likely to get mixed signals from different food and farm constituencies. When members of Congress cut the final deals in the final hours of a session, one group's win can often be another group's loss.

The federal government is a powerful force for food system change. As someone who's been an active participant in federally funded food programs, Hugh Joseph says, "Federal funding cycles have influenced the food movement since the 1960s." Democratic administrations tend to make more money available than Republican ones, which since 2009 has meant a significant increase in federal support for some of the smaller, regional food system-oriented food programs. Many of these emerged or were expanded under the umbrella of the Obama-era USDA signature initiative "Know Your Farmer, Know Your Food." According to Elanor Starmer, former special assistant to former USDA secretary Tom Vilsack, the Obama administration had made over $1 billion in investments (USDA likes to refer to grants as "investments") available for regional food systems from 2009 to 2015 (Starmer, 2015).

Yes, the availability of money that is targeted for food system purposes influences what I'll do as a food program operator; more programs and more money expand my choices. But as Hugh Joseph said, "there's never enough." As the demand grows—a demand that is fragmented by numerous interests—and the political will increases, so does the size of the funding pie. But all those fragmented interests, when they do their work well and are successful, only receive a small sliver of that pie; enough to give them a taste—never enough to share with other interests—but just enough to make them hungry for more.

But in spite of the perennial tug of war over federal food and farm money, baby steps occur that occasionally bring different interests together. While such cooperation would never entail one interest voluntarily giving up existing funds for another, agreement is occasionally reached that allows one pot of money to be used to meet the needs of multiple interests. I've already discussed the Community Food Projects Grant program and Farm to School initiatives as examples of these. Another program that was first authorized by Congress in 2014 and launched by USDA one year later pushed the envelope a little further in the direction of cooperation and hence, more unity. It is called the Food Insecurity Nutrition Incentive (FINI), and is another one of USDA's small grant programs ($16.8 million in grants in 2016). By providing low-income families, who are participants in SNAP, with incentives—educational as well as financial—to purchase healthy food, especially at farmers' markets, federal policy is tilting at several objectives with one program: encourage healthier eating, reduce poverty, and strengthen local and regional food systems and their economies.

Like most other "small" USDA programs that have multiple objectives, FINI sprouted from local and state models developed by nonprofit organizations, including Fair Food Network and Wholesome Wave. The original concept was called "Double Up Food Bucks," or sometimes just "Double Bucks," to indicate that SNAP users could expect either a doubling of amount, or at least a bonus amount, when their SNAP benefits were used at farmers' markets. The local roots of the concept gave it a fair amount of grassroots support, which helps with Congressional approval, but it also makes for an immediate and relatively smooth roll-out of the program once USDA approves applications and makes grants.

In New Mexico, FINI funds were granted to the New Mexico Farmers' Marketing Association to increase SNAP use and healthy eating at the state's numerous farmers' markets. The federal funding leveraged funding from the state of New Mexico Legislature (and state commitments can sometime leverage federal funding) that will expand program's impact by serving more farmers and low-income families. Another feature of FINI is flexibility—grant programs that allow variations within broad programmatic themes can be very helpful to discovering the best approaches to difficult problems. One grant in 2016 went to Wholesome Wave in Bridgeport, Connecticut, for an innovative approach that will be used in both Hartford, Connecticut and northeastern Vermont. In these two cases—one urban and one rural—local grocery stores will be the place where SNAP recipients will use their benefits and incentives to purchase fresh fruits and vegetables, not farmers' markets. This is based on a very successful pilot project run by the Hartford Food System in 2015 using foundation dollars to test the use of an independent, medium-sized grocery store as a place to promote year-round purchase of produce by nutritionally vulnerable residents (personal communication with Martha Page, executive director of the Hartford Food System). One might call this one strong step in the direction of more unity since it applies a concept that was designed to link local farmers to the nutritional needs of lower-income families to a concept that seeks to strengthen conventional grocery stores in lower income, sometimes food desert communities.

The foregoing description represents a selective historical review of the evolution of a few federal food programs and a consideration of the impact of intergroup dynamics ("interorganizational politics") on the policy-making process. The key point is that rather than seeking alliances between two or more organizations and their respective, but different, program interests in hopes of enhancing existing efforts and providing additional benefits for their clients or constituents, groups tend to secure their borders and mark their turf. When a new approach to addressing a food or agriculture program emerges, and it appears as if federal support is warranted, the stakeholders behind the new idea generally create a brand-new organization, largely because no willing partners invite them into their tent. The results are more federal programs and usually a little more money, which is spread out over a greater variety of funding needs. None of this, unfortunately, builds pathways to a unified, joined-up, and interconnected strategy that will meet the nation's food, farm, environment, and health needs in a holistic fashion.

# CHAPTER SIX

# Moving toward Unity

Alexis de Tocqueville, the French chronicler of the early 19th-century American experience, made no secret of his admiration for the way "Americans of all ages, conditions, and all dispositions constantly unite together" (1835/2002, 628). Before those of us who see the United States differently wonder just what narcotic Alex was concealing in his snuff box, let's look for a moment at the world through his eyes.

Coming from England and France where he experienced authoritarian governments, nobility, and landed gentry exercising top-down forms of control, de Tocqueville witnessed a budding and chaotic nation that was inventing itself from the ground up. With a weak federal government, a steadily growing number of barely cooperating states, and thousands of local communities spread across a large land mass, the only way anything could get done would be if the people pulled together. "In the United States," he said, "you can count on finding an association" to not only see to various commercial and industrial activities but also "to hold fetes, found seminaries, build inns, construct churches, distribute books, establish hospitals, prisons, and schools" (1835/2002, 628). The so-called voluntary association was the vehicle around which people united at a local level to meet the country's increasingly diversified needs.

Whereas the "old world" comprised wealthy aristocrats who had "the ability to perform great enterprises single-handed" and could virtually compel others to join them, or often needed no one at all, a democratic nation in the form of 1830s America developed the ability "to set a common aim to the efforts of a great number of men and to persuade them to pursue it voluntarily." De Tocqueville did not mean to suggest that this collective rabble of cast-off Europeans, indentured servants, and the stolen people of Africa collectively possessed some noble strain of humanity that allowed them to pledge their souls to the common good. Not at all. Instead, he saw the spirit of association as an expression of "how an enlightened regard for themselves constantly prompts them to assist one another." In other words, working together toward a commonly agreed-upon end was a matter of survival in a rough land where there was not yet even a cavalry to come to your rescue. Conversely, "A nation in which individuals lost the capacity to achieve great things . . . without acquiring the means of doing them in a shared enterprise would quickly revert to barbarism" (De Tocqueville, 1835/2002, 630).

Where do the acute observations of this ahead-of-his-time Frenchman leave the food movement some 180 years later? De Tocqueville's essay conjures up images of citizen groups raising steeples, cutting timbers for new schoolhouses, and raising funds to construct a building or two on what is to become a region's first college campus. Perhaps in scale if not also with a singular kind of purpose, I see rough parallels between the forging of America's early community infrastructure and the tens of thousands of local food enterprises like farmers' markets, food pantries, community gardens, and larger, more complex operations like community-owned supermarkets and organizations that advocate for the rights of food and farm workers. A felt need is based on the existence of a problem; two or more people articulate the need, offer leadership of varying degrees of intensity; a group from a specific place or industry sector forms, a project is defined, funds are raised, and noses are set to the grindstone.

But de Tocqueville didn't live long enough or revisit America more frequently to study the performance of these associations over time. In the parlance of researchers, there was no longitudinal survey. If he had a university department available to him, it could have sent generation after generation of researchers to follow up on his observations. At the very least, they would have seen America's Civil War, the ever-unfolding trauma associated with the oppression of Native Americans and African Americans, and community after community divided by class, religion, wealth, and all the numerations of that great human list that we draw upon when we need a reason to exclude someone. His acolytes would no doubt discover as well that government— local, state, and national—would gradually assume more responsibility for providing the goods, services, and capital infrastructure that a growing nation would require. In other words, associations, whose members are so well organized as to achieve an ambitious, but limited task, did not have the capacity to carry out larger, more complex functions. Neither could they create an "association of associations" capable of bridging significant divides between themselves and taking on more complex tasks.

It is in these strengths and weaknesses of America's early associations that I find uncanny comparisons with the food movement—with one important exception: the food movements' ability to overcome the limitations of associations and their everyday parochialism. Voices from the food movement— colleagues I cite throughout this book—agree and disagree that we are capable of achieving something far greater than the sum of our parts.

Hank Herrera, a long-time food activist from New York and California, former president of the Community Food Security Coalition (CFSC) Board of Directors and currently the president of the Center for Popular Research, Education and Policy, has witnessed enormous changes in the food movement since he entered it over 27 years ago. Through his involvement with the CFSC (to be discussed in more depth in a later section), he saw a "tremendous exchange of knowledge" between different sectors of the food system and a phenomenal amount of enthusiasm marked by the 200 people who came to the organization's first annual conference in 1997 and the 1,200 people who came to its last conference in 2011 (personal communication).

As a person who advocated tirelessly for the inclusion of people of color in the food movement, he notes two things. The first is that the food movement as a whole has failed to bridge the racial divide in the sense that leadership of the movement's many organizations is still largely white and that leadership is still not in touch with the roots of racism and oppression. The second thing, which largely accounts for Herrera's continuing enthusiasm for the movement, is that there has been "a huge increase in the number of people of color doing food system work, especially in the area of urban agriculture." He attributes this to the rise of important African American role models like Will Allen, founder of the Milwaukee-based Growing Power, and Malik Yakini, cofounder of the Detroit Black Community Food Security Network. In a larger sense, however, Herrera finds the goals of community food security (CFS)—a more embracing and comprehensive food system concept—consistent with the goals of community development. "Food is a pathway to change that supports self-reliance and resilience, and it's also consistent with people of color's deep connection to the land," he says.

This mixed review of enthusiasm for the movement's progress and disappointment with its shortcomings remains tethered to a profound uncertainty about the future. "Americans don't know how to collaborate and cooperate; we have a culture of individualism," he notes after informing me that he is also a member of a farm coop. He quotes the psychiatrist Harry Stack Sullivan (Herrera is also a psychiatrist) as saying, "Cooperation is the highest form of maturity, and competition is derived from an adolescent state." In short, Herrera aspires to a higher level of collaboration between movement groups—like just about everyone I've discussed the subject with—but remains skeptical that it will ever be achieved.

Michael Rozyne of Red Tomato is another food movement leader and activist who understands the promise of a more collaborative food movement. As described in an earlier section about communication, Rozyne wants a "bigger tent" that is more inclusive of different food system interests. His experience has led him to believe that collaboration between various groups is currently hindered by ineffective and even dysfunctional communication. With respect to questions of race and equity, Rozyne has also taken a strong position in favor of far greater inclusivity of people of color in the regional organization he works with, the Northeast Sustainable Agriculture Working Group (NESAWG). But he makes a point, which perhaps sets him apart from others who passionately advocate for greater attention to racial equity in the food movement, stating "Diversity is not an end in and of itself nor is it a 'product'—it is in fact a means to democracy." In his mind, diversity means more food system stakeholders are essential to success, perhaps drawing a line of exclusivity when it comes to "Big Food," but making it clear that it should not exclude "bigger food." This distinction has merit and the potential to bring more clarity to the discourse over race, because too often the argument hits a dead end over the question of "Okay, we have more people of color at the table. Now what?" If we respect the means for what it is—not the end—and we work hard to identify common goals and share responsibility for achieving them, then we have something that looks like a working democracy, which is certainly one prerequisite for success (personal communication).

This leaves open the question of a context, and even a location, for the operation of a diversified food movement. For Tom Kelly, a professor who heads up the Sustainability Institute at the University of New Hampshire, the context is the food system and the place is a state and a region. Within a defined region like New England with its six relatively small states, there is ample opportunity for collaboration to occur, according to Kelly. "Fragmented interests are a problem," he says, "because they are focused on only one thing. When we talk about the 'food system' we have a framework for bridging the gaps between us." By way of example he offers the challenge, some food advocates have had working with farmers who have been "freaked out" by terms like "food access" and "sustainability." For farmers, increasing access to affordable food, that is, cheaper food for lower-income families, can mean lower farm prices. Running a farm in a sustainable fashion, which everyone agrees is a desirable goal, can mean higher operating costs for the farmer. In other words, to meet all consumer demands, the farmer could face lower product prices and higher operating costs (personal communication).

But according to Kelly, when the food system frame is imposed on this divisive, either/or debate, participants begin to understand how the parts connect to one another. They see, for instance, what the consequences are of placing one goal, for example, affordable food for all, above another goal, for example, the viability of local and regional farming. When this conversation takes place, relationships develop that promote trust among the different food system actors. Even "Big [or bigger] Food" can take part because advocates realize that even large commercial retail interests are not *against* good food access for all.

This regional food system approach has been given voice over the past few years by a project called "Food Solutions New England," which Kelly oversees through the Sustainability Institute. Through a process that involved both extensive outreach to all six New England states and in depth research into the region's food and farm conditions, goals were set and ratified at a New England Food Summit. As a comprehensive, food systems approach, the summit stands out as singular advancement for the practice of food movement democracy. Each of the six states had to identify 20 delegates to attend the conference, which brought 120 people together to ratify proposals and set some direction. While the summit (which has continued to be held annually) created many concrete goals with respect to food production, food access, and food security, it also placed racial equity and justice goals at its core, goals that Kelly told me were enthusiastically adopted by all the delegates. This means, for example, that the region's food chain workers are at the planning and implementation table, one immediate outcome of which has been Vermont dairy workers speaking directly to dairy owners.

Kelly is very excited about the entire Food Solutions New England process. "There is a yearning to connect and to learn about what others are doing," he tells me. Good facilitation and purposeful, structured networking opportunities like Food Solutions are enabling more food system stakeholders to satisfy that yearning. As evidence of this surging desire to both connect and to strengthen the region's food system, Kelly points to the Boston Local Food Festival, which was attended by 60,000 people in 2015. But he doesn't let his exuberance get ahead of him, making it clear that good management and appropriate structures are necessary for success. "We need to be cognizant of how fast the food movement is growing. While it could be a force for change that raises all ships, it could just as easily be a source of division and continuing inequity."

Samina Raja sees the food movement hanging in the balance in a manner similar to Tom Kelly. As a planning professor at the University of Buffalo, Raja has been active for many years in bringing the eyes and the skills of professional planners to food system work. She has done this nationally as a member of the CFSC's board of directors, regionally as the principal investigator in a U.S. Department of Agriculture/National Institute of Food and Agriculture (USDA/NIFA)-funded project called Growing Food Connections, and locally as an organizer and consultant to the City of Buffalo Food Policy Council. She characterizes the food movement as a "Pope-less religion that has no singular voice." While she doesn't advocate that the movement elect a Pope, Raja feels it could benefit from a good orchestral conductor. She says, "There are many smaller voices clamoring to be heard, and many feel left out such as African-American groups," echoing Kelly's fear of "division and continuing inequity." She goes on to say that "people are often talking past each other" and that with better coordination the movement might find a way to define numerous shared roles that could come together in at least a loose coalition. And like many others whom I interviewed for this book, she said "the Community Food Security Coalition was an incredible example" that deserves some form of regeneration.

**

So far, I've reviewed some of the practical arguments for joining together, creating appropriate organizational structures, and constructing communication frameworks. Having personally experienced the joy of working in successful coalitions and the heartbreak of failed ones, I know there is a high degree of emotional content and ego that transcends the rational arguments of organization and communication theory. Though we may not be standing at the altar exchanging vows, sacrificing some degree of our individualism for the sake of a group may require a good deal of heart and no small measure of faith.

Before we move into some of the models of cooperation and collaboration that show promise of unifying the food movement—models that grow out of careful observation if not solid evidence—let's briefly consider the moral and theological argument for working together. Norman Wirzba in his book *Food and Faith: A Theology of Eating* (2011) puts the matter of denying our need to belong in no less dramatic terms than mankind's fall from grace. "We know that we belong to others, that they need us just as we need them," writes Wirzba, "but we can't bear the responsibility or the gift [of God]." In what he calls the "anxiety of membership" (p. 77). Wirzba asserts that the human propensity to stand alone and not recognize our essential interdependence, preferring to think that we are self-reliant individuals capable of weathering any storm, is not only a denial of God's gifts, but a forfeiture of the joy that comes from belonging.

As one might expect, our pride is often the culprit when we get into trouble. Invoking our independence rather than celebrating our interdependence leaves us, according to Wirzba, flailing and falling, unable to stand on our own. Even worse, "It is also to die by starvation" because we refuse to participate in "the multiple food webs that constitute and circulate through every living organism. Eating is the daily confirmation that we need others and are vulnerable to them." Membership is not a burden but a gift. "God calls humanity to a life of membership informed by mercy and care, fidelity and love."

Hank Herrera may be right, "Americans don't know how to collaborate and cooperate; we have a culture of individualism." Perhaps knowing full well of this design flaw in His human creatures, God gave us the scriptures to guide us as well as the theologians to interpret them. It may very well be part of the reason that there were so many clergy present in that Hartford church on that day when the members of the nascent anti-hunger coalition set aside their individualism and affirmed their faith in the group. Regardless of one's faith or spiritual practice, or the complete absence of both, belonging and standing together still may be the shortest route back to the Garden.

## Community Food Security

At the 2015 NESAWG annual meeting in Saratoga Springs, New York, Carolyn Mugar, the executive director of the national farmer action organization Farm Aid, compared the food movement to a high school dance. "Everyone's out on the gym floor listening to the same song and moving around, but no one's dancing with anyone," she told the audience at the conference's opening plenary.

It seemed like an apt metaphor—bodies gyrating to a commonly heard tune but everyone doing their own thing. By contrast I wondered what things would be like if the food movement more closely resembled formal dance traditions like the waltz or square dancing. Could we learn to dance first as couples who would move as one unit making carefully timed and syncopated steps around a crowded dance floor, hopefully free of mashing each other's toes? Once this two-way partnership was mastered could we then move on to the larger group dances that often require a caller to set the directions and connections for their many participants? When done well by practiced feet, these formations are a thing of beauty, like synchronized schools of fish swirling and diving in the shallows of coastal shoals.

Though my own dance moves were most assuredly of the high school gym variety, I always admired those choreographed formations typical of modern dance or Broadway performances. They combined the elegance and power of many energized bodies moving through space with a shared purpose across a stage, but they also recognized and optimized the individual strength of each dancer. They would evoke in me W.B. Yeats' wonderful poetic question, "How can we know the dancer from the dance?" It may have been this inherent appreciation of artistic order that inspired me to think about food systems and the food movement in a similar way. As food projects of many shapes and hues were organizing themselves across the United States from the 1970s to the early 1990s, it became apparent to me through my work at the Hartford Food System (HFS) and as a result of contacts throughout the nation that more and more communities were developing the same cluster of food projects. There were food banks, farmers' markets, community gardens, and various anti-hunger initiatives of one kind or another no matter where you went. But while they all had vaguely similar goals, they lacked a coherent framework within which to work. It was out of this unchoreographed mélange that the concept of CFS began to emerge.

CFS was a relatively new food security-promoting concept when it first emerged in the early 1990s. What differentiated it from previous initiatives was that it considered all the factors within a region or community's food system that influenced the availability, cost, and quality of food, particularly among lower-income households.

Since CFS focuses on regional and local food systems, it is concerned with the full range of food chain events including agriculture, the availability of supermarkets and other affordable retail food outlets, community participation in activities that shape the food system, the involvement of local and state governments in seeking solutions to food and farm problems, and the activities that encourage healthy food choices including schools, nutrition service providers, and commercial food operations.

CFS is now practiced implicitly and sometimes explicitly by thousands of organizations and communities across North America. These practitioners have engaged countless numbers of groups, volunteers, government and nongovernment representatives in projects and activities that have improved their communities' capacity to meet their own food needs. Projects and activities include farmers' markets, federal food assistance program outreach, community gardens, youth food and agriculture programs, farmland preservation and farm viability projects, food system planning and food policy councils, nutrition education and health promotion strategies, transportation projects, farm-to-school projects, economic development activities, and a range of food and farm-related public education and awareness campaigns.

## Some Definition

CFS is as much an anti-hunger strategy as it is a community development strategy as it is a public health strategy. It addresses multiple needs and problems within a local food system and attempts to integrate all these strategies under one large tent. You might say that CFS is both a goal and a method because it is clearly about achieving a state of food security for all people, but it must embrace the full range of food system activities and relationships to get there. This requires consideration of natural resources and agriculture, food processing and distribution, nutrition and health, public policy and all the government programs, budgets, and regulations that relate to food. In short, CFS employs a systems approach to food problems. While the goal of CFS is the same as other approaches—ending hunger and food insecurity—it also wants to build a robust local food economy, encourage healthy eating and a reduction in obesity and diet-related illnesses, protect the environment, and avert global warming. CFS, in its fullest expression, draws on a range of community food system resources while inviting the participation of many individuals and food system stakeholders to the table.

Let's continue the discussion with a comparison of CFS to other anti-hunger strategies to determine what it *is* and what it *isn't*. CFS is an extension of food security, which occurs when all households have available nutritionally adequate and safe food, or the ability to acquire food in socially acceptable ways. CFS places the concept of individual or household food security directly in a community context, which implicitly recognizes the importance the larger food system plays in ensuring food security. The most commonly used definition of CFS is a "condition in which all community residents obtain a safe, culturally acceptable, nutritionally adequate diet through a sustainable food system that maximizes community self-reliance, social justice, and democratic decision-making" (Hamm and Bellows, 2002).

For CFS, the community is the unit of analysis, which is often why the first step a local or state food coalition might take is a community food assessment to determine what is wrong, what is needed, and what is already in place. CFS assigns a high level of importance to developing community-based resources that improve access to quality, affordable food, particularly in lower-income neighborhoods. It also addresses a broad range of problems such as inadequately funded and staffed food assistance programs (Supplemental Nutrition Assistance Program (SNAP), Women, Infant, and Children Program (WIC)), lack of quality, affordable food outlets, especially in urban and rural areas, loss of small- and medium-size family farms and the farmland base needed to support food production, diet-related health problems associated with local food environments (prevalence of healthy vs. unhealthy food choices), and the overall vitality of the local food economy and its ability to generate additional community wealth and jobs through new food enterprises.

Three other components of the CFS definition—sustainability, social justice, and democratic decision-making—deserve brief explanations. Since CFS is concerned with the viability of the natural resource base that produces our food, as well as the food system's current dependence on nonrenewable energy sources (i.e., fossil fuels), it advocates for sustainable farming practices. Likewise, CFS supports strong marketing channels between consumers and farmers that share the same region to decrease the distance that food travels from field to plate (and it might be said as well to enhance the pleasure that can be from the enjoyment of locally produced food and beverages). Social justice refers to the injustice of hunger and food insecurity that is so unfavorably weighted toward lower-income families while almost avoiding entirely more affluent families. But it also includes the inadequacy of wages and the poor working conditions of those who earn their livelihoods from the food system. This includes farmers certainly, and also farm, food processing, and restaurant and food service workers. Democratic decision-making, a key principle of the CFS movement, means that all participants in the food system have the right to participate in decisions that affect the availability, cost, price, quality, and attributes (e.g., organically grown, GMO-free) of their food.

In contrast to anti-hunger approaches that primarily focus on federal food assistance programs or emergency food distribution (e.g., food banks), CFS encourages progressive planning that addresses the underlying causes of hunger and food insecurity. Planning itself encourages community-based problem-solving strategies and promotes collaborative, multisectoral processes. And finally, while CFS embraces all approaches, even if they only provide short-term hunger relief, it places special emphasis on finding long-term, system-based solutions.

With most domestic anti-hunger models, the key indicators of food security/insecurity are the size of the need, which is usually defined by the area's poverty rate, the pool of eligible federal food program participants (the number of "eligibles" is almost always higher than those who actually participate), and those defined as "food insecure" by the USDA. For emergency food providers, the primary indicator is the number of people who request food and the units of food distributed.

If one were to operate under a CFS model, a broader set of indicators would be examined to determine the relative food insecurity/security of a given community or region. For example, a typical community food assessment—a common planning tool of CFS—might evaluate the following indicators:

- The number and accessibility of affordable retail food stores that carry a wide range of healthy food choices in or near lower-income neighborhoods (beginning about 10 years ago, the USDA began to identify the number of people who lived in so-called food deserts, which as of this writing stands at 23 million)
- Public transportation systems and their ability to easily connect residents of lower-income communities to affordable, high-quality food stores and farmers' markets
- Rates of diet-related health problems including obesity and diabetes as well as infant mortality, low-birth weight babies, and iron-deficient anemia
- The prevalence, adequacy of funding, and the coordination between public health and nutrition education efforts that are designed to address diet-related health issues (obesity reduction coalitions have arisen as one way of bringing a sharper focus to this problem)
- The amount of time that a school system devotes to nutrition education in their standard curriculum; and the degree to which the school systems promote healthy eating through the food choices in their cafeteria and vending machines (so-called wellness policies that were supposed to be adopted by every school district have been one vehicle to accomplish this goal)
- The adequacy of funding and staff to do outreach for food assistance programs

- The viability of the local and regional agriculture sector, use of sustainable farming practices, and the availability of distribution channels to make local and regional farm products available to all residents, businesses, and public institutions (the growth in farmers' markets, farm-to-school programs, and community supported agriculture (CSA) marketing efforts are examples)
- The average age of farmers, the loss of prime farmland, and other measures of farm viability
- The ability of emergency food providers to meet demand; the availability of healthy food within the emergency food system; progress in addressing the underlying causes of food insecurity such as assisting clients with SNAP applications, providing job training programs, and engaging in local, state, and national policy work
- The existence of active venues for local and state food system planning, such as food policy councils that are inclusive of a diverse mix of stakeholders including government representatives

## Philosophical and Social Perspectives on Community Food Security

Before turning to some concrete examples of CFS, I will discuss three underpinnings of CFS that grow out of philosophical and social analyses. They are the role of compassion in contemporary American society and how it shapes public response to hunger issues; the manner in which social networks and citizen participation influence local food security; and the application of systems theory to hunger and food insecurity.

One can argue that if sufficient compassion for the hungry and impoverished existed today among even a significant minority of the American public, it would create the political will and public resources necessary to effectively eliminate these problems. Such is not the case. Local and state hunger news stories that use to run on page one of daily newspapers in the 1990s barely rate "Other News Items" buried on page 17 today. In spite of the evidence that hunger and food insecurity continue at significant levels, the public's sympathy for the fate or condition of those less fortunate appears to be waning. According to the food bank community, demand at emergency food sites grows from year to year. But without a continual drumbeat of public concern, few elected officials will advocate for the hungry (Lieberman, 2003) nor is the issue included in public debate during political campaigns. While changes in national political leadership and the economy influence the need for and availability of federal food assistance funds, it is perhaps more telling to ask why the electorate cannot muster or sustain the degree of compassion and passion to make domestic hunger a major public policy issue.

## The Role of Empathy

While "donor fatigue" and the public's frustration with approaches that appear to fall short may be factors, a good part of the problem lies with our diminished capacity to experience empathy for others in need (Nussbaum, 2010), or to imagine the possibility that similar circumstances could befall us. Related to these emotional and psychological factors is a collective disinterest in a more cognitive and deliberate exploration of the circumstances that spawn poverty and hunger. If we readily accept the position that one's condition, for example, hunger, is that person's fault, or assume that the condition can be addressed with a one-time hand out of food, then we will not devote adequate time to probe more deeply into the social, political, or economic forces that shape the lives of needy people and their communities. The philosopher and ethicist Martha Nussbaum says, "Only when we can imagine the good or ill of another can we extend to that other our moral concern" (*Upheavals of Thought*, 2001). Without that moral concern, viable and sustained public policy remedies are not likely to follow.

It may be that our social welfare system has become so institutionalized that the needs it addresses are effectively removed from the sight of most Americans—that we can no longer connect in our minds and hearts the problem with a range of possible solutions. The reader of Steinbeck's *Grape of Wrath* cannot help but feel compassion for the hungry and the homeless, and then respond with some degree of outrage toward the conditions that spawned them. But lacking such imaginative forms of comprehension or more direct ways of experiencing poverty, we either abdicate our responsibility for solving these problems to the so-called welfare bureaucracy (and then criticize it when the problems don't seem to disappear, or worse, occasionally flare-up), or we cultivate an indifference to the suffering of others. Either way, when the public is not constructively engaged in social welfare debates, the result is the gradual erosion of safety net programs and an insufficient will to find new and hopefully improved publicly supported methods of addressing these problems.

## Citizen Participation and Social Capital

We also need to understand why human participation contributes to better social outcomes. Research from the community development field provides ample support for community participation as a central component of urban problem-solving strategies. When community development corporations connect neighborhood people to each other and to the programs that are trying to better their community, there is a higher rate of lasting community improvement (Briggs et al., 1997).

The importance of community participation is reinforced by the growing body of literature on social capital—how social networks contribute to a community's health and well-being (Putnam, 2000). In the field of CFS, research on the relationship between food security and social capital by Dr. Katie Martin found correlations between low-income households' ability to secure sufficient food and their connection to neighbors, friends, and helping services (Martin, 2001). The study, which took place in Hartford, Connecticut, had three major findings:

- Low-income families were more likely to be food secure if their social capital, that is, connections to local social networks, was high.

- A high percentage of food insecure families do not participate in food programs (45% did not receive food stamps, 67% did not use food pantries, and 37% of the respondents who were eligible for the WIC program did not participate in it).

- Lack of access to large supermarkets and/or transportation to get to large supermarkets was significantly associated with food insecurity (55% of the respondents did not have a car).

The study also found that lower fruit and vegetable consumption was associated with limited access to supermarkets and transportation. This finding corresponds with a large study (data on food intake from 10,600 participants in the Atherosclerosis Risk in Communities survey from four states) by Dr. Kimberly Morland who correlated the dietary recall data with the participants' census tracts, proximity to supermarkets, race, and income. She found that there are four times more supermarkets located in white neighborhoods compared to black neighborhoods, three time more supermarkets in higher-income neighborhoods compared to lower-income neighborhoods, and that the further the distance to a supermarket, the lower the resident's intake of fresh fruits and vegetables (Morland et al., 2002).

## Systems Thinking

Systems theory tells us that a single intervention designed to address a specific problem is not likely to produce satisfactory results in the long term (Senge, 1994). The primary anti-hunger strategies in the United States fall into this category. Food assistance programs and food banks have mitigated the worst effects of poverty, that is, hunger, yet as has been stated repeatedly throughout this book, the need only grows and the programs never have enough funding or food to adequately keep up with demand. Additionally, the burden for ending hunger has been shifted to the intervenor, namely the federal government (public bureaucracies) and private food banks. The larger community and with it a larger range of solutions and interrelationships do not participate (with the possible exception of canned food drives and hunger walk fund-raisers which may draw thousands of people for very short and generally superficial forms of participation). While conventional anti-hunger interventions have provided important and necessary relief for needy people, they have not substantially reduced the need because they rely on a linear cause-effect approach. An unintended consequence of this approach is that the recipients too often become dependent on the providers (Winne, 2008).

We need to look to the larger system, particularly those interrelationships within the food system, to find longer-term and more comprehensive solutions. Systems theory, drawing as it does on our growing understanding of ecology and natural systems, recognizes that each of us has an impact on the world around us. Therefore, each of us shares responsibility for problems generated by the system. While it may take longer to achieve specific results, a systems approach to food insecurity will have a longer-lasting and more enduring impact. A systems approach will take the time to rebuild a spirit of compassion among the general public, a compassion that may generate a stronger national consensus for food assistance programs and other strategies that might, for instance, link those programs to nutritional health and economic development. It will recognize the importance of social networks and community participation in problem solving. And, in the words of the natural resource expert and writer, Donella Meadows, it will "strengthen the ability of the system to shoulder its own burden."

## Community Food Security in Action

Let's now consider some examples of CFS that are drawn from projects and communities across the country. We will briefly examine Hartford, Connecticut, the state of Oregon, and East Harlem, New York.

Hartford is Connecticut's capital city, with a population of 120,000. Over 35 percent of the residents live below the poverty level (nearly half the city's children live below poverty), making Hartford one of the poorest cities in the United States (*Hartford Courant*, 2015). Under the leadership of the HFS, the city developed numerous food projects and public policy initiatives. These included a Feeding America food bank (Foodshare), farmers' markets, community gardens, a CSA, new retail food outlets (the city lost 11 supermarkets since the early 1970s and currently only has one chain supermarket), new bus routes that connect low-income neighborhood residents to suburban supermarkets, a state anti-hunger coalition (End Hunger Connecticut!), farm-to-school programs, farmland protection programs, diet and health initiatives (city residents suffer from obesity and diabetes rates that are twice as high as the state average), improvements in federal food assistance programs, a City of Hartford Food Policy Commission, and a State of Connecticut Food Policy Council.

HFS took a systems approach from the very beginning because it saw that the food problems facing city residents were complex, deep, and often interrelated. For instance, small- and medium-size farmers in the region were going out of business because they could not get a good price for their products. Low-income city residents could not find affordable retail outlets where quality, fresh food could be purchased. HFS opened the state's first farmers' market in 1978 in downtown Hartford, which gave farmers a retail outlet and consumers an affordable and accessible place to purchase healthy food. To encourage farmers to sell in low-income neighborhoods across the state, HFS combined on-the-ground project organizing work with a policy initiative (an approach that it would often repeat) that established the Farmers' Market Nutrition Program (FMNP) (the origins of which were discussed earlier). The FMNP provides federal and state funding for vouchers that low-income mothers and senior citizens use to purchase produce at farmers' markets. Today, there are 130 farmers' markets across the state serving hundreds of Connecticut farmers and over 60,000 low-income individuals (and, of course, hundreds of thousands of non-low-income residents).

With regard to food assistance programs, HFS saw that more needed to be done at the local and state levels to deliver those services more effectively. Though it advocated for more national funding, the responsibility for actually delivering the services to Connecticut residents rested with the Connecticut Department of Social Services (SNAP), the City of Hartford Health Department (WIC Program), the City of Hartford Recreation Department (Summer Meals), and the City of Hartford School Department (school breakfast and school lunch). At various times, the quality of services delivered by these government agencies was compromised (sometimes severely) by poor management, local and state governments' indifference, and public apathy (lack of awareness, lack of understanding of who operated the programs and how).

To address these barriers, HFS took the lead in establishing the City of Hartford Food Policy Commission, which comprises representatives from government and nongovernment food sectors. Not only did the commission let the general public know that there were program deficiencies adversely affecting the food security of city residents, they let the city manager, mayor, and city council know as well. They convinced the appropriate city authorities and agencies to accept responsibility for the problems and engaged them in processes to find solutions. As a result of these processes and the subsequent improvements in program delivery, the quality of the service increased as did the numbers participating in all the programs (Report of the City of Hartford Advisory Commission on Food Policy, 2002).

But another way to understand how a comprehensive CFS strategy can work is to look at the performance of one organization doing work in one place over an extended period of time. To that end, the HFS, operating in one medium-size city since 1978, is a good candidate. With its obvious commitment to systems thinking, HFS has always pursued its program and policy work, if not in a coalition framework with other organizations, at least in partnership with one or more groups. While not always successful with every initiative, it always learned from its failures, built on its successes, and continued to seek innovative solutions. And through its commitment to the principles of CFS, it has strongly joined its food security interests to health and economic development interests.

Among its recent innovations, HFS is currently operating a mobile produce market, a healthy food coupon initiative in existing independent grocery stores (these are stores in the 10,000–20,000-square-foot range, much smaller than the 40,000-plus-square-foot chain supermarkets located in Hartford's suburbs), and an old factory building retrofit for a community food center. HFS also staffs the City of Hartford Advisory Commission on Food Policy, which is made up of a dozen local organizations as well as several unaffiliated city residents. Much of the Commission's work has focused on improving the delivery and utilization of federal food programs such as summer meals.

HFS plays a leading role with the projects mentioned earlier, but all of those projects require multiple partners to be successful. Conversely, HFS will assume a partnership role (as opposed to a leading one) in other projects that are attempting to improve Hartford's food landscape. These include Fresh Place, a food pantry program that gives needy clients a choice of food, job and life coaching, and intensive counseling services. The lead partners for this are the Chrysalis Center, the Junior League, food pantries, and Foodshare—all Hartford-based programs. In a similar vein, HFS collaborates with the Kitchen at Billings Forge, which is a combination food catering, job training, and employment opportunity program. Additionally, Billings Forge is part of a community development initiative within the largely lower-income Frog Hollow neighborhood of Hartford.

Two people who have been played various roles in the evolution of Hartford's food security collaborations for more than 15 years are Martha Page, HFS's executive director, and Katie Martin, a professor of community nutrition at St. Joseph College. Martha is a strong believer in collaboration and says, "Conversations about working together are more common now than they were five years ago." She notes that while the Advisory Commission on

Food Policy may still be the only place where "we in Hartford's food community do food planning," there is a greater commitment from local stakeholders to agree on their immediate goals.

Martha cites the former Swift factory project (the Swift Corporation was formerly one of the country's leading makers of gold leaf, an example of which coats the state's capitol dome) as an example of community collaboration. Community Solutions, a community development organization based in New York City, partnered with HFS, the Knox Parks Foundation (Hartford's lead community gardening organization) and other groups to retrofit the building and its grounds into a community kitchen, youth and community gardens, and a center for food enterprise development (their project's slogan is "Good Food Is Good Business"). They received funding for the project from the City of Hartford largely on the grounds that their funding application demonstrated a high degree of community collaboration.

Not only was the Swift project partnership well-defined and clearly delineated, it also included a strong community engagement component. And that wasn't just window-dressing. The location of the Swift building is in the middle of not just one of the poorest census tracts in Connecticut but also one of the poorest in the country. Unemployment, poverty, and crime rates in what is called Hartford's Northeast neighborhood are astoundingly high, which "earned" it a Promise Zone designation by the federal government. This makes the area eligible for additional public funding but also places a higher emphasis on the importance of developing good paying jobs. This broader economic focus is key to the "bigger tent" that Martha and other Hartford collaborators are trying to erect, one that will, as she put it, "make food an economic development engine," noting for example that "8 of 10 restaurant owners started in entry level food jobs."

Katie Martin, who began her work in Hartford in the late 1990s as a PhD student researching the relationship between social capital and food insecurity, sees the progress Hartford has made with more collaboration between organizations. In Katie's mind, collaboration is not just a noble concept that espouses a more virtuous form of human behavior, it's a necessary form of community and organizational interaction that is necessary to achieving ends that no single player could achieve. To that end, she scrupulously evaluates projects looking for the multiple benefits that can be derived from a collective impact approach.

Fresh Place, with its emphasis on healthy food and healthy behaviors, is one such project she's been evaluating for almost two years. So far, she's found promising results from the five food pantries in Hartford she's studied as well as two in Rhode Island, and one El Paso, Texas. Following the line of thought that multiple interventions are better than a single intervention that only meets one client need, for example, the short-term need for emergency food, Fresh Place is offering a variety of services, which require several collaborating organizations to deliver.

According to Katie, the same thinking also applies to HFS Mobile Market and the healthy food coupon program that operates in grocery stores. The mobile market is a converted, brightly colored and illustrated school bus that takes fresh food supplies (many of them sourced from area farms), nutrition information, and SNAP outreach to many Hartford neighborhoods, none of which have easy access to affordable supermarkets. She sees significant value in this approach, but she's particularly intrigued by HFS's newest venture, which is offering bonus coupons to SNAP recipients to purchase fresh produce in a small number of Hartford's independent supermarkets. This concept builds off the "Double-Up Buck" programs that target farmers' markets and have proliferated around the country over the past several years. The value of the Hartford model, as Katie sees it, is the year-round opportunity to increase the purchase and consumption of a wider range of fresh produce (most of which is not locally grown) (personal communication with Katie Martin). After HFS ran a successful pilot project in two Hartford stores, it received a substantial USDA FINI grant in 2016 to expand the program.

What is happening with Hartford projects is similar to another project in Baltimore, Maryland, that was conducted by Johns Hopkins Bloomberg School of Public Health. The researchers selected two different Baltimore grocery stores of similar size and format. Both stores were well stocked with healthy food. In one store, multiple interventions such as nutrition information, cooking demos, and extensive signage were implemented. The store without these interventions—having only a good supply of fresh produce—had only a 6 percent increase in its purchase. The store with multiple interventions had a 28 percent increase in the purchase of healthy food (Surkam et al., 2016). Simply put, it is very difficult for one person or one action to change another person's behavior, and that is certainly the case with the food system. The more we learn about the impact of CFS, the more we understand that multiple interventions are often needed to change human behavior.

Let's take a look at another community that gives us a more complex example of the potential application of collective impact. In this case, it is East Harlem, New York, where a 2015 report by the City University of New York (CUNY)/New York City Food Policy Center looked at food security progress since 2000 in one of America's most challenging high-poverty food environments. What it concluded was that in spite of much outside investment and an explosion of new food businesses and food-related nonprofits, East Harlem still has "the worst health statistics in the city [of New York] and experiences high levels of food insecurity and diet-related diseases." Most people still depend on SNAP and emergency food sites to get food (Freudenberg et al., 2016).

The report says there has been modest improvement in closing the diet-related health gap—more consumption of fruits and vegetables, some reduction in childhood obesity, and far more retail outlets, but overall East Harlem's health and food security numbers lag behind New York City's and the nation's. The report recommends that the following actions be taken:

- The creation of more community-based and -owned alternative food outlets
- A reduction in the promotion and availability of unhealthy food
- Developing creative ways to use SNAP to encourage purchase of healthier food
- The creation of a food hub that will facilitate purchase of healthy, affordable, and sometimes local food by city agencies, day care and senior centers
- Making food a part of *all* city department policies, in other words, integrating food throughout all municipal functions
- The organization of an East Harlem Food Policy Council
- Free school food for all
- And the establishment of a centralized public database that lists and describes all food and nutrition education programs

The report summarizes its findings and recommendations by saying that a substantially more coordinated and diversified public and private partnership is required to have a broad and significant impact on the community's food security.

While much work remains to be done to make significant improvements in the food security of the nation's lower-income communities, one indication of progress is that funders are seeing the value of these multiple and joined-up strategies. As Martha Page told me, "Private funders are starting to get it," meaning that they are making more grants for collaborative projects like Hartford's Mobile Market, which is now funded by Harvard's Pilgrim Health Care Foundation. The interest in collaboration is also driving public sector funding as is the case with the City of Hartford, which is effectively requiring multiple organizations to collaborate on their grant applications to the city.

## There Are Still Limits

As much as food movement groups are beginning to demonstrate more cohesion—or at least an understanding of the value of more cohesive approaches—even collective impact strategies and thoughtful food project and advocacy interventions are not always enough. Too many American cities and rural regions remain mired in economic doldrums, having never revived from the Great Recession (in some cases, never reviving from the economic woes that began after World War II). In many cases, including Hartford's, they have experienced a steady decline since the 1960s when their primary industries (heavy manufacturing in the Midwest, insurance in Hartford) started to shrink, leave town, or move off-shore. Entrenched poverty and structural economic problems can be an albatross around the neck of any well-intentioned and well-run food system approaches. According to the Economic Innovation Group, which created a new tool for measuring economic and social health called the Distressed Communities Index, places like Camden, New Jersey, Cleveland, Ohio, and Hartford have the country's highest indexes, which means they are among the most distressed. In the Hartford zip-code area that is known as the Northeast neighborhood (the neighborhood noted earlier), the distress score is 98.9 (100 being the worst). Compared to Connecticut as a whole, the statistics for the Northeast neighborhood are found in Table 6.1.

Hartford's inability to generate tax revenue sufficient to meet the high cost of services required by a large low-income population has brought it perilously close to bankruptcy (its bond rating was significantly downgraded in 2016, which may require further cuts in city services). Due to the kind of numbers found in the Distressed Communities Index, poor communities have greater food security problems and require more services of all kinds, yet they often have fewer resources to draw upon, creating what is sometimes a downward social and economic spiral.

As much as it has tried, Hartford has not been able to attract a new chain supermarket in over 20 years. City government does what it can to draw new public and private investments to ignite the local economy, but oftentimes those investments are not enough, or unfortunate compromises must be made. For instance, Hartford has been trying to attract a minor-league baseball team for decades as one way to draw more people to the city. It finally succeeded by offering to build a new stadium for a consenting team. In order to make the finances work, the city sold the naming rights to the Dunkin' Donuts chain, which, in a city that suffers from high rates of diet-related health problems, is the wrong nutrition message to be sending the community.

Table 6.1  **Northeast Neighborhood Compared to the State of Connecticut**

|  | Northeast (%) | Connecticut (%) |
|---|---|---|
| No high school degree | 37 | 11 |
| Housing vacancy rate | 18 | 7 |
| Adults not working | 63 | 39 |
| Poverty rate | 47 | 11 |

*Source:* Economic Innovation Group, 2016.

Nevertheless, Hartford's food organizations appear to be collaborating in a way that links food security, health, and economic development in a manner that may make a modest contribution to the city's hoped-for revival. They see the necessity of conducting their food work in such a way that it will also benefit the city's economy and the health of its residents. Yet even then there are glitches in community-level collaboration. Lucy Nolan of End Hunger Connecticut! reports that they have been unable to develop a common advocacy campaign and resource-sharing plan with Foodshare, Hartford's food bank, that could leverage more public funds for a city hobbled by poverty (personal communication). Overall, however, reasonable strides have been made with interorganizational collaboration. But realistically, a vastly improved food system is only part of the solution, one that needs to be integrated into improved housing and education programs as well as a more comprehensive and diversified economic development strategy.

Many other cities and states have implicitly or explicitly adopted CFS as their conceptual model for addressing food system challenges. Oregon had routinely ranked among the states with the highest rates of food insecurity and hunger (USDA). In spite of three decades of work on the part of advocates and food banks, the problem remained stubbornly persistent. According to Sharon Thornberry of the Oregon Food Bank, the goals and language of CFS helped all the stakeholders reframe the issues (personal communication). Simply using the term "food security" rather than "hunger" made the problem more real to more Oregonians because they understood that people are not actually starving but are often unable to stretch their dollars far enough to secure adequate food on a regular basis.

But adding the word "community" to "food security" brought another set of tools and options to the table. Over ten years, for example, over 30 diverse organizations with an interest in the food system came together in Tillamook County, Oregon. Together, with assistance from the Oregon Food Bank, they started a farmers' market, expanded community gardens, developed entrepreneurial food projects (producing, selling, or processing food for commercial sale), and began a strategic planning process. The Oregon Food Bank was also a member of the City of Portland/County of Multnomah Food Policy Council. Though that body fell prey to local political squabbles and was forced to stop its work in 2012, during its lifetime, the Food Policy Council grappled with a wide range of food system issues including food insecurity in low-income communities, farmland preservation, urban gardening, improvements in the Summer Meals Program, and the development of farmers' markets. Perhaps the council's most important achievement was making food system planning a part of government's routine work. Thornberry credits this progress for bringing "together many diverse partners from both the public and private sector [who are] talking, compromising, planning, and collaborating."

In summary, what CFS does is:

- Address the food and nutrition needs of low-income households and communities.
- Synthesize two or more fields, for example, food production and nutrition education.
- Unite rural and urban/producer and consumer concerns.
- Achieve multiple benefits, for example, create new supermarkets in low-income areas and provide job opportunities for neighborhood residents.
- Make community food system assessment, research, and planning part of its work.
- Take a systems approach to tackling food-related problems.
- Create a broader constituency for food system issues.

## The Community Food Security Coalition

Over 1,200 people attended the last conference of the CFSC held in 2011 in Oakland, California. This was twice as many people as attended its 2003 conference in Boston, and six times as many as attended its first conference in Los Angeles in 1997. The national organization that was founded in 1996 as a hub for the CFS movement and experienced steady growth in interest, participation, and funding from across North America until its sudden and unexpected demise in 2012.

Why did CFSC grow at such a strong pace, and just as important, why did it attract so much interest from diversified elements of the food movement? CFSC's emergence was due to two factors. The first was a recognition by food organizations across the nation that food insecurity could not be remedied by any single approach or policy. Multiple approaches—holding aside questions concerning the efficacy of any one of them—were probably necessary to resolve the many causes and symptoms of food insecurity. The second factor, and the one that speaks to the many dimensions of the food movement discussed so far in this book, was an inchoate need to provide a space, a table, even a conceptual framework for much of the activity that constituted the food movement.

While it may be a wobbly astrophysics metaphor, one could imagine many stellar bodies moving randomly within rough proximity of each other in some remote corner of space. As their numbers grow and their relative density in a portion of the great beyond increases, they begin to display more predictable patterns of movement. Inevitably, they exercise a gravitational pull on each other drawing them into more cohesive orbits with their own hubs and solar systems. In the case of organizational bodies working separately but in near proximity, they come together locally and statewide to form food policy councils, coalitions, and networks; nationally, they begin to form national associations from among their own interest groups, for example, Feeding America (food banks), the Farmers' Market Coalition, and occasionally (rarely) they start to form more diversified food coalitions, for example, the National Sustainable Agriculture Coalition. Through these processes, they discover from one another that there is a wider menu of options available to them than what each one first realized. Again, CFSC became a gathering place—both virtually and physically, even if it lacked a crystal-clear vision—for hundreds of then-current and emerging food projects, programs, and policies, represented by people who felt some inner urgency to cross the boundaries imposed on them by their single-interest orientation.

Another factor that fueled the growth of interest in CFS was, frankly, money and the public policy that made it possible. During the 1996 Farm Bill debate, the newly formed CFSC successfully advocated for the development of a small competitive grant program ("Community Food Projects Competitive Grant Program") within USDA to support the work of communities who were trying to become more food secure. All the subsequent Farm Bills reauthorized the program and funding, which expanded by 2016 to $9 million annually (a minuscule amount by Washington, D.C., standards, but large enough to stimulate interest in the concept of CFS). Since its inception, CFPCGP has provided, by my estimate, $100 million to hundreds of nonprofit organizations across the country. (Note the earlier arguments made in this book with regard to the small, specialized federal funding streams that have contributed to disunity within the food movement. While CFSC, with its creation as a national association and a USDA funding program dedicated to supporting one approach—albeit a broad one—namely CFS, wasn't the first to use this strategy, it certainly contributed momentum to a trend of similar funding strategies for other specialized approaches over the next 10–15 years). More private-sector funding for CFS (a term that would later morph into other designations like "food justice") joined the small but growing band wagon. Large national foundations like W.K. Kellogg and smaller ones like Jessie Smith Noyes would collectively add hundreds of millions of dollars in support.

As the first executive director of the HFS, I began to see how numerous food activities were emerging in Hartford and elsewhere in New England from the late 1970s to the early 1990s. I was attempting to put the concept of multistakeholder food system work into practice by developing and connecting farmers' markets, urban gardens and farms, food coops and other retail groceries, food pantries and food banks, and the early stages of food policy and food policy councils. Looking about the country for useful models, I found very little that could instruct me in effective coalition building, but I found that larger communities almost everywhere were nurturing the same kind of activities that we were in New England. With some funding support from W.K. Kellogg Foundation, I set off on my own little voyage of discovery to see what I could learn from places like Philadelphia, Austin, Chicago, San Francisco, and Los Angeles.

My visits confirmed my assumptions—there was a tremendous amount of food project activity everywhere I landed, but nowhere had anyone tried to connect the dots—that is, until I reached Los Angeles. Robert Gottlieb, a planning professor at UCLA and a few of his graduate students, one of whom was Andy Fisher, had been commissioned by a southern California food organization to ascertain how food issues may have contributed to the Los Angeles civil disturbances of 1992. The riots had followed from the police beating of Rodney King and the subsequent acquittal of four police officers. UCLA's report, *Seeds of Change* (Ashman et al., 1993) would lay the groundwork for a more food system-oriented approach to addressing the food needs of Los Angeles County's lower-income residents.

After touring food projects with Fisher for a few days, I sat down with him and Gottlieb and another student, Billi Romain, for lunch in then Los Angeles mayor Richard Riordan's restaurant to bat around some ideas. What bubbled to the surface immediately was our shared belief that something greater could be accomplished if different local food system stakeholders—like the ones I was seeing in Los Angeles, Austin, Hartford, and so on—could develop a common agenda for action and form more effective local, and possibly state, coalitions. The "actionable" portion of this idea was that it needed to be supported by a national organization, one that comprises similarly diverse stakeholders that could become a voice for community-based, food system-oriented approaches to promoting food security. The results of this lunch, which transpired over two hours, several cups of coffee and tea, and were recorded on not much more than a few paper napkins, provided the foundation for the formation of the CFSC.

What followed from this conversation, in rapid succession, was a commitment by Fisher to write a white paper describing the concept (still without a name), a commitment by me to raise some money for what was then a bootstrap operation, and an agreement to convene some food system thinkers and doers from around the country to review the paper and recommend possible next steps. Within a few months, Fisher, with input from various people including Gottlieb and me, had written a document titled "The Community Food Security Empowerment Act." I raised $10,000 from Share our Strength, and 30 people assembled for a day-and-a-half meeting in late August of 1994 in Chicago.

The term "community food security" grew out of report-title brainstorming sessions that included the aforementioned players. But some specific suggestions from Kenneth Dahlberg, a political science professor at Western Michigan University, gave the growing group the hidden-in-plain-sight nugget it had been dancing around for several months. "Food security" was a term that had gained currency among those who had been doing agricultural development work in developing countries. The term was also in the early stages of becoming USDA's defining measure for domestic hunger. By simply making "community" the antecedent to the emerging term "food security," the "inventors" found that bigger food system context that had been so sorely lacking in efforts to describe the work of multiple local food projects and organizations.

Following the review and enthusiastic approval of the "Community Food Security Empowerment Act" (in retrospect, a somewhat ponderous title) by the 30 people gathered in Chicago, a team started the wheels in motion to organize what would become the CFSC. This required the "nitty-gritty" work of building a nonprofit organization from scratch: incorporating the organization, writing by-laws and forming a board of directors, securing a 501(c)(3) Internal Revenue Service designation (required to accept tax-exempt grants and donations), raising funds, and first and foremost, defining the new organization's purpose.

Since work was already underway at the national level to pass a new Farm Bill, a CFSC legislative team (all volunteers drawn from those who attended the Chicago meeting as well as some people who did not attend) moved full-speed-ahead with advocacy efforts to implement the provisions of the Empowerment Act that required congressional action. Full-speed-ahead, that is, until November, 1994 when the lofty goals of the emerging coalition collided head-on with the newly elected Republican majority (Newt Gingrich) Congress. The election profoundly altered the political landscape. The Democratic majority and its leadership that CFSC's advocates were planning to work with were now a relatively powerless minority. But some portions of the Empowerment Act proved to have bipartisan appeal, especially the proposal to establish a small USDA funding program to promote integrated community-based approaches to ending hunger and promoting the concept of food self-reliance. With the help of Julie Paradis—formerly the head staff person for the House Agriculture Committee but relegated to a minority role by early 1995—Congressmen Kiki de la Garza (D-Texas), Sam Farr (D-California), and Bill Emerson (R-Missouri), the Community Food Projects Competitive Program found its way into the 1996 Farm Bill where it has remained ever since.

In broad strokes, those are some of the factors that contributed to the development of CFSC. There were many other milestones along the way including an annual conference whose popularity grew from year to year, the development of new programs (e.g., farm-to-school) and federal policies (e.g., farm-to-school initiatives within the Childhood Nutrition Program, the Senior Farmers Market Nutrition Program), and other initiatives such as the food policy council program that began the process of expanding the number of North American councils from a few dozen in 2006 to over 300 in

2016. The organization's budget and staff would also grow significantly. While it had managed to stretch its first $10,000 grant over an entire year and then some, CFSC would eventually reach a $2 million annual budget by the mid-2000s comprised of numerous foundation grants and federal contracts. Likewise, the staff would grow until Andy Fisher, initially a half-time private contractor, would become the executive director until 2011 overseeing a dozen employees working across the country.

**

My cell phone rang as I was driving home from the Albuquerque airport at the end of a brief summer vacation in 2012. At the other end was CFSC's executive director who had only started her job that Spring. Since I was a part-time CFSC staff person at the time, she was calling to inform me that the board of directors had decided to cease operations and shut the organization down permanently. She said that she was very sorry, but CFSC's coffers were nearly dry, and there were insufficient funding prospects on the horizon to warrant the organization's continuation. By that fall there was nothing left of an organization that had become the hub of the CFS movement but a dumpster full of office detritus. Everything else from desk chairs to Xerox machines to stacks of reports had been sold for parts.

Why had an organization that had garnered so much support, attracted so many followers, and envisioned a profoundly new way of thinking about the nation's food and farm problems suddenly closed up shop? Much can be learned of course from the ascent of CFSC—its practices and the ideas it embodied—but the real lessons, the ones that have the most import for the future of the food movement, can be found in a discussion of its descent.

"The Community Food Security Coalition provided a meeting place for people who had a large food system perspective to work with people who had a narrower, more conventional anti-hunger perspective, but in the final analysis it failed to be inclusive." This was how Jim Hanna, a community food activist from Maine and former CFSC committee member summed up the strengths and weaknesses of CFSC. He was saying that the food movement, prior to the evolution of CFSC, was often divided by methods and different program preferences. The organization, in his estimation, provided a constructive table around which to gather with the intent of finding common ground among food system stakeholders. But while it may have partially succeeded in including the food movement's many sectors, it failed to adequately include, as he put it, "the voices of the most vulnerable, those who were most affected by America's inequalities" (personal communication).

The question of "voices" and how well they are heard is an increasingly common metaphor among advocates for more inclusionary and participatory forms of democratic organization, especially among those that purport to address the needs of disenfranchised groups. Though the heart of these groups is generally sincere and their heads are willing, with few exceptions, the rhetoric regarding their commitment to the task most always exceeds the reality. Echoing Jim Hanna, Samina Raja, a former CFSC board member, said "CFSC is an incredible example of a group that tried to create a big orchestra of food organizations, but ultimately some voices felt left out."

To once again quote from my conversation with Hank Herrera, a founding CFSC member and past board president, "I was proud to be part of CFSC from the start. The organization and its dynamics offered a tremendous exchange of knowledge. But what hasn't changed over the 26 years I've been involved in community food work is the divide in race and class in America." In other words, CFSC did not succeed in overcoming that endemic schism that has haunted the nation for 400 years. Though it attempted to vault the divide, it effectively fell into the abyss of racial tumult. Herrera added, "Challenge of race and class and anti-racism were never handled well, and as a result one major group [Growing Food and Justice] split off from CFSC [in 2007]."

"CFSC didn't clearly see the rapidly changing food system landscape," is how Thomas Forster, CFSC's former policy director, described the growing waves that were starting to crash on the organization's shores during the first decade of the 21st century (personal communication). The landscape he's referring to started taking shape early in the 1990s when those that the food movement purported to represent—people of color, lower-income communities—began to develop and lead their own organizations, or at the very least, look for more seats at the table where the decision makers sat. The absence of people of color and the food insecure from most of the major sub–food movement organizations is truly stunning. Unlike leadership in the civil rights movement (Dr. Martin Luther King Jr.), the farmworkers movement (Caesar Chavez), and the women's movement (Susan B. Anthony), the food movement's leadership has stood out for being decidedly unrepresentative of the people those organizations serve. With few exceptions, it was extremely rare to ever see a person of color in a leadership role at a food bank meeting, a farmers' market gathering, an antihunger convening, or a food policy council meeting. Far and away, the leadership of these submovements—whether at local or national levels—was white, privileged, and well-educated.

With the emergence of groups like People's Grocery in Oakland, California and Growing Power in Milwaukee, the food movement began to see, at least at the local level and sometimes even in geographically smaller areas such as at a neighborhood level, groups and initiatives that were led by people who lived there, or at least by people of color who had strong connections to those constituencies. CFSC got a loud wake-up call at its first annual conference in Los Angeles in 1997 when it sought ratification from a then ill-defined membership for about a dozen people who had agreed to serve as the organization's first official board of directors (prior to that, a few people had served as interim board members). Most of the organizers, including myself, anticipated that the ratification process would be a pro forma action that wasn't going to produce much discussion. But when it became obvious that there were no more than one or two people of color on the proposed board slate, hands started shooting up and murmurings among the crowd of 100 or so participants turned to angry groans. When a couple of audience members stood up and questioned the selection process and asked why the board was so lacking in diversity, one by one each of the proposed board members removed themselves from consideration. The acting chairperson decided that it was best to suspend the election and seek a new process.

This immediately sent CFSC's early organizers (all white) into a panic, which in turn led to some frantic caucusing. A fairly rapid decision was made to start the board nomination process from scratch by throwing out the old slate and asking for new candidate nominations from the floor. This resulted in the nomination of about 20 people of whom 12 were elected. Several of those were from the original slate, but many were brand new and included at least five people of color. While this participant/member "revolt" (it should be noted that even the definition of "member" was vague at that time, which had implications for who was eligible to vote) caused considerable stress and awkwardness, it did precipitate a reexamination of the purpose of CFSC and embedded concepts like "inclusion" and "diversity" into the organization's framework.

At that moment in Los Angeles anyway, the ethnically and racially mixed board that emerged from this nascent organization's first annual meeting arguably made CFSC the most diversely led national food organization in the country. And while an internal war was averted by the quick reactions of CFSC's founding mothers and fathers, it did not mean the cessation of all hostilities. The debate would continue, the conflict would simmer, and the unresolved issues of race and racism would eventually contribute to CFSC's demise.

Race and diversity are often the third rail of organizational, community, and national conversations. Touch it and you're likely to be burned or worse; avoid it and the issue crackles and sizzles until something spontaneously ignites. For CFSC, a vague racial tension was always lingering in the air and would reveal itself in different ways. At times, there would be angry rants from black or Hispanic directors as well as white sympathizers during board meetings, sometimes directed at nobody in particular and sometimes at Andy Fisher, the executive director. Rarely was a tangible agenda articulated or specific request made; the dissatisfaction was expressed more as a general annunciation that CFSC wasn't doing enough to meet the needs of people of color.

There were moments that rose to the level of "Mau-mauing," a practice brought to light by Tom Wolfe's nonfiction 1970 piece "Mau-mauing the Flak-catchers" that described how the Black Panthers would use angry and aggressive behavior to gain concessions and support from white liberals. One action the organization took to address its alleged negligence with respect to race concerns was to hold its 2004 conference in Milwaukee, a severely segregated city, to partially highlight the work of Will Allen's organization Growing Power. The following year it would hold its conference in Atlanta, which has a large black population and history of a black-led political structure.

Feeling that not enough was being done to focus CFSC's attention on people of color, the board decided to push ahead with a process called "dismantling racism," which required the staff (by this time numbering about ten) and board members to engage in a weekend long retreat that analyzed such things as "white privilege" and the sources of each person's racial views. In the session that I participated in, having become a staff member in 2005, I was told by CFSC's dismantling racism consultants that I was a racist because "all white people are racist." While I found the analysis of white privilege and the sources of oppression eye-opening, such an accusation leveled against me, a person who had devoted 35 years of his life at that point to actively fighting oppression, didn't go over well. While the reactions of other participants were mixed—some feeling that it was liberating, others that it was ridiculous—an uncomfortable and decidedly negative pall began to settle over the organization. Schisms erupted between segments of the board and staff that culminated in one group of dismantling-racism adherents, roughly aligned with Will Allen and Growing Power, splitting off from CFSC. This would partially contribute to the founding of Growing Food and Justice, an initiative inspired by Will Allen and his daughter Erika Allen that hoped to pick up where CFSC had supposedly failed.

Anyone who has found themselves in the middle of an intraorganizational conflict knows that it is not just a difference of opinion that drives the debate. Strong personalities, entrenched interests, word-choice, and an organization's culture can obscure the legitimacy of the ideas and hinder the resolution of troublesome issues. There is a political life of sorts that grows up in any organization, no matter how small, that if not balanced with a shared commitment to common principles and values, will allow powerful people and internal factions to overwhelm the process. This was the case with Will Allen who filled a power void created by the organization's racial conflicts to elevate the importance of his own organization, Growing Power, as well as its national spin-off, Growing Food and Justice. A certain faction of CFSC's member coalesced around Allen and his work, and together they parted company with CFSC.

Now, none of these tensions or political struggles should detract from the successful work that Allen and organizations like his have done. In Allen's case his agricultural projects and his persona have been inspirations to thousands who see promise in smaller-scale, intensive food production methods that are especially appropriate for densely developed areas. In particular, Allen has been a role model for other people of color who have been flocking to urban agriculture as one expression of food and racial justice. He has also contributed to a modest resurgence of young African Americans who have been returning to the land to take up farming. But as one former Growing Power employee told me, and as evident from Allen's actions with CFSC, he is not a team-player, at least in the sense of wanting to work in partnership with other organizations. He's an "evangelist" for intensive and sustainable food production and for racial justice, but he sees both himself and Growing Power as "brands" unto themselves.

In effect, Allen is a force unto himself who is worshipped by many and who has lifted up a necessary part of the food movement. But he falls into a large category of older food movement leader around whom a cult following develops and takes on a life of its own. Similar personalities can be found in other sectors of the food movement including food bank executive directors/CEOs, some of whom have been in the same position for 30 years or more (Big Hunger, 2017). Extreme longevity by itself is not always a negative, but too often it is associated with leaders who become their own institutions. They defend their organization's mission (and sometimes their own legacy) with a singular tenacity, but rarely set aside some of that zeal to serve a broader food system vision. Their strong wills and high profiles are not put to work in service to a bigger cause that extends beyond their own boundaries.

These were some of the challenges that faced CFSC—conflicts that arose over race and diversity, the presence of strong egos and personalities, and an inability of some members to commit to a larger purpose if it meant temporarily holding aside one's individual interest. It's important to be mindful of the perilous currents that run through a broad coalition as well as those that swirl just beyond its perimeter. The elephant in CFSC's room was always race, but there were other forces as well that would dull the organization's impact. For instance, competition with other individuals and interests was always something that had to be taken into account. Nothing drives competition like a new idea that appears to have discovered a special market niche, and in the social action marketplace, CFS was the idea that a lot of people and organizations wanted a piece of. As Hank Herrera told me, "[The members of CFSC] really collaborated and we really worked well together from 1997 to 2004. But because [CFSC] had built a better mousetrap, 100 imitators soon came along to challenge us and to siphon off our energy." And noting how the organization's success may have ironically contributed to its failure, he said, "We generated something really valuable, but we didn't know how to manage our growth or how to work with the competition—those who wanted to get their piece of the pie."

Part of that growth came in the form of the farm-to-school movement that started picking up steam in the late 1990s. The impetus for farm-to-school grew out of other direct marketing initiatives, such as farmers' markets, that wanted to develop more outlets for locally produced food. School cafeterias were a logical place but for a variety of logistical and costs reasons—as well as a simple lack of awareness—schools were not buying locally produced food. Starting with some pilot projects in places like Santa Monica, California and Hartford, Connecticut, farm-to-school would eventually be operating in over 42,000 U.S. public schools, or about 42 percent of all schools (Farm to School Census, 2015). CFSC served as an incubator for the emerging program during the early 2000s, and took the lead in Washington, D.C., to enact policy and regulatory changes within the federal Child Nutrition Program (Schools Meals) and Farm Bill to increase the likelihood that public schools would use locally produced food.

The policy work was critical to the ultimate success of farm-to-school since its expansion faced so many federal regulatory and financial hurdles. In his book *Civic Engagement in Food System Governance* (2015), Alan Hunt provides a detailed account of the legislation, advocacy efforts, and attempt to build alliances with different national food associations to strengthen and expand farm-to-school. During these times, from roughly 2003 to 2010, CFSC and the National Farm to School Network (NFSN) worked very closely to gain farm-to-school funding and untie the federal regulatory knots. But they often did it in the face of headwinds generated by important Washington-based organizations. Hunt says, "Funding support for the farm-to-school program was initially resisted by the anti-hunger and nutrition policy communities" (p. 51). He goes on to chronicle the many ways that groups such as the National Alliance for Nutrition and Activity (NANA) and the Child Nutrition Forum (CNF) withheld support for a very small program innovation (for farm-to-school program, federal spending would be in the very low millions compared to the billions for other nutrition programs). This was a continuation of the same pattern of opposition to innovation that has characterized the inside-the-Beltway public interest food establishment, from its opposition to the Farmers Market Nutrition Program (1989) to Community Food Projects (1996), and then farm-to-school. It is another measure of the frustration that has plagued the food movement's attempt to build a bigger and stronger tent.

But in spite of the ultimate policy successes of the CFSC/NFSN, it wasn't enough to keep the alliance intact. As I've indicated earlier, new food movement initiatives like farm-to-school pick up their own momentum, attract a dedicated crowd of adherents, and take steps to galvanize their own identity, such as seeking separate funding and organizing their own national conferences. This is what happened with the formation of the NFSN, which grew up in the CFSC nest and left once it was able to fly. But unlike cute, fuzzy fledglings whose exit is strongly encouraged by mom and pop bird, the separation of the NFSN from CFSC was a conflicted affair. Not unlike the Growing Food and Justice exit from CFSC, NFSN's decision to go its own way was driven by strong personalities intent on creating their own national organization. Yes, there were practical reasons for the separation, and leaving CFSC did not do any intrinsic harm to CFSC in the way that Growing Power's leaving did, but the promise of unified movement was further diminished.

Some will blame the dissolution of CFSC on a "power-grabbing" mentality of a few people who saw the coalition as an opportunity to advance their own interests. Others will place the fault on Andy Fisher and some board members who failed to navigate the organization (and the movement) through the stormy waters of racial conflict and heated competition from emerging organizations and submovements. As a witness to much of CFSC's events and as a participant in the organization's development and some of its programming, my conclusion is that there's plenty of blame to go around. But blame is worthless without lessons that can be learned from a closer, dispassionate analysis. Going forward and for those wanting to build more resilient and necessary multistakeholder coalitions, I would offer these intermediate thoughts (a more comprehensive look at building the bigger and more impactful tent will follow).

- The strengths and weaknesses of individuals—their flaws, skills, and personalities—will always be factors in the success or failure of any organization. Bookshelves everywhere are lined with advice from so-called great and not-so-great leaders replete with tales of how they alone made (or unmade) a corporation, an organization, or nation. Attributing the success or failure of an entity to one person is part of the compounding American myth of the self-made man and heroic individualism. In the case of a broad-based coalition, however, we cannot allow its success or failure to be dependent on one person. The coalition's vision, structure, and governance systems must be relatively immune to human vicissitudes, as it must also assume that the whole is greater than the sum of its part.

- Coalitions, like organizations and nations, cannot be expected to change as rapidly as the society around them. Just as the formation of new laws always lags behind social change, coalitions and organizations need time to process the events and people that are always knocking at their doors. Just as a deliberative process is needed to assess new needs and opportunities, a clear organization vision, understood and agreed to by all from the outset, not only keeps members united around their cause, it also allows them to determine when to make changes. Discipline balanced by flexibility can bring clarity to the murkiest of situations.

- While it is impossible to anticipate all the challenges that may confront any newly forming democratic organization 5 or 10 or 20 years down the road, the more an organizational structure can be designed from the get-go to manage change, include new voices, and perhaps above all, know how to manage conflict the more resilient and effective it will be. Speaking as a professor, CFSC board member, and food activist, Samina Raja said, "We all need more training in group process and conflict management" (personal communication).

Looking at the final chapter in the CFSC story, Raja's point stands out as both an understatement and a clarion call for the food movement to take more thoughtful action. By the summer of 2011, CFSC's board of directors had reached its limit of tolerance with Andy Fisher and his management of race issues and the organization's financial management. Though there is a significant difference of opinion surrounding both of those topics, the majority felt the board must intervene. Seeking advice from human resource lawyers, the board took the unprecedented action of summarily dismissing Fisher from his job as executive director. Based on varying accounts, he was given anywhere from one to eight hours to clean out his desk, turn over account passwords and office keys, and vacate the premises. The operation of CFSC was turned over to a temporary nonprofit management consultant who would try to steer the ship until the board could find a permanent replacement. Staff, past board members, and many CFSC members were shocked and horrified by the board's abrupt and harsh reaction. As one long-time food activist remarked when told of Fisher's firing and the way it was handled, "We [nonprofit food organizations] don't do that!"

The board's action had profound ripple effects. It adversely affected staff morale and left the organization without the capacity to raise funds, something that by all accounts Fisher excelled at. For instance, Fisher was fired on a Tuesday, and there were two federal grant applications due that Friday, which, based on CFSC's track record with securing similar grants in the past, were virtual shoe-ins. According to Fisher, those grants would have brought $2 million to CFSC. Even after being fired, Fisher told me that he had offered to the board members who had fired him to voluntarily write and submit those applications because there was no one else available to do it in the short period of time available. They refused his offer, presumably on advice of their counsel.

If true, that refusal, with the benefit of hindsight, would be the ticking time-bomb that sunk the organization's ship. Virtually no grant applications were submitted after Fisher's firing, and a nine-month delay in finding his replacement left the organization's bank account nearly empty. Starting as late in the game as she did, the new executive director simply did not have enough time to get up to speed. Hence the decision to close the CFSC's doors 13 months after Fisher's firing was taken.

The full extent of the damage—both psychological and financial—would begin to come to light at CFSC's 2011 annual conference in Oakland that fall—the one that drew a record number of people. During the proceedings, the board president announced that, due to both limited staff resources and CFSC's financial challenges, there would be no 2012 conference. This announcement was greeted with substantial anger and consternation by those in attendance.

To gain an understanding of how important the CFSC conference was to the food movement, both for its substantive content and method as well as its symbolic value—it might be helpful to hear the perspective of an outsider. In Alan Hunt's book, he shares a lengthy interview with a person he describes as a well-known British environmental interest group leader who had attended her first CFSC conference in Oakland and found herself making comparisons with similar British social movements. Her enthusiasm for what she experienced in Oakland is best characterized by her following remarks: "At the conference . . . I felt that kind of edge, that confidence, [people] trying to find a collective voice of a movement. [Oakland] felt like a movement whereas [in the United Kingdom] it feels . . . disparate [as if people are saying] 'that's a nice thing to do to help our communities' but not a serious way of building an alternative system. And I loved it. I really loved . . . the hopefulness, the confidence, the sense of agency, and a sense [that] . . . we are in it together" (pp. 178–80).

That sense that "we are in it together" still has a grip on the food movement. It's just that the "hub" that connected those spokes had collapsed. But because that unique brand of American confidence and hopefulness is alive and well, one can be optimistic that a new hub (or hubs) will sprout from the ashes of CFSC. As we move forward in our understanding of the U.S. food movement and the forces that can strengthen or undercut it, let's examine some generic models and specific illustrations that hold promise for building a unified movement for stronger local and national food systems.

# CHAPTER SEVEN

# Strategies for Unifying: Building a Bigger Tent That Won't Fall Down

There are methods, models, and perhaps a little magic required to build a stronger and more unified food movement. The good news is that these options don't need to be assembled from scratch. They exist already, though they may need to be modified to suit current realities and situations; some may require reinvention or perhaps adaptation from a different but related field; and still others will perform best after some practice and experimentation. Examples and illustrations are also available from different parts of the country and different settings—urban and rural, big and small. None of this is to say, of course, that all you have to do is add water and heat. Any commitment to use these methods, whether at local or national level, may require a sea change in how business is conducted and a commitment to a longer time horizon. But small steps are allowed as long as the direction is clear and the commitment strong.

In this section, I'll examine some of those methods and models, and I'll consider where and how that magic—let's also call it imagination—may need to be applied. To begin, I'll look at the concept of collective impact and its application to community food system settings. While the term has been overused and the concept criticized in some quarters (the criticism will be considered as well), collective impact does provide a broad and logical framework in which to undertake food system work. Next, I'll examine the role of food policy councils (and similar food coalitions) as a pragmatic tool for organizing food system stakeholders in a given city, region, state, or tribe. Along with food policy councils, I'll include a discussion of food charters and plans that have been used locally and statewide to organize stakeholders around an agreed-upon set of principles and actions. The third piece, and one that's roughly related to the second, is how multiple food system stakeholders can begin and have begun to work together at the national level, specifically with regard to shaping federal food policy. Though the emphasis is usually on existing federal programs and budgets, there is evidence of sustained and broader (food systemwide) initiatives that are looking for more "joined-up" forms of food policy. Finally, I'll provide additional examples and illustrations that demonstrate how individual food movement sectors have built bigger tents both locally and nationally.

Let's begin with collective impact. There are two reasons that the concept should be considered in the context of the food movement, and especially at the level of organized community action. The first is because it offers a set of tasks that, if adhered to by all the participants, provides a clear path to working together effectively. The second reason is that collective impact is particularly well adapted to food system thinking, which considers the connection and potential integration between the many parts of our food supply. A short paper by John Kania and Mark Kramer (2011) describes the concept's basic elements. I'll follow their outline to provide a summation.

The justification for the use of collective impact is that, "Large-scale social change requires broad cross-sector coordination, yet the social sector remains focused on the isolated intervention of individual organizations." Nothing describes the state of local and national food movement activity more accurately than that statement. Whether you're working in Seattle, Washington, or Washington, D.C., food sector activists will recognize both the immensity of the social change they want to bring about and the state of rampant disconnect that exists among those who have something to contribute to that change. Food banks are busy distributing food, urban garden advocates are trying to expand local food production, nutrition educators are teaching people to make healthier food choices, and farmers' market coordinators are working to strengthen the small farm sector. Everyone's work is needed but every sector is "doing its own thing" without expending enough time to join forces with other sectors.

Collective impact argues that these divides and participants' myopia can be bridged if the stakeholders practice five central tenets.

1.  Develop a common agenda: If we consider a community food system approach, all of the major sectors would come together to establish a shared vision, "one that includes a common understanding of the problem and a joint approach to solving it through agreed upon actions." For food system work this means that residents of a community will be food secure (presumably using standard definitions and measurements), the natural resources necessary for a substantial measure of regional food production

are protected and assured for long-term use, and residents will have adequate access to reasonably priced sources of healthy food. No matter which food sector you work in, participants in a collective impact scenario will understand and support all the elements of that vision.

2. Create a shared measurement system: If we agree to work together toward a common agenda, we need to know if we're making progress—what's working and what's not. As Kania and Kramer put it, collecting data and measuring results consistently, "enables the participants to hold each other accountable and learn from each other's successes and failures." If a food bank, for instance, says they distribute 900 bags of food each week, the other participants need to know what that means in terms of reducing food insecurity, and how it aligns with the collective's larger goals—in other words, is it a useful measure of our shared commitment to promoting food security. If the group had also agreed that they want to increase the amount of fresh fruits and vegetables that needy families were receiving, and that half of that perishable food would be purchased from local farms, then the food bank would alter its practices in accordance with the group's larger nutrition and farm goals. But beyond those outputs—ones they have already presumably agreed to—they want to know if they are contributing as well to longer-term outcomes. In other words, is food insecurity being reduced in the community? Are BMI rates lower in the city's schools? Are more farmers showing signs of greater prosperity by increasing their incomes?

3. Organize mutually reinforcing activities: The power of collective impact comes not from everyone doing the same thing, "but by encouraging each participant to undertake the specific set of activities at which it excels in a way that supports and is coordinated with the actions of others" (Ibid.). Multiple skills and multiple interventions are required to address a big problem whether it's health, education, or food insecurity. No one person, group, or strategy—in isolation and not working in synch with others—can address complex problems in modern society, and especially in the food system. If my group is very well experienced at developing and managing urban farms, it doesn't mean I also have the knowledge to operate an emergency food distribution program. But we know in advance that those activities contribute to the realization of the collective's larger vision, and perhaps most importantly, we each will know who's responsible for implementing that portion of the larger program.

4. Conduct continuous communication: Going back to earlier discussions of communication and the importance of relationship building, the need for effective and frequent communication between partners can't be overstated. The more participants there are, the more need there is for regular communication. Communication isn't just a way to share information about what each other is doing; it is also a means to build trust, an essential part of any collective enterprise. Additionally, it allows everyone to develop a common vocabulary. While not as challenging as learning a new language,

understanding the terms, jargon, acronyms, and even the culture of the other groups in the collective is something that takes a considerable amount of time and attention. Technology can greatly enhance the ability of groups to communicate with others, but it shouldn't be relied on as the only means. Regular meetings—real facetime, in other words, with everyone—are a must. These meetings or other in-person forums should be at least once a month if not more often. Frequent communication expedites that process and is also essential to developing shared measurements.

5.  Use a backbone support organizations: Kania and Kramer emphasize that coordination of a collective impact effort takes time, skill, and money. Without those ingredients, and otherwise left to their own devices, it is unlikely that the collective will be able to manage the above four components effectively. By "backbone support," we are essentially talking about organizational infrastructure that will support the collaborative. This is not the same as a traditional nonprofit organization with a board of directors and executive director that has sole responsibility for one organization. In this case, the reference is to a body and/or person who can provide thorough coordination, administration, research, and fund-raising. Usually, dedicated staff—even if it's only half-time—are needed by the collective (the amount of time is related to the size and the complexity of the undertaking). Trying to assign or absorb the collective tasks within the already existing work of one of the collective's members is not generally effective, though some limited work, for example, writing a grant, managing a website, can be taken on by members with a little surplus capacity.

How is collective impact different from other forms of collaboration? Looking over the list of collective impact activities, people will likely say they do some of them or parts of some, but rarely all of them together in an integrated fashion. That typifies most of what passes for organized, coalition-like process—we get together on a periodic basis with other groups who share some of our interests, and we may attempt to undertake some joint activities. When I give a talk, or conduct a workshop, I often ask the audience by show of hands how many people belong to a coalition of some kind, and how many have been disappointed or seriously frustrated by coalitions they have belonged to. Between 90 and 100 percent of the hands go up in response to both questions.

As the results of my own survey of food system participants suggest (cited earlier), there is a strong urge to cooperate. But there is a sense that cooperation is not as fulfilling as it should be given that respondents overwhelmingly indicated that there was a need for improved cooperation (and coordination). Like human relationships, especially mid-stage romantic ones, there is often the belief that they should be more fulfilling than they are, or that something is missing. Ideally, belonging to a relationship, whether personal or professional, is an experience that should be adding value to my life and/or that of my organization. In other words, the maxim that you get out of something as much (at least) as you put into it still generally holds.

The current state of our organizational and coalition lives may be a large part of the reason that we "can't get no satisfaction." As Kania and Kramer point out, most forms of collaboration commonly practiced by nonprofit organizations come up short in comparison to collective impact. The three most relevant types of collaboration in this regard are public-private partnerships, multistakeholder initiatives, and social sector networks.

Public-private partnerships are typified by government and private sector entities that are designed to develop a specific set of services, including physical development, for example, new housing. In the food world, I would also add that such partnerships can take place between a nonprofit organization and for-profit organization. These are narrowly targeted collaborations with a single goal or set of goals to be achieved in a defined period of time. Their limitation is that they "don't engage the full set of stakeholders that affect the issue," thus denying themselves a deeper and/or wider impact across a community. A large food bank seeking a major facility expansion may turn to local or state government to support that effort, or a major urban agriculture organization may receive a significant donation from a large corporation to expand their organization. While these partnerships expand their respective programs, they don't represent a commitment to or the larger interest of the community they purport to serve, nor do they necessarily provide any value or enhancement to numerous other groups operating in the same food system who were probably never consulted. Essentially the "need" that was identified and the response that was developed is entirely the separate product of the food bank and urban farm.

Multistakeholder initiatives fall into the category of a classic coalition whose members join it voluntarily and because they support a common cause such as ending hunger in their community. They meet regularly, have a modicum of leadership, and find ways to support commonly agreed upon action which might include testifying in favor of a legislative bill to provide funding for the state's food programs. What groups like these—and there are many of them in the food movement, particularly among food policy councils—"lack is any shared measurement of impact and supporting infrastructure to forge any true alignment of efforts or accountability for results" (Ibid.). In other words, the members may have succeeded or failed in passing the bill, but there will be no evaluation of the why or why not, nor will members be held accountable for the level of commitment they made to the process.

Social sector networks have coalition-like qualities as well, but often have more purposeful and professional relationships and connections between members. This kind of collaboration tends to be more ad hoc and often forms around a specific funding opportunity (obesity reduction coalitions where one or more of its members have received a large grant, often fit this model). Their function tends to be more information sharing, and their collaborative activity is "targeted short-term actions, rather than a sustained and structured initiative."

The concept of collective impact is reinforced from a slightly different direction in a paper that also appeared in the *Stanford Social Innovation Review* (Shore et al., 2013) and later reviewed in the same journal (Gibson et al., 2013). Bill Shore, himself a major political and anti-hunger activist who founded the national food organization Share Our Strength, and his coauthors argue that the social sector needs to "shift its attention from modest goals that provide short-term relief to bold goals that . . . provide long-term solutions by tackling the root of social problems." Problems as deep and "multidimensional" as poverty, which are at the root of many food insecurity issues, "require an array of approaches to resolve" (Shore et al., 2013).

In their critique, Cynthia Gibson and her coauthors take a dim view of what they refer to as "simplistic," single-solution organizations "built on flawed foundations focused on symptoms, rather than on deeper system change." The social-entrepreneur cult with its mantra to "innovate, prototype, refine, and scale" is challenged as well because the problems we/they face are dynamic, not static—they are always changing and moving and, therefore, not easily remedied by a new approach no matter how innovative. I would illustrate this mindset with food banks and Supplemental Nutrition Assistance Program (SNAP), which are the most dominant private and public, respectively, food security programs both locally and nationally. While they have been effective at doing one thing well for a long time—mitigating food insecurity for the past 50 years or so—they have changed little in response to the growing awareness that poverty is the cause of hunger, and to the evidence that their approaches have serious deficiencies in addressing the nutritional needs of the people they serve. If focused on the "bigger problems" and working diligently and collectively with others, their respective impacts would be greater because more facets of people's lives and the intricacies of their communities would be addressed as well. "We've learned the hard way," states Gibson and her coauthors, "that the more an organization positions itself—or its model—at the center of a resolution, the less sustainable the progress it creates." She adds that at least some of this tendency to focus on the single model—apart from the larger "ecosystem" it inhabits—is driven by funders who are anxious to attribute success to one intervention.

Shore and his coauthors identify two other failures in the current service and social-entrepreneur sectors: their lack of interest in addressing big problems through public policy and, at the grassroots levels, an inability (not a lack of interest) to "authentically engag[e] the community in every step of the process—including identifying issues, creating plans to address them and rolling them out." Utilizing these two critical elements effectively, in tandem, within a collective impact framework is summed up with the statement: "the best advocacy brings together nonprofits, affected constituents, and forward-thinking policymakers and their staff to drive change." In the food world, the evolution of food policy councils, which will be discussed shortly, is an opportunity to embrace this holistic approach.

## A Collective Impact Counterview

It was strange to come across the article "Ten Places Where Collective Impact Gets It Wrong" (2016) by a long-time hero of mine, Tom Wolff. His piece attacks both collective impact and the article by Kania and Kramer that I have cited earlier. I say "strange" because Wolff's work, including his seminal manual on developing community coalitions *From the Ground Up!* (1997) have instructed and informed my community work for nearly 20 years. I regard *From the Ground Up!* as something like a bible for those of us who have banged our heads against the many brick walls of community organizing and the domineering institutions who arrogantly claim to speak for the community. When I first read *From the Ground Up!* this statement by Wolff and his coauthor, Gillian Kaye, offered me assurances that I wasn't insane or incompetent: "Involving grassroots citizens in the work of coalitions is one of the thorniest issues that coalitions grapple with. Again and again, we hear coalitions bemoan the lack of real citizens and residents as participant in their coalition efforts."

Let me briefly describe Wolff's criticisms, not to enter into a debate, but to suggest that Wolff's ideas add value (and already have) to collective impact's *impact*. His criticisms boil down to his beliefs that *collective impact does not:* (1) meaningfully engage those in the community most affected by the issue, and instead represents a top-down approach to community problem solving; (2) include policy change, systems change, nor a core focus on social justice; and (3) have a realistic understanding of the difficulties coalitions face in raising funds to support backbone organizations, nor accept the fact that backbone organizations, when they do exist, must also *build* leadership, not just *provide* it. Wolff also alleges several methodological and research shortcomings in the Kania and Kramer article, which I will let them fight about, but I will note that Wolff adds six principles of highly effective collaborations. They are:

1. Engage a broad spectrum of the community.
2. Encourage true collaboration as the form of exchange.
3. Practice democracy.
4. Employ an ecological approach that emphasizes the individual in his/her setting.

5.  Take action.

6.  Engage your spirituality as your compass for social change.

Many of the "failures" that Wolff assigns to collective impact are failures one can easily assign as well to multitudes of coalitions, collaborations, and partnerships, which include the shortcomings that Kania and Kramer identified in their own article. But to say that collective impact "does not include policy change and systems change," however, is dead wrong. Many organizations that attempt to apply some form of collective impact thinking to their work are doing policy and systems work, for example, food *policy* councils that also utilize *food system* thinking. Either way, there is no inherent reason or structural flaw within the collective impact model that prohibits both policy work and a systems approach.

Where I think Wolff gets it mostly right is identifying the failure to engage the community of those most affected by the problems, and that funding backbone organizations, as well as simply funding any kind of collaboration at all, is extremely difficult for reasons stated throughout this book. But again, collective impact should not be singled out for these faults. As Wolff himself said 20 years ago, "Involving grassroots citizens in the work of coalitions is one of the thorniest issues that coalitions grapple with." Every coalition and food policy council I've worked with identifies the need for core or backbone funding, and they attempt—some more successfully than others—to engage the community. On the latter point, a body of practice is emerging that is sharing "lessons learned" about the multiple approaches to community participation (see "Food Policy Councils for All . . ." for a compilation of community engagement techniques: McCullagh and Santo, 2014).

Rather than be put off by Wolff's somewhat strident assault on collective impact, practitioners should embrace his critique and, if not doing so already, give serious consideration to how the community they are serving can be more thoroughly a part of the work of the coalition, council, or collective. There is no better source of know-how for this purpose than *From the Ground Up!* And for funders, once again, they must take stock of how their limited funds can best be deployed. There is recent evidence that they are funding more of the "glue" that can hold together the groups that see the value of working together.

## Techniques for Improving Group and Coalition Performance

Before we move on to a review of examples of collective impact in action, especially in the context of the food movement, I want to share some techniques that I have found to be useful in group and coalition settings. Though my formal training in group dynamics has been limited, I've observed and participated in dozens of groups and coalitions over the past 45 years that have succeeded or failed due in large to their ability to manage their own dynamics. Good meeting facilitation, effective group leadership, and thoughtful strategic management are at the heart of every successful organization, partnership, and coalition I've ever worked with. While many people will unfortunately only pay these topics lip-service or dismiss them as secondary to the "real work" of the group—securing public policy wins or developing new programs—they are like the "poems" in the William Carlos Williams's line: "It is difficult to get the news from poems, yet men die miserably every day for lack of what's found there."

Again, one piece of theory to get us started, and this one in the form of the classic tale known as the "Tragedy of the Commons." As the story goes, there is a large common pasture in the village where the residents can graze their cows. The common is a finite size and only has the capacity under normal weather conditions to graze a set number of cows. However, there are no limits on how many cows each of the resident herdsmen can pasture there, relying on their own individual goodwill and collective common sense to self-regulate. One day, one herdsman decides to add one additional cow to his grazing herd, thinking perhaps that no one would notice or that there would be nothing more than a marginal impact on the pasture. But he's wrong. First one herdsman notices and then another, and thinking along the lines of the first herdsman to transgress the limit, they too add one additional cow each until all have done the same. With no controlling mechanism and each increasingly desperate herdsman trying not to lose ground, the common is overgrazed and soon decimated.

The lesson is probably obvious: without proper controls and regulations, ultimately no one will benefit, or a very small number will benefit at the expense of all the others. Without a force greater than the individual (and I will add an organization or a member of any collective) that all will subscribe to, submitting freely to mutually agreed upon rules, regulations, laws, or contracts, then some form of universal ruin will befall all the participants. Though the consequences of a member of a food coalition "going their own way" and ultimately snubbing their nose at the group may not be as severe as what might befall the herdsmen, the practical benefit for everyone to submit to group rules and procedures can't be overstated. I have seen more than one coalition crumble, sacrificing months and even years of collective work, when one of its members decides to jump ship, or finding a way to add one cow to their paddock at the expense of others. This has happened in national coalitions working on the farm bill and in local coalitions working in small cities.

Brian Gunia, a professor at the Johns Hopkins Carey Business School who studies group behavior, negotiations, and decision-making, recommends that any team, coalition, or other group made up of voluntary members establish formal statements of how they will work together. He recommends that the following components be contained in these state-ments (personal communication):

- Members: who are we as individuals and as a team; how do we define our membership; do we know each person's talents?
- Mission: what are we trying to accomplish; does everyone in the group understand and share our goals?
- Definition of success: how will we gauge progress and goal achievement; what are we measuring?
- Division of labor: what will be our various roles and responsibilities; are there subgroups or committees that have defined roles and responsibilities?
- Expectations: what do we expect of each other?
- Syndication: how will we ensure that we routinely communicate (frequent communication)?
- Decision-making: what procedure will we use to make decisions; are we voting, using a consensus model, and do we need to follow certain proto-cols, for example, can't decide on an issue without a quorum and without the item appearing in advance on the agenda?
- Accountability: how will we hold each other accountable and deal with con-flict or contract violations?
- Contingencies: what might change with task/team/environment; how will we adjust?
- Revision: Under what conditions will we revisit or revise the contract?

Additionally, Gunia recommends that each group establish the following procedures:

- Everyone should participate; if members start to not show up, they must be reminded of their commitment.
- Everyone should sign the contract/agreement.
- The contract/agreement should be actively and frequently referred to.
- The contract should be "alive" but not "slippery" (it can be flexible but not manipulated to allow members to escape responsibility).
- The team should formally review the contract periodically
- The contract should include *just enough* detail—not too much.
- The contract should be aligned with the mission.

At first glance, this list might appear onerous. People who are used to work-ing in free-flowing, *ad hoc* environments, or who are very task-oriented and get fidgety when they feel there is too much process may revolt at this much structure. At a practical level, the costs of developing and maintaining an organization or coalition that takes its contract seriously are higher than they are for a similar entity that has a looser approach. Like ensuring that a backbone organization is well-funded and capable of serving its purpose in a collective impact structure, additional costs can be expected. It will take more staff time to honor and monitor the contract, and it can be expected that the work of these teams may move at a slower pace, which can also translate into higher costs.

Yet Gunia makes it clear that two things, at a minimum, come from such a diligent process. The first is that groups with contracts simply do better than those who don't have them. Their "up-front" investment costs may be higher but so is their return on investment. They perform at higher levels, produce more outputs, and are more successful at achieving their goals. The second outcome from groups that develop and adhere to contracts/agreements is that they build and sustain higher levels of trust among members. Trust is one of those ephemeral human qualities that is hard to measure, but you sure know when you don't have it. I also think of trust in the sense of the importance of relationship building in a group or coalition. The stronger and more extensive the relationships are between people in the group, the more likely it is that you'll have high levels of trust. And, of course, we know the downside of weak relationships and distrust.

Here are a few more thoughts about group dynamics from Brian Gunia and me and some recent research that should help leaders and facilitators manage effective coalitions and organizations:

- Groups whose members participate a lot and contribute more equally, rather than allowing one or two people to dominate, are more effective and have a higher level of commitment to the group.

- Reading the emotional state (emotional intelligence) of other members can help facilitators and participants guide or focus the discussion in ways that help to manage stress and conflict. Research suggests that groups that have more women do better in this regard because they are better at reading emotional states of others.

- "Social loafing" is a term that describes a condition when one or more members don't carry their own weight as part of the team. They decide for whatever reason—boredom, frustration, feelings of powerlessness—to let others do more of the work. This is a condition that group leaders should keep an eye open for, and it's also one that participants need to be aware of. Asking yourself why you might be feeling disengaged can lead to steps that may change the way you work with the group, or you may use it as an opportunity to improve the group's process

- "The Abilene Effect," which is not a sociopsychological phenomenon common only to the Texas city, occurs when everyone in the group decides to go along with an idea just to go along with the idea. In other words, they don't really believe the idea has merit or would add any value to the group but for the sake of preserving group harmony, they decided to go along with the group. When the suggested action is challenged by someone brave enough to question "group think," they often discover that no one else is that excited by the idea either.

- Information asymmetrically held, or information unevenly distributed among group members and not openly shared, is a common problem in groups. The term "asymmetrically held" comes from the field of economics where, by way of example, as a manufacturer of a product I know how much it costs to make it, but this is information not shared with the buyer. As the sole "keeper" of this knowledge, I have an inherent advantage in setting the price (in certain quarters of the food movement, consumers have been willing to pay a certain price for locally produced food once they understand from the farmers what all of their costs are). But in group work, we often find that individual members hold back certain pieces of information that the collective needs to make the best decision. When one or more members decide to withhold their "piece of the puzzle" then everyone is at a disadvantage.

- "Mountain climbing" is a term that simply refers to the steps that groups take to acquire greater knowledge that builds on what has happened in the past. We are always building on what we know, what we've learned, and our previous actions, successes, and failures. But oftentimes we forget that past, even the immediate past, and neglect valuable lessons as well as the opportunity to celebrate how far we've actually come. Not staying in touch with that past information and experiences, which sometimes takes the form of a group being demoralized because they think they haven't accomplished anything, can be a mistake. Taking time as a group to reflect on past achievements, even if they are minor, builds confidence in where the group is now as well as in its plans for the future.

- "Hard listening" and telling the clock to "shut up" are ways of strengthening one's commitment to the group and especially to each other. Too often, we grow impatient with someone who's having difficulty making a point in a meeting. This is especially true if the meeting is conducted in English, and the speaker's English skills are weak. If time and the agenda can't be altered to allow for people who may need more time to express themselves, then an effort should be made to communicate with those people outside the meeting. Creative listening skills such as restating or paraphrasing someone's statement is also an effective way to be certain that you are "hearing" what they are saying. Similarly, the clock is often an oppressive force in many meetings. "We've allowed two hours for this meeting and that's all!" is the refrain we often hear. Sometimes people need more time to be heard, and when working in community settings, being heard is often what matters most. If adequate time is not allowed, or if those who run meetings are not flexible, then many necessary voices may be lost.

## Thoughts on Vision, Leadership, Management and Communication

The success of a collective impact initiative or a coalition that has many stakeholders with a broad, communitywide or national focus is directly linked to the strength of its vision, leadership, management, and communication. In a single organization or in an initiative largely led by a single, often charismatic person, the vision is the product of that one group or person; it is not "owned" by any other group or persons. As I have maintained throughout this book, a single organization or person is not enough to bring about the sweeping transformation that our food system needs. The work must be done by many who share a common vision, can provide their own leadership, and are capable of developing a management structure capable of keeping everyone working without a hierarchical, top-down structure.

I like the following diagram (See Figure 7.1) as a guide for developing and monitoring the progress of multistakeholder organizations like food policy councils. It follows a logical planning path from its inception to gathering the data ("community food assessment") to determining the direction of the group to developing and implementing a plan based on collective impact to

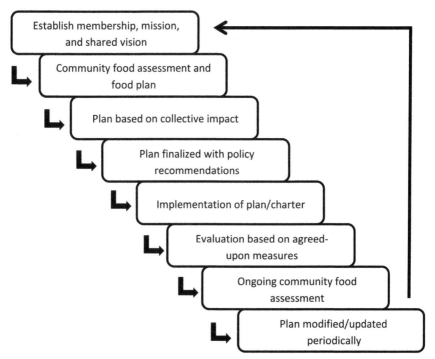

Figure 7.1

evaluating the work based on common measures to the feedback loop that assesses the need to change the plan if not the mission and vision.

The first step is to establish a vision. For the vision to be inspiring and to ensure everyone's commitment, it must be shared by everyone. A shared vision is a desired future state shared by a collective of persons that is physically possible, not necessarily easily imaginable, but owned, even "felt" by the members of the group. When done right, shared visions cause people to invest in the organization/coalition that articulated that vision. Without a shared vision, it is possible to achieve success, but those who have responsibility for implementing it will be far less invested in the work of the organization, which will require higher levels of control, supervision, and expendable resources.

Leadership and management in a collective impact model also follow a somewhat unconventional path. Looking at the two leadership and management diagrams in Figure 7.2, we can see distinctive differences.

The upper "hierarchy" model diagram depicts a traditional top-down approach to leadership and management. There is one person who promulgates policies and directives that are then implemented ever lower along the chain of command. All the people, except the president, are looking "up" at what's coming down to them, and they in turn are looking "down" to see who they are passing some part of the work load to.

The more desirable approach for purposes of collective impact, food policy councils, and active coalitions is the lower "flat (self-managing)" diagram. Here, the work and responsibility are firmly positioned in the lower-level boxes, which are usually any number of committees, work groups, teams, and so on that the collective has decided to establish. In a food-related collective,

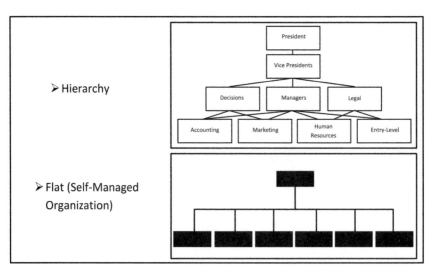

Figure 7.2

like a food policy council, these groups may be committees focused on issue or topic areas like food security, food access, food production, or health and diet. They can also be committees that are focused on organizational maintenance issues like governance and membership, communication, and fundraising. Everyone, whether an individual or organizational member of the collective, should be on at least one of these committees because they are "where the action is." As such, the chairs or cochairs of these committees are important and relatively powerful in the life of the collective.

The top box is occupied by a chair, cochairs, and staff, possibly from a backbone organization. Their "leadership" roles are decidedly different than those of the president in the hierarchical mode. They are there to facilitate, to serve as a resource to the committees (primarily a staff function), and to keep the organization focused on its vision, plan, and/or goals.

Here are a few of my tips for good leadership in a collective-impact-style coalition:

- Meetings should be interesting and engaging; inviting outside speakers to give presentations can have multiple benefits.
- Leadership should focus on facilitating, active listening, and coordinating.
- Keep in mind that everyone's worth and contribution should be acknowledged; allow space to voice feelings.
- Try to make agenda items "actionable," for example, some resolution or follow up is clearly defined at the end of an item's discussion, even if it's only to table the item until the next meeting.
- Make sure there is food, especially something that has a "message," for example, locally produced and/or made by a culinary training program.
- Leadership needs to be responsive to emergent needs, trends, and people who are ready to become leaders themselves; there is no one "right leader" for all occasions; it's situational in that the group's needs change and certain people are ready rise to the task.
- Leaders don't know everything; members provide leadership to the network based on their skills, knowledge, and experience.
- Leaders should be communicating the vision to members constantly; encourage members to contribute, ask questions, share stories and resources, maintain transparency.
- Build the capacity of the group to achieve its goals.

## Food Policy Councils

A growing category of coalitions that come close to embodying the principles of collective impact are food policy councils. The first one came to life in the early 1980s in Knoxville, Tennessee. They grew by fits and starts, and slowly leveled out at 110 in 2011. Suddenly, for reasons that are difficult to determine, their numbers swelled rapidly to 246 in the United States in 2016. This figure does not include another 50 or so food policy councils across Canada, and a smaller number starting to emerge in Europe and Australia. Of those 246 U.S. councils, about 30 are state councils and about 6 are active with Native American tribes. The rest are primarily focused on local food and farm issues at a city, county, city and county, or regional level. Let's take a closer look at how food policy councils operate.

The term "food democracy" had become an interesting but still abstract concept for me until one of the regularly scheduled monthly meetings in 2001 of the City of Hartford Advisory Commission on Food Policy (what is today the second longest continuously operating food policy council in the country). At one of its regularly scheduled meetings, a council member briefed the group on the status of Women, Infant, and Children Program (WIC) run by City of Hartford, which provides nutrition benefits to lower-income mothers, infants, and children under the age of five. Apparently, enrollment in the program had dropped in only one month from 10,000 people to 6,000. The Commission's 15 members (I was a member) gathered around the table were stunned. We all knew that Connecticut's poorest city had not experienced a sudden explosion of prosperity sufficient to lift thousands of people out of poverty. Something was amiss, and we determined to find out what it was.

The "culprit" was discovered in the form of an indifferent city bureaucracy, which closed one of Hartford's two WIC clinics in order to make some building renovations. When Commission representatives contacted the city's public works department they were told the repairs were "likely to take several months." Neither current nor future "WIC moms" had been given any information other than a handwritten sign on the clinic's door that said "Closed for repair." When the Commission began to dig deeper into the WIC program's management, it discovered a chronic pattern of poor customer service including unanswered phones, rude staff, and clinic hours that were totally unaccommodating to the needs of WIC participants.

A quickly arranged meeting between the Commission, Hartford's mayor, and the city health department (the WIC program administrator) ensued. The Commission apprised the mayor and health department of the problems and offered its assistance, but the members made it abundantly clear that the situation was intolerable and that the media would be alerted if action wasn't taken immediately. Lo and behold, the clinic reopened in a week, the former caseload of 10,000 was restored soon after, and commission members worked with city staff to correct the management and customer service issues.

What were the lessons learned? Reflecting the Nobel laureate economist Amartya Sen's statement on how to avoid famine, "When a government is accountable to the public, and when there is free news-reporting and uncensored public criticism, then the government too has an excellent incentive to do its best to eradicate famines" (2011, p. 343), the Commission relied on its multistakeholder membership to report and ultimately fix a problem that was adversely affecting the city's most vulnerable citizens. In its most concrete form, this is what "food democracy" should be—watchful, informed citizens and organizations working together, in partnership with government, to ensure food security for everyone.

Food policy councils are a vehicle for food democracy and an engaged food citizenry. When we let money and the marketplace pursue their own ends unfettered, the public interest and the most vulnerable, in particular, are relegated to much lower levels of importance. Yes, the marketplace will shift slowly to accommodate changing food preferences and better informed consumers, for example, more organic, less fat, but unless citizens, various food system stakeholders, and the public sector speak up, preferably in an organized fashion, the food system will not serve the people equitably.

My stories are many. In addition to the lackadaisical city bureaucracy whose clumsy actions denied several thousand low-income mothers and children access to WIC benefits, there was a vengeful New Mexico state bureaucrat who had decided unilaterally to deny thousands of elderly access to the Senior Farmers' Market Nutrition Program; the regional public transportation authority that ignored the needs of low-income, car-less urban residents to travel to distant suburban supermarkets for food; and the Connecticut governor who had castrated his state's farmland preservation program to enable developers to run rampant over prime agricultural land.

These few examples of challenges, and countless more, were favorably resolved when food policy councils and other watchful advocacy groups intervened. As the food movement has grown and diversified, local and state groups have expanded their capacity to include those new interests and to work collaboratively for food policy change.

More and more, however, local and state food challenges have become less confrontational as governments see the value to their social, environmental, and economic interests in working in partnership with private for-profit and nonprofit groups to shape a more robust, healthy, and secure food system. As the report from Michigan State University indicates (2013), each city is reporting an average of three food policy actions. Similarly, states have stepped up their food policy games as the National Conference of State Legislatures report found: 36 states passed 90 bills between 2012 and 2014 to improve food access, local agriculture, and food policy councils.

Trying to make national food and farm policy more amicable toward food security, health, and sustainability has never been an easy process. Although progress has been made (see the example from the 2008 farm bill in the coming section), it typically takes the form of relatively small programs and budgets, as well as preventing cuts in existing programs, for example, SNAP. Reliance on big national policy moments like the Farm Bill or the Child Nutrition Act that come along every five years can be enormously frustrating. For those seeking faster, small "p" policy wins, local and state governments have been offering more attractive playing fields to both elected officials and advocates. It might be said that democracy, at least in the way that Amartya Sen envisions it, works best when the people and policy makers are in close proximity to one another.

Generally, a food policy council consists of a designated set of individuals representing various sectors—government and nongovernment, food production to consumption, grassroots to grass-tops—from a geographically and politically defined area. Some food policy councils operate in a looser, open-ended fashion when it comes to defining memberships (New Mexico Food and Agriculture Policy Council), others have a very clearly defined membership that is appointed by elected officials (Hartford), while others have a combination of both (the Los Angeles Food Policy Council (LAFPC) has hundreds of members but very well-defined committees and governance structure).

A food policy council (sometimes simply called a council, an advisory council, a commission, or food system network) gathers and analyzes food system information, makes recommendations on program and policy issues, educates the public about needs, and fosters coordination between various food system actors. As the previous flow chart diagram indicated, following a logical process of understanding the problem, creating a plan, and implementing it is the preferred form of action. In the case of food policy councils, however, the council itself is not necessarily the entity that puts individual food projects into action. They are not generally project oriented but in fact are policy oriented. Rather than start a new community garden, for instance, they will work with the city council to change zoning regulations that make it easier for others to start many community gardens.

Closely associated with this growth in food policy councils is the phenomenon of local and state food planning. From Seattle to New York City, and in states like Minnesota and Michigan, food policy councils and other public and private entities have come together to construct formal food documents often known as "food plans" or "food charters," which are designed to guide the evolution and growth of their respective food systems. A parallel trend, one that further reflects the interest of cities in food policy, has been the number of cities that have one or more staff within city government that are dedicated to food issues. These include Boston, New York, Baltimore, and most recently, Washington, D.C. The U.S. Conference of Mayors reports that about 23 cities have food policy advisors working on food issues (Holly Freishtat, personal communication). This doesn't include a much larger number of city and county staff, often in planning or health departments, that dedicate a substantial portion of their time to more food system topics addressed by food policy councils.

Food charters like the one passed in Detroit several years ago articulate a set of principles and values that are designed to guide the city's policy makers and its nongovernmental organizations. It prescribed the creation of the Detroit Food Policy Council, which has used the charter to advocate for a more robust urban agriculture sector and improved access to healthy food outlets. Charters and plans should not be mistaken for actual implementation documents or even detailed work plans. When done well, they set a vision for the community's food future and identify clear goals, targets, and measurable outcomes. Perhaps most importantly, they indicate who is responsible for each action or goal. In effect, the process of establishing a charter or plan, particularly with respect to who's responsible for each step, is just as important as the content of the plan. If the process for establishing the plan has been good—it has adequately engaged the community, key stakeholders, and decision makers—the more likely that the key stakeholders will "own" the plan. The more that those stakeholders "feel the plan in their gut"—in other words, there's a palpable form of commitment—the more likely the plan will be successfully executed.

Sometimes in concert with government and sometimes independently, food policy councils have asserted their will in ways both big and small to shore up the critical links between health, food production, the food economy, planning, and citizen participation. The Connecticut Food Policy Council, founded in 1998, secured a commitment from the state's economic development agency for a $1 million investment in a new supermarket project in a low-income New Haven neighborhood, the first new supermarket in that community in 20 years.

The New Mexico Food and Agriculture Policy Council, founded in 2003, established working partnerships with state agencies and legislative leaders to expand funding for farm-to-school initiatives (state funding averaging about $300,000 per year) and to halt the sale of sugary soft drinks in New Mexico's public schools. In 2015, they added significantly to their list of "wins" after they secured over $400,000 from the state legislature to double the value of SNAP benefits used to purchase fresh produce at the state's farmers' markets. It should be noted as well that state food policy councils like New Mexico's also maintain strong ties to federal food and farm issues. By advocating for and keeping tabs on federal funding sources, they've been able to both influence federal policy as well as benefit from it. To this end, a group affiliated with the New Mexico council also secured over $2 million in federal Food Insecurity Nutrition Initiative funding (personal communication with Pam Roy, NMF&APC Coordinator).

The achievements of the Cleveland-Cuyahoga Food Policy Council exemplify both the opportunities and challenges that an engaged food citizenry face in promoting a healthier food environment. Starting in 2005, the Food Policy Council forged a close, working partnership with members of the Cleveland City Council as well as key city administrative staff to use food as way of engaging both Cleveland's economic and health problems. This resulted in changes to the city's zoning code and economic development strategies to promote urban farming and gardening, new food purchasing preferences to support local agriculture, and better access to healthy food outlets.

But Cleveland went further. Like many other cities over the past decade, they proposed a ban on the use of trans-fats in restaurants and food shops. As one of the initiative's prime sponsors, City Councilman Joe Cimperman referred to the ban as one of "the more common-sense things we're trying to do in terms of public health" (personal communication). Catching wind of this new regulation, the state's restaurant association promptly secured passage of a bill from the Republican-controlled Ohio legislature that pre-empted the authority of the state's municipalities to regulate food ingredients, an action that Cimperman fervently denounced as "pro-obesity, pro-diabetes, pro-death" (Winne, 2012). (The state action was later overturned in an Ohio court).

Cities and states are becoming more frequent battlegrounds in the growing food wars. While some are deploying incentive-based strategies that make it easier for SNAP participants to use their benefits at farmers' markets, others are taking more aggressive approaches like banning trans-fats or taxing sugar-sweetened beverages. In all cases, there is clearly a welling-up of citizen concern over the long-term health, safety, and sources of their food. Increasingly, this includes concerns over the work conditions that people must labor under to produce and process food. Public officials are listening and acting. Mayors and county officials are "getting religion" when it comes to food realizing that their constituents want action on issues where the federal government may be falling short. But as the stakes grow, so does the pushback from large food industry forces that regard regulations or oversight of their businesses as an impingement on their "right" to run a business. In this environment, the role of food policy councils and the voice of food citizens will become ever more critical.

Resources: For more information about food policy councils and related coalitions go to www.foodpolicynetworks.org at the Johns Hopkins Center for a Livable Future. Particularly appropriate are the following documents:

- *Doing Food Policy Councils Right: A Guide to Development and Action.* Michael Burgan and Mark Winne. September 2012.
- *Framing the Future: A Planning Resource for Food Policy Councils.* Center for a Livable Future. 2016.

- *Good Laws, Good Food: Putting Local Food Policy to Work in Our Communities.* Harvard Law and Policy Clinic. November, 2012. (Harvard also has a separate document devoted to state food policy.)

## Food Charters, Food Plans, and Food Councils

When food policy councils began organizing in the 1980s and 1990s, the idea of food planning *per se*, as a formal planning function, was barely on the table. Robert Wilson, the founder of the nation's first food policy council in Knoxville, was a professor of planning at the University of Tennessee. It was his simple but compelling idea that communities could bring the discipline of professional planning to bear on food systems in cities, counties, and even states.

While the idea of food policy councils began to slowly take hold, the idea of doing systematic planning with respect to food did not. Too many obstacles that would take time to overcome were in the way. The concept of a food system, for instance, with it multilayered and interconnected parts, was too new and unfamiliar to most people. Policy makers didn't see the value in devoting significant resources to food, which, as far they were concerned, was a private marketplace issue with a small role reserved for the federal government (e.g., food stamps, school lunch) and nonprofits (e.g., food banks). After all, cities that had the greatest food problems were also overwhelmed with more traditional public sector issues like crime, education, and housing. Food policy councils, at least during the first decade or two of their existence, were left to slowly chip away at issues like food deserts, public transportation, the local and state operation of federal food programs, and farmland loss. Instead of a holistic approach to the food system, they were relegated to a piecemeal one.

With the emergence of state food policy councils, however, a considerably bigger palate upon which to work was laid before food advocates. Both state and local food activists would later be joined by the American Planning Association, which gave its imprimatur to its member planners during the early 2000s to directly engage in food system work. Partially as a result of a growing understanding of the connection between diet and health problems like diabetes, local and state health officials would also begin to feel some urgency to develop more systemic programs and policies. Though some groups (the Connecticut Food Policy Council in the late 1990s and the north central Connecticut Capitol Region Council of Governments) tried to integrate food system planning into state and regional planning documents (*A Plan of Conservation and Development for the Capitol Region—Achieving the Balance*, 2003), it wasn't until 2009 that Michigan would take the first big step in the direction of comprehensive, statewide food planning (it should be noted that some Canadian jurisdictions such as Toronto had developed earlier food plan/charter models).

Starting in 2009, Michigan State University Center for Regional Food Systems (CRFS), the Food Bank Council of Michigan, and Michigan Food Policy Council joined forces to produce the Michigan Good Food Charter in 2010. The charter includes a vision and set of goals for the state's food system, and its implementation is overseen by a steering committee, which works to further coordination between the charter's partner organizations and oversee what is now known as the Michigan Good Food Initiative (Shapiro et al., 2015). Their vision statement is worth noting: "We envision a thriving economy, equity, and sustainability for all of Michigan and its people through a food system rooted in local communities and centered on good food." A selection of the charter's goals includes the following: by 2020, 20 percent of food purchased by public institutions will be locally grown; 80 percent of Michigan's residents will have easy access to affordable, healthy, fresh food (20% of which will be local); Michigan's schools will incorporate food and agriculture into their kindergarten to 12th grade curricula.

The Food Charter partners and steering committee have used a set of unique strategies that rely largely on convening and coordinating other existing food and farm networks including the Michigan Farm to Institution Network, the Michigan Food Hub Network, the Michigan Local Food Council Network, the Livestock Work Group, and the Food Justice Work Group. In other words, the steering committee, which employs a collective impact framework, serves as a hub itself for these various statewide networks that collectively cover a large swath of the state's food system. While not exactly a "backbone organization," the steering committee does promote communication between the state's food stakeholders (they host a biannual statewide summit—the 2016 convening drew 500 people), facilitate the creation of a shared measurement system, and provide technical assistance and, recently, some funding to improve food access and foster viable food businesses.

What Michigan has set in motion has three important components. The first is the charter itself, which many hands created and now serves as a beacon for the network. The second component is the networking and coordination of other networks and coalitions that collectively represent an array of Michigan's food sectors. Finally, and perhaps most importantly, is Michigan State University's Center for Regional Food Systems, which provides a host of important technical, support, research, and evaluation services. While not unique among the country's land-grant university systems, CRFS provides an extraordinary reservoir of talent, value-based commitment, and institutional stability that can make all the difference to early stage, often fragile collective impact initiatives.

Over the course of the five or so years of operation, and with CRFS's assistance, the Michigan Good Food Initiative has reflected on what is working and where work needs to be done, especially with respect to its role as a hub. Among their "lessons learned" is the recurring need for education and capacity building at the start of almost every new project. As has been noted several times throughout this book, communicating your purpose and method of operation can't be done once and simply put on a website in hopes that everyone will read and understand it. Restating and explaining your work frequently is necessary. In a similar vein, racial equity can't just be a slogan or a slot on the board of directors; it must an explicit focus of the group. This may mean, for instance, that new leaders must be constantly cultivated. As seems to be the case throughout the food movement, collaboration is something that food movement groups are hungry for. The trick is facilitating and harnessing the power of collaboration so that it adds to the strength of the movement without consuming more resources than it produces. Finally, these "lessons learned" shouldn't be taken as absolute prescriptions by other practitioners without those practitioners taking into account their own food system contexts—agricultural systems, local politics, funder and nonprofit infrastructure, and public policy advocacy. There is a role, in other words, for "local knowledge" and the history of people and organizations, to say nothing of the unique cultural context of a place.

Minnesota took a similar path with the development and implementation of the Minnesota Food Charter. Perhaps what stands out is the lengthy (two years) and in-depth community engagement process the organizers followed to create the charter. Starting a couple of years after Michigan, the organizers, which included among others the Blue Cross, Blue Shield Foundation of Minnesota, and the University of Minnesota Cooperative Extension Service, held meetings and reached to thousands of people, organizations, and agencies across the state. The numbers alone are impressive: 2,500 individuals offered input into the contents of the charter; 400 online worksheets were completed; 144 separate events were held to gather information; and 90 interviews were conducted. All of this was overseen by a steering committee of 27 people (personal communication with Alison Rotel, Blue Cross, Blue Shield Foundation of Minnesota; www.mnfood charter.com).

In comparison to Michigan, Minnesota places somewhat more emphasis on food access themes than on the development of a local food economy, although both charters cover many of the same issues (actual issue content of any particular charter will always be influenced by who's around the table). In the course of assembling Minnesota's document, the organizers had a particularly keen eye open for policy opportunities, and as such engaged government officials to ascertain which policies might receive the most favorable responses. According to one official from Blue Cross, Blue Shield, they made a strategic choice to avoid highly controversial topics (e.g., a sugar tax in Minnesota would have been vigorously opposed by the state's large sugar beet industry) to secure as much general and advance political "buy-in" for the full charter as possible.

The statement taken directly from the Minnesota Food Charter website makes it clear that public policy is front and center as a way to change the food system. The statement also contains the charter's 2017 public policy priorities.

The Minnesota Food Charter contains 99 proven policy and system changes designed to increase reliable access to safe, affordable, healthy food for all Minnesotans. There are over twenty policy strategies contained in the Food Charter that are focused on state-level policy action. If implemented, these policies are designed to move the dial on creating healthier food environments, healthy food skills, and a healthy food infrastructure that supports the health and prosperity of all Minnesota communities.

This year (2017), the Minnesota Food Charter Network–for the first time–has selected statewide policy priorities that reflect Food Charter strategies. The Food Charter Network's Policy Action Team undertook a rigorous process to identify these priorities over the last several months. With guidance and engagement from hunger relief, healthcare, agriculture, public health, community food advocacy, economic development and other sectors, the Policy Action Team selected a series of important state-level policies that are consistent with Food Charter strategies. These policies include:

Providing state funding for mobile food shelves

Increasing resources to support hunger relief initiatives through food banks and food shelves

Investing $10 million in the 'Good Food Access Fund' to support the development of healthy food retail in areas of the state with inadequate access to healthy food

Contributing adequate funding for school meals to ensure districts have the resources they need to provide healthy food to students

Providing resources to encourage small-scale food production to develop regional economies and enhance food security in communities across Minnesota

The Minnesota Food Charter Network will collaborate with coalitions and organizations leading this work, helping raise awareness about the issues and how these policies help fulfill Food Charter strategies.

Over the next couple of years, the Food Charter Network's Policy Action Team will also undertake further work on:

Exploring concrete policy solutions to improve farmland access and farmland succession planning

Integrating and increasing funding for agricultural development, food and farm-related technical assistance, and food and farm-related enterprise development

Increasing and sustaining public support for farmers' markets, so they are able to accept SNAP/EBT and provide "market bucks" incentives to limited resource customers

Ensuring all Minnesotans have the resources they need to purchase healthy food, by supporting a living wage for all earners

Developing and implementing purchasing standards to ensure that foods purchased and served by state government-run facilities and agencies promote the health and well-being of the state's residents

Providing sustained, adequate funding to improve our understanding and treatment of tick-borne diseases that affect Minnesotans' ability to hunt and gather food

Offering adequate, affordable insurance coverage for farmers who raise healthy food for nearby markets, with a focus on healthcare, crops, and risk management

Developing a comprehensive, long-range plan to equip all Minnesotans with the healthy food skills they need to take care of their health

Generating investment and plans for a robust, profitable food infrastructure that promotes the health and prosperity of all Minnesotans, while provide resources needed by small and medium food and farm enterprises across the state

Making the healthy choice the easy choice for our state will necessitate policy work at the state level from seed to table. The Minnesota Food Charter Network is pleased to support the efforts of many partners advancing these policy changes, by engaging in issue advocacy and raising awareness of its supporters and relevant decision makers.

With their emphasis on healthy food access, the Minnesota Food Charter Network also smartly engaged its local public health infrastructure, which has a presence in every county in the state. This gives it a "leg up" when conducting public education and community outreach in a more or less equitable manner throughout the state. The "every county" approach also avoids the urban bias that sometimes creeps into food initiatives, which intend to be statewide in theory but often favor areas with much higher population densities. As such, Minnesota maintains a strong commitment to its rural counties and Tribal Nations.

Taking note of measurement—what do we measure, and how do we assign causality for results that we can measure—we see that more collective impact food system networks are attempting to make it a central part of their work. Vermont's Farm to Plate Initiative has tracked the total value of farm direct sales over time in all six New England states as an indicator of local food consumption. Between 1997 and 2012, they saw a doubling of local food consumption from $81 million to $160 million (Vermont Sustainable Jobs Fund, 2017). But networks will be the first to admit that it wasn't their backbone organization that made this happen since various forces, including those that predate the formation of the network, acted on those trends or indicators. Nevertheless, there is general agreement that individual actors within the network have played important roles—some more than others, no doubt—in sending those measures in the right direction.

One other measure consistently rises to the top in the evaluation of collective impact networks is the low levels of participation and leadership from people of color. The fact that racial equity and diversity are food system "indicators" as much or more so than dollars of local food or pounds of donated food bank food, does indicate a commitment to inclusivity and the process of community engagement. While this might sound like an overly optimistic assessment of the state of racial equity in the food system, it is in fact a highly distinguishing feature of food system work. How many organizations, businesses, or associations include diversity measures in their annual reports or single the issue out for special treatment, especially when they are falling short? While the collective impact initiatives haven't found all the answers, the issue does appear to be front and center.

## Indianapolis, Indiana

Local collective impact networks are also developing. As with state networks, the local initiatives are developing food plans and often associate with or are a part of food policy councils or similar organizations. One example is the Indy Food Council in Indianapolis, Indiana which had been operating since 2013 and officially became a collective impact organization the following year. Perhaps the strongest evidence of the Council's commitment to collective impact is its structure and extensive membership, which includes representatives from government (county health department; city office of sustainability), numerous nonprofit organizations engaged in a variety of food system activities, and larger institutions (Indiana University, Purdue Cooperative Extension, the Local Initiative Support Corporation). Participation by groups like these give the collective access to both technical know-how (universities) as well as policy makers (city and county representatives). These various groups are incorporated into a structure that emphasizes a strong role for seven committees such as community engagement and food access, which in turn are facilitated by an executive committee and supported by an advisory committee.

Their vision statement is "to create a food system that provides everyone [in Marion County] with access to healthy nutritious food, enhances ecology, and creates meaningful economic and civic opportunities" (Indy Food Council, 2013). Their mission is to connect their region's food system stakeholders. In other words, the focus is on the larger food system and the means to address the problems with multiple participants from all levels of the community.

The Indy Food Council's general assessment of food problems is comprehensive in that it takes in all the areas of their food system where attention is needed by the collective. They recognize the high rates of overweight and obesity as a reflection of the community's diet-related health challenges including a high concentration of food deserts; high rates of food insecurity, especially among children; and the existence of a very large amount (17,000 parcels) of vacant land in the city and unused farmland in the surrounding county (Marion) as an opportunity to promote more food production, local food consumption, and jobs. As such, their primary goals are to expand the market for local food, increase access to healthy and affordable food, and to promote more nutrition and cooking education.

Community engagement is a major focus of the council, which held 13 separate community meeting and outreach events during its formative year of 2013. To some extent, that engagement is reinforced with the distribution of small grants to neighborhood-based food initiatives. Over about three years, these grants have totaled $113,000. Using mini-grants distributed by a council or network can be a good technique for reaching parts of the community that can sometimes be difficult to reach.

## New Brunswick, New Jersey

New Brunswick is a small city of about 65,000 that stretches along the banks of the Raritan River in densely populated central New Jersey. Its most distinguished institution is Rutgers, the State University of New Jersey, and its best-known corporation is Johnson & Johnson. Together they are a source of higher education, wealth, prestige, and jobs. But in spite of the relative enormity of these giants in comparison to the rest of the community, New Brunswick suffers from above average levels of food insecurity (51% of the city's families) and poverty. About 56 percent of the city is Latino, but it has also become home to numerous other immigrant communities, many of which struggle to get by in the city's neighborhoods. Rents are high, services are expensive, and according to a spokesperson for Unity Square, a nonprofit community organization, the living wage for this part of Middlesex County, where New Brunswick is located, is $21 per hour. The state's minimum wage remains stuck at an inadequate $8.30 per hour (Glaser et al., 2014).

To make ends meet, most people are working two jobs and crowding into dilapidated, overpriced housing, according to Yvette Molina, a community outreach specialist for Elijah's Promise, a highly regarded multiservice community organization. Because food is one area where the community can help needy people reduce costs, Elijah's Promise focuses on food programs, including a culinary jobs training center. Struggling families will also use any of a dozen or so food pantries that are scattered around the city such as the one at Elijah's Promise that serves over 1,600 registered households. Although community service providers try to sign up people for SNAP, their efforts are often frustrated by immigrant fears that they'll be deported if they become too public. But as Molina says, "Food insecurity is just a metric for poverty."

But the other problem that bedevils New Brunswick is the lack of cohesion between the many groups that are fighting to improve the lives of its residents. As Keith Jones, a special assistant to the Mayor of New Brunswick, sees it, "there are too many organizations, including houses of worship, that are doing their own thing and not collaborating with each other." To address this problem, one that I've indicated is common in communities all across the country, Jones and others started the New Brunswick Community Food Alliance, which, according to their mission statement, "is committed to the development and maintenance of a sustainable local food system . . . so that all residents have access to . . . food" (New Brunswick Food Alliance, 2014). Interestingly, the alliance, which was started in 2012, doesn't say that residents need more food or related services, they say the community needs "a more coordinated food system . . . to use resources more efficiently."

Knowing that a lack of coordination was a big part of the problem, Elijah's Promise and the Alliance began working with Rutgers Bloustein School of Planning and Public Policy to conduct a food assessment and construct a food plan for the city. They were fortunate to have a sympathetic ally in the form of the Johnson & Johnson Foundation that eagerly joined the campaign with a generous commitment of funds for a three-year task that started in 2014 and was completed in 2017.

To tell New Brunswick's "food story" and describe its many efforts to improve food security, Rutgers undertook surveys, interviews, and data collection procedures that painted a detailed and comprehensive picture of the region's food system. While they mustered an impressive array of food information, they didn't hesitate to dig beneath the numbers to carefully explain what is meant by food security and what causes food insecurity. The report reviews the city's food and nutrition programs, its food retail environment, and the state of the community's food banks and food pantries. To round out the New Brunswick food system picture, the report also addresses community and backyard gardens, the growth of small food businesses, and efforts by local and federal agencies to expand nutrition and cooking education. The report (The New Brunswick Food System Action Plan Rutgers University Bloustein School of Planning and Public Policy, 2017) concludes with recommendations on how food- and nonfood-related strategies can reduce food insecurity in New Brunswick.

But what's more significant about the assessment and plan was its community engagement process. There are a lot of New Brunswick people, organizations, and agencies who have rolled up their sleeves over the years to address the city's food needs. But in addition to their programs, the hardest and most beneficial action that the community's stakeholders can take is to collaborate. Rutgers knew that in advance, and so as a major part of their research process they literally engaged dozens of organizations and hundreds of people as their partners. In a carefully managed fashion, this led to community members using the University's data, often gathered by community groups and people, to come up with their action steps.

A small sampling of the action steps includes the following:

- Work collectively to identify and apply for grants and others resources.
- Provide more comprehensive services at food sites including mental and physical health.
- Create workshop to increase gardening knowledge and skills.
- Identify and describe everyone doing nutrition education in the city.
- Connect farmers' markets to faith groups to promote more purchase and consumption of local food.
- Create a micro food business incubator.
- Create a mobile food truck.
- Track legislation related to food at the state level.

These steps have been reviewed by dozens of people. Through a committee structure they were brought to a community food planning forum in October 2016 that was attended by 60 people, representing most of the city's communities and food system stakeholders. They were accepted (in some cases modified) by everyone present. The final step was to bring these recommendations and a final food plan to a community food forum planned for February, 2017 that was sponsored by the New Brunswick Community Food Alliance. Preliminary indications are that the Johnson & Johnson Foundation will fund a coordinating hub that will oversee the New Brunswick food plan implementation.

## Partnership Models

Forming broad-based state and community food coalitions is not always a feasible or practical way to start. Oftentimes food activists have to simply connect two or more dots from the food system to begin the process of building bigger tents. One place where partnerships between multiple sectors and interests are becoming more common is in the anti-hunger and food bank arenas. Since operating a food program in a particular community is more than likely to put you in touch with other food programs in the same community, it's just natural that connections will be made. Though simply "connecting" is not necessarily an active form of partnership, evidence is mounting that groups are developing more substantial networking relationships.

In a 2014 survey of large food banks that are part of the Feeding America network (unpublished Feeding America data, 2014), 90 respondents (about 45% of Feeding America's members) shared how they worked with other food projects and groups in their respective geographies (these food banks generally cover large regions—multicounty—and/or highly populated metro areas of their states). The responding food banks indicated that:

- 46 percent participate in some sort of food policy council.
- 39 percent operate or support a garden(s).
- 20 percent operate or support a food hub, or are actively exploring the possibility.
- 21 percent operate or support a farm-to-school/institution program.
- 14 percent operate or support a farm.
- 14 percent operate or support a farmers' market or a mobile farmers' market.
- 34 percent advocate for Double Up Bucks programs
- 58 percent advocate for access to farmers' markets by SNAP and WIC recipients.

As one who has been in and around the food bank world for most of his career, I would say these numbers are encouraging. If almost half of the respondents (about one-fifth of all food banks) participate in "some sort of food policy council," then we see that the largest private food organizations in any community are stretching their wings beyond their singular purpose of receiving and distributing food to food insecure people. Similarly, that reasonable percentages are showing interest in food production and locally produced food also point to an expanding horizon that embraces other large sectors of the food movement.

As Andy Fisher points out (2017), there is a growing list of food banks who are expanding their food system partnerships as well as their missions. These actions are not just an attempt to be responsible community partners; they also represent a growing awareness that ending hunger will not be accomplished by food banks alone. One of the bright lights in the emerging constellation of food banks is an initiative called Closing the Hunger Gap (CTHG). Currently, this is a loosely organized collective of what can be termed "progressive food banks" and other anti-hunger activist organizations that are using WHYHunger as their backbone organization. They grew out of an initial conference in Tucson, Arizona, in 2013 that drew about 300 people. This was followed by a second conference in Portland, Oregon, in 2015 that was attended by 500 people from 41 states and Canada.

CTHG's aspiration is to "create a network to not just share information and inspiration, but to build collective power." Their message is about "creating lasting change in partnership with . . . vulnerable people" and "emergency food providers redefining their role . . . as healthcare intervention sites . . . organizers . . . trainers . . . advocates." They characterize this kind of shift in the anti-hunger world as a "sea-change," and one that reframes their purpose "as one of charity to one of justice."

Their methods, other than a coalescing of efforts and appealing to a broad swath of food system and social justice activists, have not been determined yet. Nor do they have a fully formed vision statement or governance structure in place. They have advertised for and hope to hire their first staff person dedicated to CTHG in the near future. A third CTHG conference is planned for Tacoma, Washington, in September 2017, and the expectation is that the number of attendees will exceed that of 2015. Since I know many of the leaders of this movement—their histories, the evolution of their thinking, and their high level of competency—I am reasonably sanguine as of this writing that CTHG will be a very positive force in the evolution of the food movement toward greater unity.

## Public Procurement—A Path to Partnerships and Unity

Sometimes partnerships are formed around one concept that can embody the diverse interests and goals of many groups. Such is the case with public procurement and a rapidly emerging concept called the Good Food Purchasing Program (GFPP), which grew out of the work of the LAFPC and the Food Chain Workers Alliance (FCWA) (http://foodchainworkers.org/). While GFPP builds off the buy-local trend forged by the farm to school movement, the City of Los Angeles and the L.A. Unified School District, which together serve over 750,000 meals a day, set the bar several notches higher. They have embraced a procurement standard that includes not just local food sourcing but also nutrition, animal welfare, economic development, environmental sustainability, and labor issues.

Over lunch on a balmy January day in L.A., Clare Fox, the LAFPC's executive director told me, "The GFPP is the best of what food policy councils can do." She stressed "Public procurement is a real food systems issue" because it directly addresses most of the key values that are increasingly driving food consumer choice. Fox and her colleagues shepherded the procurement plan through the large and organizationally complex food policy council, which literally engages hundreds of people and groups. Such a thorough vetting process ensured that these ambitious standards had widespread support.

Joann Lo, the Food Chain Worker Alliance's executive director, is a woman with an intuitive grasp of the food system web. She joined the environmental club in high school, converted to veganism while attending Yale University, and became a supporter of both organic food and Yale's worker unions. At that time, the workers were fighting for better wages from one of the world's most powerful institutions. And like a hybridized seed that found its way to a very fertile growing medium, Joann landed in L.A. with the FCWA, a powerful force for fundamental food system change. Fortunately, that L.A. soil was tended by then-mayor Antonio Villaraigosa, himself a former labor organizer who had appointed Paula Daniels, then a local Public Works Commissioner, to organize the LAFPC. From that point on, the council has been a very collaborative effort involving thousands of people.

As one of many food chain worker representatives on the LAFPC, Lo played a catalytic role in bringing the interests of food and farm workers to the table. When public procurement boiled to the top of the LAFPC's early agenda, a committee called the "Build a Market for Good Food Working Group" took on the task of drafting what would become the "Good Food Purchasing Plan." The plan's power is in the way it balances a web of food system issues against one another through an intricately designed five-star rating system of the food products and the companies that produce and sell them.

But what is GFPP's strength is also its challenge. In a *Progressive Planning* article coauthored by Lo and Alexa Delwiche (2013), LAFPC's first coordinator and now the director of the newly formed Center for Good Food Purchasing, the history and sometimes contentious development of the GFPP are recounted. Do we buy our food from unionized farms that are usually industrial-scale operations that also pollute? Or do we buy our food from smaller, sustainably farmed operations with lower, nonunion wages? Working this stuff out, even in the mellow air of progressive L.A., produces sparks that can badly singe the negotiators. But work it out they did, and the early evidence suggests that the GFPP may be strong enough to survive the tests that lay ahead.

With $150 million a year in public food contracts on the table (and with most contracts running for five years), L.A. believes it has the leverage to demand more in social, economic, and environmental benefits from its suppliers. Perhaps over time, its tough standards will modify the more unsavory behaviors of large industrial food corporations like Tyson Foods who need consumer demand as well as government inspectors to hold them accountable. And as the good food procurement movement spreads (similar plans are on the table in places like Chicago, Oakland, and Austin), other food outfits will have to respond to more "good food" bids worth billions in public dollars.

## Food Coops

No longer operating out of the back of your neighbor's garage, retail cooperative food stores are full-fledged business enterprises, managed by professional staff, and generally well capitalized. They are not necessarily single-store operations either. The Puget Consumer Coop in Seattle has 11 store locations. La Montanita in New Mexico has six store locations. Retail coop sales are also nothing to sneeze at. The Park Slope Food Coop in Brooklyn has 16,000 members and $48 million in annual sales. Burlington, Vermont's City Market-Onion River Coop has 8,000 members and $33 million in sales. Nationwide, combined coop sales are in the billions and official membership exceeds 1.3 million (Winne, 2013).

But it's not only growth and impressive business performance that distinguishes coops—it's their adherence to a set of inviolate principles that have also made them successful social enterprises. In the course of my research of the recent coop movement, I came across amazing stories of true democracy in the workplace and marketplace, efforts to educate and inform eaters, initiatives to reduce local hunger, and strategies to develop regional agriculture and resilient communities.

Like most food coops, the Good Foods Coop in Lexington, Kentucky holds firm to the principles of open membership, democratic control, member ownership and financing, community concern, equality, equity, and solidarity. Growing since 1972, Good Foods now occupies a lovely 12,000 square feet space that I've had the privilege to visit. In addition to selling great food, the coop makes monthly donations to local nonprofits, assists a local food pantry, and participates in nutrition and health programs.

Thanks to a survey of coop activity by Darrow Vanderburg-Wertz, I learned how coops are reaching out to low-income residents. The City Market-Onion River Coop in Burlington, Vermont accepts SNAP and WIC benefits, which represents about $1.3 million of its $33 million in annual sales, has volunteer work options that allow discounts on purchases, makes free deliveries to senior housing complexes, offers free cooking classes to discounted members, and partners with the state WIC program to offer frugal shopping and basic cooking programs, which include incentive gift cards to encourage WIC participants to shop at the Coop.

My "hometown coop," La Montanita, is New Mexico's leading buyer and distributor of locally grown food. Through their warehousing, local business investment programs, and extended partnerships, including an innovative mobile grocery program operating in vast and sparsely populated Native American Pueblos, they are sourcing 1,100 local products from 400 local producers, which now represent 20 percent of their coop's sales.

I learned from the Sacramento and Davis (California) Food Coops that coops aren't just interested in buying local food; they want to ensure that there will be sources of local food to buy from. Through a member-supported effort, the two coops raised funds to purchase an easement on the Central Valley organic farm owned by Jeff and Annie Main. A documentary film, *The Last Crop*, tells the story of the farm and the coops' efforts to preserve it.

From a paper written by Kelsey Byrd and Celeste Winston that compared food coops to Walmart (Ibid.), I was reminded of the extraordinary history and work of New Hampshire's Hanover Co-op, started in 1936. The coop intervened a few years ago to take over a failed independent grocer in the lower middle–income town of White River Junction, Vermont. In spite of the high risk associated with reopening a store in this area, the coop saw an opportunity to sell high-quality food at low prices to people who needed both. The coop saved jobs, expanded the market for local food, improved the local economy by keeping more food dollars in the community, and earned an enormous amount of goodwill.

While not every member of the Hanover Coop was excited by this investment, one board member told me, "Yes, we could have used our profits to give our members lower prices, but chose instead to open a store in a community that needed one." A similar sentiment was echoed by a Puget Consumer Coop board member who said that the coop is solicited all the time by affluent Seattle area neighborhoods that want a PCC store, but their newest store opened in a lower-income community for three reasons: the success of their earlier stores gave them the necessary resources to assume a modest level of risk, the new store is projected to be financially successful, and their values dictate that a needier neighborhood should come first.

How do coops compare overall to Walmart and other conventional supermarkets? Food coops spend 38 percent of their revenues locally compared to 24 percent by conventional grocers; source 20 percent of their products locally compared to 6 percent; keep 17 percent more money in the community; sell 82 percent of their produce as organic compared to 12 percent; and create significantly more full-time workers with benefits (Ibid.).

Now, I do find that I spend more money for food at my coop than I do for comparable items at an Albertson's Supermarket. But I know that every extra dime I spend is being reinvested in the coop, going back to members, paying workers a living wage and decent benefits, buying from local farmers, and strengthening the economic underpinnings of my community. Can Albertson's or Walmart make those claims?

Retail food coops are a unique player in as much they bring a clear-eyed business focus to work that holds values similar to those of others in the food movement. But rather than holding narrowly to their primary mission of bringing good food at reasonable prices to their members, they are also a part of a larger community that is trying to promote healthy eating, economic development, and food security.

Collective impact initiatives, multistakeholder coalitions, and multipurpose organizations don't just arise from the "airy nothing," though as indicated earlier, a little magic can help. They take hard work, and like most carefully scripted efforts, they also require invention and an adherence to local norms and situations. To recap, I've highlighted the value in using a collective impact framework to organize broad-based initiatives to bring about systemic change in our food system. It's also important to consider the model's criticisms carefully (Tom Wolff), not as a way to undermine collective impact theory, but as a way to augment it. When it comes to how people relate to one another across what are often self-imposed divides, I have yet to find any substitute for people honestly struggling to communicate to find common ground with each other. Flaws may emerge in our efforts—we are all so terribly human, after all—but where there is a genuine commitment to that struggle, light will generally break through bringing a measure of comfort to a space that was previously uncomfortable.

The number of food policy councils is growing rapidly. They take on different forms and names, and they operate in and across multiple jurisdictions, but their common thread is to provide a large table around which many stakeholders can sit. While they are only beginning to reach their potential for having a meaningful impact on their food systems, they are serving in many places as a vanguard for promoting cooperation and coordination and for promoting responsive food policies.

States like Michigan and Minnesota, and cities like Indianapolis and New Brunswick, to their credit, are going as "big" as they can to make their food systems work for all residents. They have employed sophisticated and often elaborate food assessment methods and conducted rigorous planning efforts to bring together sometimes thousands of stakeholders to "buy into" and to "own" the outcomes. Time will tell what kind of difference they will make—again, to their credit, they are also developing measures commensurate with the scope of their undertakings. But as we know, to continue "business as usual," which is based on single-project, unconnected enterprises, we should only expect more of the same, which is to say very little progress.

Having said all of that, there is still the reality, often based on where you find yourself, that those larger multistakeholder efforts just aren't where you are able to start. In those cases, take one solid baby step: form a partnership with a group or set of interests that are just outside the scope of your usual work. Food banks are becoming more engaged with food policy councils as well as gardening and farming. Those who have worked to secure a place for local food in school cafeterias are extending their moral reach by saying that a range of social, economic, and environmental impacts must be considered when it comes to the public procurement of food. Food coops as well have moved far beyond the "good old days" of granola and cut-your-own-cheese-with-a-rusty-knife to becoming platforms for expanded and diversified community food action. These and other sectors of the food movement have become intersections of interests and issues where multidimensional relationships between various food activists and organizations can develop.

These are some of the models that are paving the way to greater food movement unity. But just as important as the models are, so are the methods they employ, which must pay attention to the fundamentals of organizational development and group dynamics. Good intentions and a noble cause are not enough. Good organizational and leadership practices must also be front and center.

## National Level

Though the food movement must become more unified in the nation's cities, counties, tribes, and states—and the evidence suggests that the "arc of history" is bending slowly toward unity—it is necessary as well for national efforts to follow a similar trajectory. Hopefully, the reasons are obvious. It is at the national level where federal food and agriculture policy is made. What goes on in Washington in terms of conferences, communication, and funding matters immensely to the food movement. And because it is the nation's "bully pulpit," really big topics like hunger, sustainability, and health always get attention. How groups work together—or don't—and how the connections between these topics are articulated reverberates across the country.

For years, many advocates, Michael Pollan among them, have called for a national food policy—one that embraces the entire food system and not just pieces of its—and for changing the name of the U.S. Department of Agriculture to the Department of Food. There are at least two obstacles to accomplishing those very logical objectives. One of course is the larger and wealthier segments of the food industry, which have never taken a shine to the idea of explicitly linking agriculture, food security, sustainability, and health to one another, as we can see from the reaction of many of its sectors to the recommendations of the Dietary Guidelines expert panel. The other obstacle, however, is nongovernmental groups that advocate on these issues—ones that generally work individually on single topics and rarely, if ever, work collectively toward something as profound as a joined-up national food policy.

But as we see at the local and state levels, progress is starting to be made at the national level as well. I will briefly look at three examples, one from the recent past, and two current ones, all of which deserve consideration for what they can teach us. The first example is the Farm and Food Policy Project (FFPP) that was a collaboration made up of the Community Food Security Coalition (CFSC), the Environmental Defense Fund (EDF), the National Sustainable Agriculture Coalition (NSAC), the Rural Coalition, the American Farmland Trust (AFT), and the Northeast Midwest Institute (NEMWI). The NEMWI served as the coordinating hub for this collaboration, and the other five national organizations (all except CFSC had their headquarters in Washington) represented different areas of the food system (food security, sustainability, racial and social justice, and limited-resource farmers). The FFPP was funded by the W.K. Kellogg Foundation from 2005 to 2008, with the goal of delivering a substantial number of new and expanded policies in what became the 2008 Farm Bill. The funding portion and the outcomes of this project were discussed in an earlier section; here I will only focus on the collaboration itself. And as indicated earlier, the source of this analysis of the FFPP comes from me being a member of the FFPP team as an employee of the CFSC, and from Alan Hunt's *Civic Engagement in Food System Governance*.

First off, this project was a success. As Hunt states, "[The 2008 Farm Bill's] passage represented the largest shift in spending toward programs for environmental protection, conservation practices, socially disadvantaged producers, fruits and vegetables, and local food systems." Not all of that shift can be attributed to the FFPP, but it did secure 23 of its original 38 proposals in the Farm Bill. Of the remaining proposals, seven were partially included, and eight were not included at all. The Kellogg Foundation investment of $5.5 million yielded a "net gain of $5 billion in mandatory program funding compared with the 2002 Farm Bill."

Collaboration was at the core of the FFPP, and collaboration was what the foundation insisted on. This was evident from equally rigorous grant preparation and grantee selection processes that were conducted to pick the six participating organizations from over 100 applicants. Kellogg wanted results in the form of significant policy outcomes, but it was just as committed to the process. The grant application process effectively required the groups to work together before a final grant was made, which "resulted in significant collaborative learning about each organization's theory of policy change, strategy, tactics, messaging, and priorities." Investing this much time and energy allowed "enough trust and mutual understanding" to develop before the policy development and advocacy work even got under way.

One difference between the participating organizations, aside from their unique issue interests, was who they represented, and how they defined their own members. CFSC, NSAC (called the Sustainable Agriculture Coalition at the time), and the Rural Coalition were organizations that comprised other organizations. Today, NSAC has 116 organizational members and the Rural Coalition has over 50 (the numbers were a little lower in 2006). CFSC's membership was well over 100 groups. As such, these three entities were used to working within a coalition framework, which meant, to varying degrees, that a lot of member consultation and engagement was required to set their coalitions' respective directions.

This was not the case with EDF and AFT because they were not coalitions. They were typical large membership/subscriber-based organizations that operated in a more-or-less top-down fashion. Whereas the other FFPP organizations had to continuously consult their other coalition partners, EDF and AFT could act more rapidly. However, their styles of advocacy were different as well. The coalition groups were able to mobilize larger bases of grassroots organizations, which translated into what might be considered more democratic and transparent forms of citizen participation. AFT and EDF tended to rely on more insider engagement between lobbyists and legislators as well as mass media campaigns. Their respective decision-making procedures and organizational cultures did influence how fully and effectively each of the FFPP members collaborated with one another. Indeed, one member, EDF, decided to remove itself from the day-to-day operations of the FFPP and essentially "went it alone." However, the members did stay together long enough to present one fairly straightforward message and a suite of thematically linked policy proposals before the Members of Congress.

This mostly united front was certainly far better than the usual situation, which has too many disparate advocacy groups competing for limited amounts of policymakers' attention. But the lesson was clear: those groups that are used to playing with others in a sandbox tend to carry over their skills when they have to play in larger sandboxes with even bigger kids. And those who have never learned sandbox skills have serious cooperative deficiencies when entering the sandbox, which is often why they choose to never to do so.

In an interesting corollary to the issue of participation, Hunt includes a stakeholder-engagement rating of U.S. and U.K. food and agriculture organizations that were compiled by Jules Pretty, a U.K. academic who has studied food development strategies across the globe. Pretty assigns a "7" to those organizations that have exhibited the highest level of stakeholder/member engagement and a "1" to those with the lowest. Using this scale, CFSC and NSAC were rated 7, Rural Coalition received a 6, AFT a 5, and EDF a 2. While Pretty's rating was not connected to the FFPP, it does tend to buttress the contention that some organizations are better designed structurally to work collaboratively than others.

As important as Kellogg's funding and the initial disposition of FFPP's members were—policy experience and membership/organizational structures—NEMWI was an essential lynchpin for the project. It was as neutral, professional, and thoroughly competent a hub as anyone could ask for in a collective impact-style framework. NEMWI coordinated the preparation and writing of *Seeking Balance*, the project's comprehensive proposal that included all of the policy proposals and framed the food system problems that the proposals addressed. They served as the convener and facilitator for the countless large group and committee meetings that took place in Washington as well as the conference calls. As such, NEMWI took responsibility for the essential collective impact activity of ensuring frequent communication between all the players. It also managed the national press and communication strategies that served the larger project purposes, while the individual members ran their own targeted communications, which nevertheless remained consistent with the FFPP's message. NEMWI provided a great deal of administrative support and served as the liaison between all the members, the funder, and the outside evaluator who remained a constant and helpful presence throughout the project's life.

What did FFPP not have? While a degree of measurement was woven into the project from the beginning, it cannot be said that there were ready and ongoing indicators of success. Given the unruly nature of federal policy work, the lack of intermediate measures may be a very forgivable sin. As indicated, an evaluator was present, but the longer-term outcomes and, perhaps more critically, the "lessons learned" from the project's unique process were not learned until after the fact. This meant that the opportunity to make mid-course corrections that may have enabled the project to reach a higher standard of performance were not available.

The second shortcoming concerns which food system interests were represented and not represented in the process of developing policy proposals. The notable vacancies were groups that directly represented the anti-hunger and food bank sector as well as the nutrition and obesity prevention work that was gaining momentum at that time. Of all the project's members, only CFSC came close to representing these broad but very important sectors, and even then, that representation was tenuous at best.

The last criticism is that the FFPP was only funded for the duration of the 2008 Farm Bill process—three years of operation with a little more time prior to that for the grantee selection process. While that might be considered a more than adequate horizon for a policy initiative focused on one major piece of legislation, the food movement would have benefitted from the FFPP morphing into a permanent hub for an expanding network of organizations, coalitions, and federal policy-making activities. Instead, all the member organizations went their own ways when the project ceased, left to resume their own individual national policy work within their own relatively narrow frames of reference. Some limited networking has continued between the FFPP's former members, but nothing has filled the void left by the absence of the project's powerful coalescing framework.

**

I introduced some of the work of the NSAC earlier in this book. But again, it deserves note as the longest standing, most diverse, national food and farm coalition in the country. I'll cut to the chase to say why it is successful at so many levels. First, its membership and growth are carefully managed; its members use a rigorous process to choose the policy issues that NSAC will work on; its members contribute to the advocacy by contacting Congress both in-person and remotely; members meet twice a year, face-to-face, in numbers that are small enough and with sufficient time to ensure quality communication and networking opportunities (the January 2017 meeting had 100 of its 116 members present). Though underfunded, NSAC is sufficiently staffed and competently led. In terms of its policy advocacy strategy, if one were to compare NSAC's strengths to a basketball team, you would say that it has both an inside game (it knows how to maneuver in Congress and with the Administration) and an outside game (a constituency that can be mobilized to take action).

NSAC's members have to pay dues, which are modest in their amounts but something that many in the food movement find off-putting. Too often, nonprofit organizations with their modest budgets feel that anything more than token dues exclude some groups from participation, which opens the door to charges of "elitism." The value of paying $500 to work collaboratively and effectively with others on critically important national policy issues is not always recognized in the nonprofit world. In NSAC's case, paying dues reinforces the commitment of the members to the coalition.

While the issues that the Coalition addresses don't cover the entire food system spectrum, the major components of their policy portfolio include conservation, farm programs, agricultural research, marketing, and rural concerns. More specifically, NSAC's work supports family farmers, encourages beginning (new) farmers, builds local and regional food systems, increases access to healthy food for all, drives research innovations, and rewards farmers and ranchers who are good stewards of the land. Some of more recent advocacy work has centered on the Food Safety Modernization Act (FSMA), Farm to School, and the Food Insecurity Nutrition Initiative (FINI), both relatively new federal programs, and ones that build bridges between producers and lower-income consumers. Food security/hunger are partially addressed in this way, but NSAC doesn't engage in the more direct forms of advocacy related to such programs as SNAP, which are largely left to Food Research and Action Center (FRAC) and other explicitly anti-hunger organizations.

NSAC is also fairly unique among food movement coalitions in that it strives consistently to resolve the ongoing need to be more inclusive of and responsive to race and equity issues. They have established a Diversity Committee that "incorporates and assesses social justice and diversity as operational elements of NSAC's activities, including in the Organizational Council, Policy Council, Issue Committees . . . and other operations of NSAC [including the determination of] policy priorities, advocacy strategies, communications, and all other NSAC approved or supported activities" (NSAC, 2017).

But NSAC faces the same challenges to diversity and race as other largely white-led organizations. Its staff and members still fall short of fully including the range of communities of color whose needs NSAC attempts to address. And even when it reaches out to organizations that are led by people of color, it is sometimes rebuffed. This happened in 2014 when NSAC tried to bring the Southeastern African American Farmers Organic Network (SAAFON) into the Coalition. Discussions were held between Cynthia Hayes, SAAFON's founder and director, and Ferd Hoefner, NSAC's policy director, but SAAFON was ambivalent and finally declined. As one who was party to some of those conversations, I interpreted Hayes's resistance as one of feeling that NSAC request was somehow disingenuous. Hayes, who passed away in 2016, referred to NSAC's offer as a "token effort." Additional analysis of this exchange is no longer possible; however, it does point to the ongoing tension that exists in the food movement between black- and white-led organizations. Subsequently, SAAFON became a member of NSAC.

In terms of its communication strategy, NSAC remains pragmatic and modest in terms of its message eschewing the pronouncements of sister organizations that the "food system is broken," which according to Hoefner, "is a non-starter with Congress." Some attribute NSAC's success to the fact that there is little turnover in its membership, whose longevity rate with the organization remains unusually high. And citing its Midwestern origins (NSAC came originally out of the 1980s Midwest farm crisis) as one possible reason, trust among members and staff is also very high. The regional roots of certain human personality traits should receive their due, of course, but one should also give credit to the way the organization is managed and the considerable amount of air-time that is given to actual facetime.

Finally, its members know the seriousness of their coalition's purpose. Though NSAC may avoid the rhetoric that warns that the food system's sky is falling, it is clearly committed to transforming the food system, not just covering up its wounds with band aids. Perhaps most importantly, the policies and programs its members work for have the capacity to reach the scale necessary to make that change.

It might be helpful to compare NSAC's operational model to that of the CFSC. Three major items stand out as I hold both coalitions up for scrutiny— one in the present and one with the benefit of hindsight. CFSC did not learn how to manage its growth nor did it have a serious protocol or vetting procedure to bring in new members. NSAC has reached 116 members over the course of 30 years. CFSC reached that many in about three years. The second noteworthy difference is that CFSC often found itself struggling with how to prioritize the issues it would work on—some of which were programmatic and some of which were public policy. Again, NSAC has a very systematic, member-driven process to select issues. Part of CFSC's problem was that it took a lot of money from the federal government (NSAC has taken very little federal money in its history), which made it too dependent on one source. That dependency effectively determined CFSC's issues and also kept the members from having a say in the prioritization process. And finally, NSAC has an ongoing Diversity Committee, the job of which is to integrate race and justice issues into all facets of the coalition. CFSC had a similar committee, but it could never find a balance with the other activities, policies, and committees of CFSC. Sometimes CFSC's diversity concerns were so dominant that they literally drove the work of CFSC. Other times they were so contentious that they sent schisms running-like-spider veins throughout the organization. Perhaps unlike NSAC, with its supposed abundance of trusting Midwestern sensibilities, CFSC gradually sank into a morass of distrust.

"The spirit is willing, but the flesh is weak" would be an apt adage for the challenges associated with building bigger, broader food system alliances. We all think it's a good idea to work together, but as soon as we hit too many speed bumps, we succumb to any number of excuses that eventually lead to an abandonment of the process and a retreat into our known, single-purpose organizations and worlds. This chapter has attempted to ease the hardship and stress associated with the admittedly difficult work of operating effective, multistakeholder organizations.

There are ample numbers of models and examples from which to learn. This chapter's review of collective impact, food policy councils, food charters and plans, and smaller-scale partnerships is designed to demonstrate that much of the foundation has been laid and is ready to build upon. That doesn't mean that high-impact coalition development will be easy, but at least there are road maps to follow.

But by themselves, models aren't enough. You can follow the tracks into the forest, but once there you'll need to rely on your skills to navigate your way through unfamiliar surroundings. This is why I emphasize the importance of organizational development and group dynamic skills. While achieving their mastery requires a life-long practice, people involved in the food movement should have at least a working knowledge of their use. If you pay attention to the role of leadership, keep your ear to the ground of your group to detect its shifts and moods and be attentive to what makes for strong coalitions, you will enter what should be a long and pleasant journey to mastery.

# Conclusion

Let me first say that I love what I do. I've been loving it and this food movement of ours since I first dipped my toe into its swirling waters as an 18-year-old college freshman, certain as I was at the time that I could single-handedly end world hunger. Nearly 50 years later, as I've grown up in the food movement and watched it grow up around me, I love it even more. And what's not to love? Where else could anyone find so much quirkiness, improvisation, sensual pleasure, humanity, compassion, democracy, diversity, and righteous rage? Could any artist ever find a richer palette from which to fill a large canvass with bold patterns representing health, sustainability, as well as social and economic security? It has been so much fun that I sometimes feel guilty being paid to do this work. (Fortunately, I've gotten over that.)

As a witness and participant in the historical progression of the food movement, I have on occasion imagined a Rip Van Winkle moment where, at the age of 20 in 1970 Maine where I went to college, I fall into a deep sleep. I don't wake up until 2017, but I'm now in my current hometown of Santa Fe, New Mexico. Instead of the small Maine city's one dingy food coop, a handful of hippie organic farmers, and a fly-by-night breakfast program for neighborhood kids, I see today's community brimming with endless food options, programs, public policies, stories, conversations, and publications. Not only am I mesmerized by a dazzling array of tasty delights, many of which I barely recognize, I am baffled by unfamiliar concepts like food banks and farm-to-school programs. Overhearing conversations about "GMOs" and "trans-fats" leaves me wondering what country these people are from because I don't recognize the language. An incomprehensible newspaper headline catching my eye announces high rates of "Food Insecurity and Obesity among Children."

Seeing the white beard that has descended to my waist and the stunned look in my eyes, a young woman approaches me asking if I need help. I tell her I'm alright but that I feel very disoriented. She says her name is Judith and wants to know what in particular confuses me, so I tell her about the food I'm seeing and the words I'm hearing and reading. It turns out Judith was a "food studies" major in college, which leaves me even more perplexed, but she kindly offers to take me on a tour of her "community's food system." I accept her invitation even though I have no idea what or where that is.

Though she complimented my thread-bare, bell-bottom jeans saying "they are pretty cool," Judith noticed that I looked tired and asked if I could use a little "pick me up." Handing me a bottle of something called "kombucha," I first sniffed it and then took a few sips to be polite, but soon found my steps feeling light and my brain alert to a thousand images as I moved swiftly to keep up with her. Before my eyes, in living, breathing technicolor and rapid succession, appeared a huge farmers' market, a 50,000-square-feet food bank, a Whole Foods, and a mile-long commercial road corridor lined with fast-food restaurants. Gently and patiently, Judith explained each one to me, sharing their histories, origins, purposes, and challenges. She answered all my questions patiently, but said, "We need to keep moving because there is so much to see!" I saw a food policy council meeting that was discussing the Mayor's proposed tax on soda. She told me about the council and the tax, which was one way to use food policy to get people to reduce sugar consumption. I saw large trucks, one with the name of a local food bank and another with the name of a coop food store. Judith gave me a brief summary of all the ways government was involved with food including programs I had never heard of before such as Women, Infant, and Children Program (WIC), Farmers' Market Nutrition Programs, and Child and Adult Care Food Programs. She explained how and why private and public organizations were trying to protect farmland and encourage more farming, why lower-income people were given incentives to buy locally produced food, and why more was being done to teach people how to purchase and prepare food.

It seemed as if everywhere Judith took me people were talking about food. At the state legislature, we sat in on a hearing about how to bolster the purchase of locally grown food by public schools and to increase state funding for Supplemental Nutrition Assistance Program (SNAP) recipients (which I had known as a small program called food stamps). We walked into a meeting of the city council where they were talking about a plan to encourage urban farming. At a local book store, a cookbook author was signing copies of her newest book on how to eat locally. And at a community center, residents were having a heated discussion about how to bring a supermarket to something they called a "food desert."

All of this talk about food as well as the fact that I hadn't eaten in 46 years was making me hungry. Judith suggested that we stop at a local café, which gave her an opportunity to talk about farm-to-table restaurants while I ate an egg salad sandwich on whole wheat bread from local eggs, grain, and lettuce.

As if on cue, a parade of people orchestrated by Judith sat at our table for a few minutes to explain their work. One was a planner who was designing agricultural programs for the county; another was a teacher at the community college who had developed an aquaponics program; several were entrepreneurs who were running various kinds of home-chef and prepared-meal delivery companies; and one small group consisted of beekeepers who were trying to ban something called neonicotinoids.

When I looked up, the line of people waiting to talk and gawk at me was out the door and around the block. Even Judith, who seemed so well-versed in all of this, realized that it was too much. With a flourish of her hand, the earnest folks waiting their turn magically disappeared. She suggested that we get a beer at a local brew pub where she'd be happy to answer any other questions I had. I liked beer—having a vague remembrance of drinking too much of it before I fell asleep. I was enthusiastic until we walked into the "brewpub" where I was confronted by 57 taps with beer names I'd never heard of. Having been used to three or four brands of weasel-pee that all tasted the same, I was shocked by the array of choices as well as the incomprehensible beer prose that described each one. Judith said not to worry, and she selected one for me that was called a "pale ale." It was good—very good—and I thanked her profusely for the tour of her "community's food system," which I told her emphatically was unlike anything I could remember.

As I emptied my glass I noticed the sun was setting. Even though Judith offered me another pint, I decided to hold at one since I didn't think I'd survive another 46-year hangover. I told her that I thought it was time for me to go; after all, I needed a shave, and I was sure no one had fed my dog while I was gone. I thanked her again. As she was waving goodbye, Judith shouted out that she hoped to see me around the "food system."

Homer made lists of the Greek's ships; ornithologists make lists of the birds they spot; Bruce Springsteen makes lists of the girls, guitars, and cars he's known. We show our love for people, places, and things by the lists we make, and my list of food projects, policies, and initiatives is my Valentine to the world. But like the sick child whose parent's love may not be enough to cure him or her, all of the energy, passion, and goodwill gushing from the food movement has not yet given us the kind of food system we want. Whether the food system is sick, in need of repair, or simply not the best we can get is partly a matter of conjecture, what side of the argument you're on, and what you believe in (love) the most.

As I have argued throughout this book, the food movement is polarized and fragmented. Rather than one large, diverse, and well-functioning country, we resemble a balkanized region comprising many small nation-states whose borders may be semipermeable and between which some trade occurs, but meaningful alliances are few. In the parlance of defense treaties, we can safely say that an attack on one *is not* considered an attack on all. Offering even harsher appraisals, some food advocates have caricatured the food movement as a circular firing squad—one command to "Fire!" and we're all dead.

It's not that we lack for commitment or enthusiasm—a surfeit of both is the norm. We in fact believe sometimes too stridently, too certainly, holding to our sacred vows regardless of the facts, giving proof to Montaigne's admonition that "nothing is so firmly believed as that which a man knoweth least." But perhaps the food movement's biggest internal threat, which always appears just beneath the radar, is a kind of voluntary servitude to our cause, our mission, our institutions, and the "rules" that prescribe our thoughts and actions with regard to who or what we serve. Too often we "go along" with the crowd more out of social prudence than any heartfelt personal conviction. Simply put, my loyalty is to my group's mission, not the larger vision. The time has come to remove the blinders and take in the wider food system landscape—its beauty as well as its ugliness.

And there still is much ugliness. With food insecurity and obesity rates remaining stubbornly high, with climate change approaching a nightmarish reality, and with our farmers struggling to achieve both financial and environmental sustainability, there is more work to do than ever before. Studies, reports, and wheel-barrels full of data continue to roll in, suggesting a little improvement here or no progress there. As my writing comes to an end, yet one more report arrives in my inbox announcing another food system shortcoming. This one is a recent Harvard study (American Journal of Preventive Medicine, March, 2017) of restaurant chains that found "little progress" in meeting their pledge to make children's meals healthier. This in spite of an entirely earnest and well-publicized effort by the former First Lady Michelle Obama to modify children's diets and increase their physical activity. Before this book opens in your lap or laptop, hundreds of more food-related reports and studies will appear that affirm or deny our current assumptions.

As I write this in the winter of 2017, there is one more glaring reality I did not anticipate when I set out to describe the challenges facing the food movement. I, in fact, did not think that the work would be as enormously political as it has become with the new U.S. presidential administration. It was my hope that the food movement would have a favorable political wind for a decade or so, and not what presently looks like a gusty headwind into which we will need to constantly tack until at least 2021. If the current challenges to the food system weren't reason enough to mobilize the food movement as a unified force for change, they moved to "red alert" status on the morning of November 9, 2016.

As a closing thought, I will turn to what I think is the most critical place where food system activists must apply pressure, namely the institutions that are working, either whole or in part, on food system issues. These would include nonprofit organizations and coalitions, for-profit food businesses and enterprises, government agencies and elected bodies, academic institutions, hospitals and other health care providers, and grant-making foundations. If those institutions can adjust to the needs and complexities of larger scale, collective impact structures that genuinely engage many partners, then the food movement could achieve the level of social mobilization it needs to leverage the transformation of the food system.

For some thoughts on the role of institutions I turned to Francis Fukuyama (2011), who is one of this nation's leading scholars on governance and the development of political organization. When I ask myself, which I often do, "Why can't people just learn to work together?" Fukuyama's answer surprised me. It seems that human beings don't readily cooperate outside of their own kinship group because it is against their biological instincts. In other words, we are hard-wired to affiliate socially as members of tribes, clans, and family, and we will act altruistically toward those with whom we share a common gene pool. The closer my relationship, for example, parent to child, the more altruistically I will act. Distant relatives will, if they're lucky, get a Christmas card from me once a year.

Fortunately, our inclination to cooperate with others is not only limited to our biological relationships. We can also draw on what Fukuyama calls *reciprocal altruism* (p. 438), which means that human beings will work together with other, nonrelated people, in more or less direct proportion to how often they work or interact with any particular person(s). Fukuyama says that reciprocal altruism will "depend on repeated, direct personal interaction and the trust relationships generated out of such interactions." It seems like the more "facetime," in other words, that we have with one another, the more likely that networks will expand, trust will develop, and reciprocal altruism will emerge.

Progressing from small and insular kinship groups, we find that humans also have an inclination for creating and following rules, hence the formation of institutions because their structures and practices effectively limit individual choice, that is, the institution comes first. Referencing Samuel Huntington, Fukuyama uses his definition of an institution as an entity that has, "stable, valued, recurring patterns of behavior" (p. 450). Ever wonder why institutions change so slowly, if at all? It is because they are conservative by nature—not in a political sense, necessarily, but in the traditional sense of sticking with the status quo, resisting change because it will upset those "recurring patterns." Their rules become an extension of their values, and values of course go to the core of who we are as individuals and groups.

This is all fine if you're the leader of an institution—your job is much easier when everyone knows and accepts the rules. But when you're a small food organization that wants to work together with a number of other small food organizations, or you have a need to make an important policy change at city hall and you can't secure it without the help of a large institution, you're in for a long struggle. And while rules and a conservative environment may ensure an easy, low-hassle institutional life, they work against the organization when change and the pitchfork-toting rebels are screaming at the door.

Organizations, big and small, live and die based on their abilities to adapt to a changing world, market, political winds, or demands of their constituents. Unlike biological systems, which have the ability to adapt over time to changing circumstances through their genetic reflexes, institutions rely exclusively on humans to accept the need for action that may literally be required to ensure their survival. Institutions rarely die but they do decay, becoming calcified as an accretion of old ideas and ways immobilize their limbs and clog their arteries. Of course, institutions can adapt and remain vigorous through many generations, but good leadership and intentional management practices that facilitate change and nurture flexibility must become values as important as any other. As Fukuyama says, "An adaptable organization can evaluate a changing external environment and modify its own internal procedures in response. Adaptable institutions are the ones that survive, since environments always change" (p. 450).

No better example of poor adaptation within the food movement exists than with the inability of the Community Food Security Coalition (CFSC) to manage the changing environment brought on by the emergence of racial justice groups clamoring for a more substantive role. And no better example of institutional adaptability exists than the National Sustainable Agriculture Coalition (NSAC) with its ability to manage its growth in terms of new and diversified membership as well as an expanding menu of policy issues and interests. Fukuyama uses the term "rule of law," which is applied often to compare functioning nation states and nonfunctioning nation states, as in "we are a nation subject to the rule of law." In political settings, this means of course that no one person or group can take matters into their own hands or stand above the laws/rules that have been set forth and agreed to by all. In an institutional or organizational setting, I would take the "rule of law" as an agreed-upon set of rules that govern the operation of an organization. Again, in NSAC's case, the rules agreed to by all prescribe a way of managing growth and change the way one would expect from a politically mature country; in CFSC's case, the lack of a rule of law allowed strong people to exert their own agenda and left a governance vacuum that did not provide the guidance necessary to manage emerging crises.

There are, unfortunately, too many inflexible organizations within the food movement, some of which might be considered "gateway" institutions that, if able to open themselves up to new ideas and values, might unleash a stream of necessary new patterns. They could, if they set aside the rules that only ensure their self-preservation, and most likely only lead to their decay, bow more gracefully to the creative faculties that swim with so much vigor through the food movement's gene pool. But America is an individualistic society and, blame what you will, our society's failure to raise both cooperation and the inclusion of our ineffable diversity to a national virtue is a never-ending obstacle. Despite the sentiment expressed under the seal of the United States, *E Pluribus Unum*, we ignore the "oneness" and celebrate the disunited "many." Its transatlantic but influential counterpart can be found in Margaret Thatcher's blunt disavowal of the very concept of society, "There's no such thing," she said. "There are individual men and women, and there are families" (Deresiewicz, 2015).

Perhaps this is because, as Fukuyama suggests, humans need recognition and in a truly cooperative model, no individual is the "winner," nor does one person get all the credit (or the blame). Unlike today's youth soccer leagues where even the least talented "athletes" get a trophy lest their egos be damaged, most American institutions treat cooperation as an aspirational goal rather than a living, breathing way of conducting their work, business, and organizational lives. In these institutions, the truly cooperative person, the one who places the group above himself or herself, can easily become roadkill beneath the wheels of the hard-charging, competitive warriors. Harkening back to my opening account of food people and groups working together for their mutual benefit and for the greater good in early 1980s Hartford, I wondered if this might have been an age of innocence, undergirded perhaps by the political threat to human welfare posed by the ascending Reagan administration. But in fact, I see it, with the benefit of hindsight, as a *pre-institutional period* in the early evolution of the food movement when larger institutions didn't exist to exert dominance over grassroots efforts, where rules were few, trust was high, and the exigencies of the moment took precedent. The less contact, the less trust; the less trust, the more rules; the more rules, the more institutions.

Some might attribute America's cult of individualism, which has worked against collective enterprise, to our earliest and arguably greatest philosopher, Ralph Waldo Emerson. He is known for praising the spirit of an emerging American culture committed to geographic expansion, innovation, and self-reliance. Yet in spite of statements like, "Society everywhere is in conspiracy against . . . every one of its members," taken to mean that the free-spirited individual is always held back by societal constraints, one doesn't realize that Emerson also bore prophetic witness against the evils of his day. His writings offer clear evidence that he vigorously challenged the institution of slavery and the tragic relocation of eastern America's native tribes. In other words, not only did he uphold the principles of justice he also made evident his preference for the common good over the selfish striving of the individual. In remarks like "the man of genius apprises us not of his wealth but of the commonwealth" we feel as well an Emersonian passion for both a common vision and the will to achieve it. In those words, I find a directive for today's food movement leaders to use their imaginations and talents for the larger good of the food system, not only for the aggrandizement of themselves and their organizations.

It is now time to challenge the very institutions whose powers, if they were collectively harnessed, could provide the impact the food movement needs to upset the applecart. This is what Emerson meant by the "society" that conspires against its members. In this case, the societies are the institutions that relentlessly cling to their ways and patterns regardless of what else is going on around them, regardless of their record of failure or mediocre results, and in spite of the lip service they may utter to other food organizations who suggest a better way. Those institutions could instead, as a bold and generous gesture, provide shelter beneath an expanding tent that nurtures and supports synergistic food movement thinking and builds a collective impact framework for action. If the institutions won't bend, build a coalition of smaller entities that are in favor of change and willing to take on the larger stakeholders. Persistence, clear and thoughtful communication, and holding those stakeholders constantly accountable are likely to open the door a crack. And when that happens, turn the massed bodies of your allies into a battering ram that will bust the door from its hinges!

Yes, a more detailed list of recommendations is called for. So here are mine.

- Food organizations, coalitions, councils, and initiatives must adopt a collective impact approach to their work. This applies to the national level as much as it does at the local, state, tribal, and provincial levels. It can start with well-defined partnerships between two or more stakeholders but should escalate in a managed way over time to include a reasonably diverse selection of food system stakeholders. The precepts of collective impact as a method of management and operation don't need to be rigorously adhered to, but they should be considered and understood by all group members, adapted to fit particular circumstances, and integrated with other methods of community engagement that add value to the larger work.

- The funding and academic communities, as well as other educational and support institutions must make building the capacity of the food movement to have a larger, long-term impact its highest priority. Single organization, single issue, single project funding and support should be limited in favor of more cohesive, collaborative-favored, and long-term investments. A greater commitment, for instance, to supporting organizational development, community organizing, and coalition building will have better, long-term returns.

- A greater effort by all food system stakeholders—big and little, bad and good, rich and poor, pro and con—must be made to find common ground. While this is likely to open up a big market for professional mediators, it could result in some major breakthroughs that would save a lot of time and money in the future if successful. Trying and failing should not be regarded as a waste of time; failing to try may be far costlier.

- While implied by the above recommendations, it is necessary to make explicit the commitment to addressing racial and economic inequality in all food system endeavors. The issues that divide must be brought to the fore and worked on until agreement is found. Sincerity from all participants is necessary to finding common goals.

- Effective and frequent communication between all stakeholders must become a stronger focus of all food movement actors. This applies as much to "internal" communication between stakeholders and participants as it does to "external" recipients such as the general public and policy makers. And effective communication must include thoughtful framing and messaging techniques.

- Institutions, big and small, *live* by their rules and the urge to preserve the status quo. But they will *thrive* by their ability to adapt to changing circumstances. They can be the dull, rusty sword that maintains a meager defense, or they can be the shiny tip of the spear that leads the assault. Don't be cowered by them; cultivate their capacity to change so that they can lead the charge for change.

- Nationally, all institutions and food movement coalitions must begin to work for a "joined-up" food and farm policy. Achieving one national policy that produces healthy food for people, ensures prosperity for farmers, provides living wages and safe working conditions for all food and farm employment, and secures the benefits of a sustainable, climate-resilient food system for everyone is a component of the vision that all players must be working toward.

Learning to stand and work together will easily be the hardest thing we will ever accomplish. But to do less will mean that the few will have more, and the many will have less.

# References

Agricultural Act of 2014. United States Department of Agriculture, https://www
.fns.usda.gov/sites/default/files/Agriculture%20Act%20of%202014.pdf

Ashman, Linda, Jaime de la Vega, Marc Dohan, Andy Fisher, Rosa Hippler, Billi
Romain. 1993. *Seeds of Change: Strategies for Food Security for the Inner
City.* Los Angeles: University of Los Angeles. http://community-wealth
.org/sites/clone.community-wealth.org/files/downloads/report-ashman-
et-al.pdf

Birth, Allyssa. 2015. "Americans Split on Importance of Buying Local at the Grocery Store." The Harris Poll, December 8. http://www.theharrispoll.com/
business/Buying-Local-at-the-Grocery-Store.html

Bittman, Mark, Michael Pollan, Ricardo Salvador, and Olivier De Schutter. 2014.
"How a National Food Policy Could Save Millions of American Lives."
*Washington Post,* November 7. https://www.washingtonpost.com/opinions/
how-a-national-food-policy-could-save-millions-of-american-lives/2014/
11/07/89c55e16-637f-11e4-836c-83bc4f26eb67_story.html

Black, Jane. 2014. "Finding the Food Movement's Path to Progress." The Stone
Barns Center for Food and Agriculture, November 20. https://www
.stonebarnscenter.org/learn/jane-black-on-food-ag/finding-the-food-
movement-s-path-to-progress.html

Bovy, Phoebe Maltz. 2015. "Food Snobs Like Mark Bittman Aren't Even Hiding
Their Elitism Anymore." *New Republic,* March 25. https://newrepublic
.com/article/121374/foodie-elitism-are-mark-bittman-and-michael-
pollan-elitist

Briggs, Xaiver de Souza, Elizabeth J. Mueller, and Mercer Sullivan. 1997. *From
Neighborhoods to Community: Evidence on the Social Effects of Community
Development.* New York: Community Development Research Center.

Brown, Allison. 2002. "Farmers' Market Research 1940–2000: An Inventory
and Review." *American Journal of Alternative Agriculture* 17, no. 4 (December): 167–176.

Bruni, Frank. 2016. "How Facebook Warps Our Worlds." *New York Times,*
May 21. https://www.nytimes.com/2016/05/22/opinion/sunday/how-face
book-warps-our-worlds.html

Burt, Randy, Mike Goldblatt, and Shayna Silverman. 2015. *Firmly Rooted, the Local Food Market Expands.* A. T. Kearney. https://www.atkearney.com/documents/10192/6773369/Firmly+Rooted+the+Local+Food+Market+Expands.pdf/863737a6-0b44-40d0-b339-da25c4563dc3

Carman, Tim. 2016. "For Some Growers, Farmers Markets Just Aren't What They Used to Be." *Washington Post,* June 21. https://www.washingtonpost.com/lifestyle/food/for-some-growers-farmers-markets-just-arent-what-they-used-to-be/2016/06/21/c5d93644-3271-11e6-8758-d58e76e11b12_story.html?utm_term=.542b7feec151

Case, Anne, and Angus Deaton. 2015. "Rising Morbidity and Mortality in Midlife among White Non-Hispanic Americans in the 21st Century." *Proceedings of the National Academy of Sciences* 112, no 49. http://www.pnas.org/content/112/49/15078.full

CBS News. 2015. "New Twist on the Supermarket for Low-income Families." June 17. http://www.cbsnews.com/news/boston-grocery-store-daily-table-offers-discounted-healthy-food-low-income-families/

Centers for Disease Control and Prevention. 2016. Adult Obesity Facts. https://www.cdc.gov/obesity/data/adult.html

City Seed. 2017. http://cityseed.org/

Closing the Hunger Cap Conference. 2015. September 13–16.

Coleman-Jensen, Alisha, Matthew P. Rabbitt, Christian A. Gregory, and Anita Singh. 2016. *Household Food Security in the United States in 2015.* United States Department of Agriculture. https://www.ers.usda.gov/webdocs/publications/err215/err-215.pdf?v=42636

College and University Food Bank Alliance. 2017. http://www.cufba.org/

De Tocqueville, Alexis. 2002. *Democracy in America.* New York: Bantam Books (Original work published 1835).

Deresiewicz, William. 2015. "The Neoliberal Arts: How College Sold Its Soul to the Market." *Harper's Magazine,* September. http://harpers.org/archive/2015/09/the-neoliberal-arts/

Diedrich, Sara. 2015. "Food Is Community: UI Study Finds Local Food Movement Rooted in Relationships and Values." *Iowa Now,* August 24. https://now.uiowa.edu/2015/08/food-community

Dietary Guidelines Advisory Committee, 2015. *Scientific Report of the 2015 Dietary Guidelines Advisory Committee.* United States Department of Agriculture. https://health.gov/dietaryguidelines/2015-scientific-report/10-chapter-5/

Echevarria, Samuel, Robert Santos, Elaine Waxman, Emily Engelhard, and Theresa Del Vecchio. 2011. *Food Banks: Hunger's New Staple.* Feeding America. http://www.feedingamerica.org/hunger-in-america/our-research/hungers-new-staple/hungers-new-staple-full-report.pdf?s_src=W171ORGSC&s_referrer=google&s_subsrc=http%3A%2F%2Fwww.feedingamerica.org%2Fhunger-in-america%2Four-research%2Fhungers-new-staple%2F%3Freferrer%3Dhttps%3A%2F%2Fwww.google.com%2F

Economic Innovation Group. 2016. *The 2016 Distressed Communities Index: An Analysis of Community Well-Being across the United States.* http://eig.org/wp-content/uploads/2016/02/2016-Distressed-Communities-Index-Report.pdf

Environmental Protection Agency. 2017. National Summary of Impaired Waters and TMDL Information. https://iaspub.epa.gov/waters10/attains_nation_cy.control?p_report_type=T

Essex, Amanda, Douglas Shinkle, and Mindy Bridges. 2015. *Harvesting Healthier Options: State Legislative Trends in Local Foods 2012–2014.* National Conference of State Legislatures. http://www.ncsl.org/Portals/1/Documents/environ/HarvestingHealthierOptions.pdf

Farm to School Census. 2015. United States Department of Agriculture. https://farmtoschoolcensus.fns.usda.gov/

Farmers Market Coalition. 2017. https://farmersmarketcoalition.org/

Farmers Market Directory Search. 2017. United States Department of Agriculture. https://search.ams.usda.gov/farmersmarkets/

Feeding America. 2017. http://www.feedingamerica.org/about-us/how-we-work/food-bank-network

Fisher, Andy. 2017. *Big Hunger: The Unholy Alliance between Corporate America and Anti-Hunger Groups.* Cambridge: MIT Press.

Fisher, Andy, and Robert Gottlieb. 2014. "Who Benefits When Walmart Funds the Food Movement?" Civil Eats, December 18. http://civileats.com/2014/12/18/who-benefits-when-walmart-funds-the-food-movement/

Food Insecurity Nutrition Incentive (FINI) Grant Program. 2017. United States Department of Agriculture. https://nifa.usda.gov/program/food-insecurity-nutrition-incentive-fini-grant-program

Frameworks Institute, IPM Voice, and Red Tomato. 2016. The Food Narrative Project: Toward a More Informed Conversation about Food and Farming. Proposal Draft.

Freudenberg, Nicholas, N. Cohen, M.R. Fuster, S. Garza, D. Johnson D, J. Poppendieck, A. Rafalow, M. Sheldon, M. Silver, and A. Srivastava. 2016. *Eating in East Harlem: An Assessment of Changing Foodscapes in Community District 11, 2000–2015.* New York: CUNY School of Public Health and New York City Food Policy Center at Hunter College. http://eatingineastharlem.org

Fukuyama, Francis. 2011. *The Origins of Political Order: From Prehuman Times to the French Revolution.* New York: Farrar, Straus and Giroux.

Galanes, Philip. 2016. "Barack Obama and Bryan Cranston on the Roles of a Lifetime." *New York Times*, May 6. https://www.nytimes.com/2016/05/08/fashion/barack-obama-bryan-cranston-table-for-three.html

Gibson, Cynthia, Katya Smyth, Gail Nayowith, and Jonathan Zaff. 2013. "To Get to the Good, You Gotta Dance with the Wicked." *Stanford Social Innovation Review*, September 19. https://ssir.org/articles/entry/to_get_to_the_good_you_gotta_dance_with_the_wicked

Gilpin, Lyndsey. 2016. "In the Shadow of Silicon Valley, a New Crop of Tech-savvy Farmers." High Country News, April 4. http://www.hcn.org/issues/48.6/in-the-shadow-of-silicon-valley-a-new-crop-of-tech-savvy-farmers

Glaser, Francine, Ruthie Goldstein, Ashley Mena, Kellie Palomba, Saad Shamshair, Daniel Chibbaro, Julene Paul, Matthew Rigney, Patricia Voltolini, and Kathe Newman. 2014. *Improving Community Food Security in New Brunswick.* Ralph W. Voorhees Center for Civic Engagement, Edward J. Bloustein School of Planning and Public Policy, Rutgers University. http://rwv.rutgers.edu/wp-content/uploads/2015/01/F2014-Voorhees-Food Security-Report.pdf

Guthman, Julie. 2011. *Weighing In: Obesity, Food Justice, and the Limits of Capitalism.* Berkeley: University of California Press.

Hall, Billy. 2015. "Food Stamps and WIC." In *The SAGE Encyclopedia of Food Issues,* edited by Ken Albala, 625–630. Los Angeles: SAGE Reference.

*Hartford Courant.* 2015. "Hartford's Report Card: 10 Ways to Measure The City." January 24. http://www.courant.com/opinion/editorials/hc-ed-where-is-hartford-datawise-20150123-story.html

Heid, Markham. 2016. "Experts Say Lobbying Skewed the U.S. Dietary Guidelines." *Time,* January 8. http://www.time.com/4130043/lobbying-politics-dietary-guidelines/

Hesterman, Oran B. 2011. *Fair Food: Growing a Healthy, Sustainable Food System for All.* New York: PublicAffairs.

Hladik, Maurice J. 2012. *Demystifying Food from Farm to Fork.* Bloomington, IN: iUniverse.

Holt-Giménez, Eric, ed. 2011. *Food Movements Unite!* Oakland, CA: Food First Books.

Hunt, Alan R. 2015. *Civic Engagement in Food System Governance: A Comparative Perspective of American and British Local Food Movements.* New York: Routledge.

Indy Food Council. 2013. http://indyfoodcouncil.org/about-ifc/vision/

Jenkins, Willlis. 2014. "Worrying about the Food Movement." *Reflections.* http://reflections.yale.edu/article/risk-our-food-our-water-ourselves/worrying-about-food-movement

Johns Hopkins Center for a Livable Future. 2015a. Food Policy Councils in North America: 2015 Trends. http://www.foodpolicynetworks.org/food-policy-resources/?resource=834

Johns Hopkins Center for a Livable Future. 2015b. Unpublished survey conducted by staff and students.

Kania, John, and Mark Kramer. 2011. "Collective Impact." *Stanford Social Innovation Review,* Winter. https://ssir.org/articles/entry/collective_impact

Kaye, Gillian, and Tom Wolff. 1997. *From the Ground Up! A Workbook on Coalition Building & Community Development.* Amherst, MA: AHEC/Community Partners.

Lehrer, Nadine. 2015. "Farm Bills." In *The SAGE Encyclopedia of Food Issues,* edited by Ken Albala, 453–458. Los Angeles: SAGE Reference.

Lieberman, Trudy. 2003. "Hungry in America." *The Nation*, July 31. https://www.thenation.com/article/hungry-america/

Lo, Joann, and Alexa Delwiche. 2013. "Los Angeles' Good Food Purchasing Policy: Worker, Farmer and Nutrition Advocates Meet . . . and Agree!" *Progressive Planning* no. 197 (Fall), 24–28.

Local Food Directories: National Farmers Market Directory. 2017. United States Department of Agriculture. https://www.ams.usda.gov/local-food-directories/farmersmarkets

Martin, Katie S. 2001. *Food Security and Community: Putting the Pieces Together*. Hartford, CT: Hartford Food System.

McCullagh, Molly, and Raychel Santo. 2014. *Food Policy for All: Inclusion of Diverse Community Residents on Food Policy Councils*. Tufts University and the Johns Hopkins Center for a Livable Future. https://assets.jhsph.edu/clf/mod_clfResource/doc/Food%20Policy%20For%20All%204-81.pdf

Michigan State University Center for Regional Food Systems. 2013. *Local Government Support for Food Systems*. http://foodsystems.msu.edu/uploads/files/local-govt-survey-brief.pdf; http://foodsystems.msu.edu/resources/brief/2015%20ICMA-MSU%20local%20government%20food%20survey%20results%20summary.pdf

Michigan State University Center for Regional Food Systems. 2016. National Food Hub Survey. http://foodsystems.msu.edu/our-work/national_food_hub_survey/

Minnesota Food Charter Network. Minnesota Food Charter for Our Healthy Future. http://mnfoodcharter.com/

Moran, Alyssa J., Jason P. Block, Simo G. Goshev, Sara N. Bleich, and Christina A. Roberto. 2017. "Trends in Nutrient Content of Children's Menu Items in U.S. Chain Restaurants." *American Journal of Preventive Medicine* 52, no. 3 (March): 284–291.

Morland, Kimberly, Steve Wing, and Ana Diez Roux. 2002. "The Contextual Effect of the Local Food Environment on Residents' Diets: The Atherosclerosis Risk in Communities Study." *American Journal of Public Health* 92, no. 11 (November): 1761–1768. http://ajph.aphapublications.org/doi/full/10.2105/AJPH.92.11.1761

Moskin, Julia. 2016. "When Community-Supported Agriculture Is Not What It Seems." *New York Times*, July 19. https://www.nytimes.com/2016/07/20/dining/csa-farm-share-community-supported-agriculture.html?_r=3

Myers, Todd, and Steven Sexton. 2015. "A Contrarian View of the Local Food Movement." *Wall Street Journal*, July 16. http://blogs.wsj.com/experts/2015/07/16/a-contrarian-view-of-the-local-food-movement/ta...

Nash Information Services. 2017. The Numbers. http://www.the-numbers.com/movies/genre/Documentary

National Sustainable Agriculture Coalition. 2017. http://sustainableagriculture.net/about-us/organizational-structure/

New Brunswick Food Alliance. 2014. http://www.nbfoodalliance.org/about/mission-vision-goals/

New Brunswick Food System. 2017. Action Plan. New Brunswick: Bloustein
     School of Planning and Public Policy, Rutgers University.
New Mexico Department of Health. 2016. New Mexico Childhood Obesity
     Update: 2015. https://nmhealth.org/data/view/chronic/1861/
New Mexico Farmers' Market. 2017. Bring the Harvest Home. http://farmers
     marketsnm.org/
Nussbaum, Martha C. 2001. *Upheavals of Thought: The Intelligence of Emotions.*
     New York: Cambridge University Press.
Nussbaum, Martha C. 2010. *Not for Profit: Why Democracy Needs the Humanities.*
     Princeton, NJ: Princeton University Press.
Obenchain, Janel, and Arlene Spark. 2015. *Food Policy: Looking Forward from the
     Past.* Boca Raton, FL: CRC Press.
O'Connor, Clare. 2014. "Report: Walmart Workers Cost Taxpayers $6.2 Billion
     in Public Assistance." *Forbes*, April 15. http://www.forbes.com/sites/clare
     oconnor/2014/04/15/report-walmart-workers-cost-taxpayers-6-2-billion-
     in-public-assistance/#be654137cd84
Penn State College of Agricultural Sciences. 2017. Enhancing Food Security in
     the Northeast. http://agsci.psu.edu/research/food-security/about
Philip Morris International. 2011. Annual Report. http://phx.corporate-ir.net/
     External.File?item=UGFyZW50SUQ9NjM4NDQ4fENoaWxkSUQ9MTM
     xODkzfFR5cGU9MQ==&t=1
Piketty, Thomas. 2014. *Capital in the Twenty-First Century.* Translated by Arthur
     Goldhammer. Cambridge, MA: Belknap Press.
Pirog, Rich, Crystal Miller, Lindsay Way, Christina Hazekamp, and Emily Kim.
     2014. *The Local Food Movement: Setting the Stage for Good Food.* Michigan
     State University Center for Regional Food Systems. http://foodsystems
     .msu.edu/resources/local-food-movement-setting-the-stage
*A Plan of Conservation and Development for the Capitol Region—Achieving the Balance.*
     2003. Capitol Region Council of Governments, Hartford, Connecticut.
Pollan, Michael. 2006. *The Omnivore's Dilemma: A Natural History of Four Meals.*
     New York: Penguin Press.
Poppendieck, Janet. 1999. *Sweet Charity?: Emergency Food and the End of Entitle-
     ment.* New York: Penguin Books.
Power, Elaine. 2015. "Food Banks." In *The SAGE Encyclopedia of Food Issues,*
     edited by Ken Albala, 552–557. Los Angeles: SAGE Reference. https://us
     .sagepub.com/en-us/nam/the-sage-encyclopedia-of-food-issues/book
     239023
Public Comments to the Federal Government on the Scientific Report of the
     2015 Dietary Guidelines Advisory Committee. Department of Health
     and Human Services. https://health.gov/dietaryguidelines/2015/public-
     comments.asp
Putnam, Robert D. 2000. *Bowling Alone: The Collapse and Revival of American
     Community.* New York: Simon & Schuster.
Real Food Challenge. 2017. http://realfoodchallenge.org/about-real-food-challenge

Reese, Stephen D. Reese, Oscar H. Gandy Jr., and August E. Grant, eds. 2001. *Framing Public Life: Perspectives on Media and Our Understanding of the Social World*. New York: Routledge.

Report of the City of Hartford Advisory Commission on Food Policy, 2002. Hartford Food System, Hartford, Connecticut.

Rohleder, Anna. 2014. "The Nation's Largest Food Hub Is Coming to Louisville, Kentucky." Civil Eats, December 3. http://civileats.com/2014/12/03/the-nations-biggest-food-hub-coming-to-louisville-kentucky/

Rozyne, Michael. 2016. "Announcing the Food Narrative Project." Red Tomato, April 7. http://www.redtomato.org/announcing-food-narrative-project/

Santo, Raychel, Anne Palmer, and Brent Kim. 2016. *Vacant Lots to Vibrant Plots: A Review of the Benefits and Limitations of Urban Agriculture*. Johns Hopkins Center for a Livable Future. http://www.jhsph.edu/research/centers-and-institutes/johns-hopkins-center-for-a-livable-future/_pdf/research/clf_reports/urban-ag-literature-review.pdf

Saul, Nick, and Andrea Curtis. 2013. *The Stop: How the Fight for Good Food Transformed a Community and Inspired a Movement*. New York: Melville House.

Sen, Amartya. 2011. *The Idea of Justice*. Reprint. Cambridge, MA: Harvard University Press.

Senge, Peter M. 1994. *The Fifth Discipline: The Art & Practice of the Learning Organization*. New York: Random House.

Shapiro, Lilly Fink, Lesli Hoey, Kathryn Colasanti, Sue Ann Savas. 2015. *You Can't Rush The Process: Collective Impact Models of Food Systems Change*. East Lansing: Michigan State University Center for Regional Food Systems. http://foodsystems.msu.edu/resources/collective_impact_models_of_food_systems_change

Shore, Bill, Darell Hammond, and Amy Celep. 2013. "When Good Is Not Good Enough." *Stanford Social Innovation Review*. Fall. https://ssir.org/articles/entry/when_good_is_not_good_enough

Simon, Ben. 2015. "No Time to Waste." *U.S. News & World Report*. October 1. https://www.usnews.com/opinion/blogs/policy-dose/2015/10/01/we-need-more-than-usda-goals-to-reduce-food-waste

Spurling, Carol Price. 2015. "Community Supported Agriculture (CSAs), Consumers' Perspective." In *The SAGE Encyclopedia of Food Issues*, edited by Ken Albala, 266–270. Los Angeles: SAGE Reference.

Starmer, Elanor. 2015. Speech delivered at the Enhancing Food Security in the Northeast Conference, Greenbelt, Maryland. December 10.

Stiffman, Eden. 2015. "Giving to Food Causes Is Increasingly Popular—and More Complicated," *Chronicle of Philanthropy*, November 18. https://philanthropy.com/article/Giving-to-Food-Causes-Is/234258/

Supplemental Nutrition Assistance Program (SNAP), 2017, United States Department of Agriculture. https://www.fns.usda.gov/sites/default/files/pd/SNAP summary.pdf

Surkam, Pamela J., Maryam J. Tabrizi, Ryan M. Lee, Anne M. Palmer, and Kevin D. Frick. 2016. "'Eat Right–Live Well!' Supermarket Intervention Impact on Sales of Healthy Foods in a Low-Income Neighborhood." *Journal of Nutrition Education and Behavior* 48, no. 2 (February): 112–121. http://www.jneb.org/article/S1499-4046(15)00670-3/fulltext#sec1

Szymanski, Ileana F. 2015. "Blogging." In *The SAGE Encyclopedia of Food Issues*, edited by Ken Albala, 136–140. Los Angeles: SAGE Reference.

*2015–2020 Dietary Guidelines for Americans*. 2015. Department of Health and Human Services. https://health.gov/dietaryguidelines/2015/

United States Department of Agriculture. 2015. "USDA and EPA Join with Private Sector, Charitable Organizations to Set Nation's First Food Waste Reduction Goals." September 16. https://www.usda.gov/wps/portal/usda/usdahome?contentid=2015/09/0257.xml

United States Department of Agriculture. 2016. "USDA Celebrates Progress during National School Lunch Week and Farm to School Month." October 11. https://www.fns.usda.gov/pressrelease/2016/0219-16

University of Oregon Food Studies. 2017. http://foodstudies.uoregon.edu/

Vermont Sustainable Jobs Fund. 2017. Farm to Plate. http://www.vtfarmtoplate.com/plan

Wallbridge, Rob. 2014. "Organic Farmer Viewpoint: Has the 'Food Movement' Become a Religious Cult?" Genetic Literacy Project, September 14. https://www.geneticliteracyproject.org/2014/09/14/organic-farmer-viewpoint-has-the-food-movement-become-a-religious-cult/Has the

Walmart Foundation. 2017. http://giving.walmart.com/our-focus

West, Rachel, and Michael Reich. 2014. "The Effects of Minimum Wages on SNAP Enrollments and Expenditures." Center for American Progress, March 5. https://www.americanprogress.org/issues/economy/reports/2014/03/05/85158/the-effects-of-minimum-wages-on-snap-enrollments-and-expenditures/

Williams, Tate. "An Interesting Twist in the Growing Feast of Food Philanthropy: Creative Placemaking." *Inside Philanthropy*, June 7. https://www.insidephilanthropy.com/grants-for-parks-gardens/2016/6/7/an-interesting-twist-in-the-growing-feast-of-food-philanthro.html

Winne, Mark. 2008. *Closing the Food Gap: Resetting the Table in the Land of Plenty*. Boston: Beacon Press.

Winne, Mark. 2010. *Food Rebels, Guerrilla Gardeners, and Smart-Cookin' Mamas: Fighting Back in an Age of Industrial Agriculture*. Boston: Beacon Press.

Winne, Mark. 2012. "Food Democracy on the March." *Harvard Health Policy Review* 13, no. 2 (Fall): 24–25.

Winne, Mark. 2013. "Food Corps: A Faith Renewed." June 19. http://www.markwinne.com/food-coops-a-faith-renewed/

Winne, Peter. 2017. "Coordination in the U.S. Food Movement." (Survey Report). New York University, New York.

Wirzba, Norman. 2011. *Food and Faith: A Theology of Eating*. New York: Cambridge University Press.

Wolff, Tom. 2016. "Ten Places Where Collective Impact Gets It Wrong." *Global Journal of Community Psychology Practice* 7, no. 1 (March). http://www.gjcpp.org/en/resource.php?issue=21&resource=200

World Health Organization. 2008. *WHO Report on the Global Tobacco Epidemic, 2008*. Geneva: World Health Organization. http://whqlibdoc.who.int/publications/2008/9789241596282_eng.pdf?ua=1

# Index

## About the Author

**Mark Winne**, from 1979 to 2003, was the executive director of the Hartford Food System, a Connecticut nonprofit food organization. He is the cofounder of the Community Food Security Coalition, where he also worked as the Food Policy Council program director. He was a Kellogg Foundation Food and Society Fellow, a Johns Hopkins School of Public Health Visiting Scholar, a member of the U.S. delegation to the 2000 Rome Conference on Food Security, and currently serves as a senior advisor to the Center for a Livable Future at Johns Hopkins. He is the author of *Closing the Food Gap: Resetting the Table in the Land of Plenty* and *Food Rebels, Guerrilla Gardeners, and Smart-Cookin' Mamas*. Through his own firm, Mark Winne Associates, Mark speaks, trains, and writes on topics related to community food systems, food policy, and food security. He resides in Santa Fe, New Mexico.